Families AND Communities AS Educators

HOPE JENSEN LEICHTER

Teachers College, Columbia University

Editor

Teachers College Press
Teachers College, Columbia University
New York & London   1979

Published 1979 by
Teachers College Press
Teachers College, Columbia University
1234 Amsterdam Avenue
New York, N.Y. 10027

First published by
Teachers College Record
May 1978, Vol. 79, No. 4

Library of Congress Cataloging in Publication Data:

Main entry under title:

Families and communities as educators.

  Originally published as Teachers College record,
v. 79, no. 4, May 1978.
  Includes bibliographical references.
  1. Community and school—United States—Addresses,
essays, lectures. 2. United States—Intellectual life—
Addresses, essays, lectures. I. Leichter, Hope Jensen.
II. Teachers College record.
LC221.F35   370.19'31   79-63
ISBN 0-8077-2560-9 Cloth
ISBN 0-8077-2559-5 pbk.

Manufactured in the United States of America
6 5 4 3 2 1 79 80 81 82 83 84

Dedicated
to the memory of
MARGARET MEAD

Contents

HOPE JENSEN LEICHTER   vii *Foreword*

HOPE JENSEN LEICHTER   3 *Families and Communities as Educators:*
                                   Some Concepts of Relationship

J. W. GETZELS   95 *The Communities of Education*

LAWRENCE A. CREMIN   119 *Family-Community Linkages in American*
                                   Education: Some Comments on the
                                   Recent Historiography

MARGARET MEAD   141 *The Conservation of Insight—Educational*
                                   Understanding of Bilingualism

ELIOT D. CHAPPLE   158 *New Directions in Education in Advanced*
                                   Technological Societies

PETER R. MOOCK   173 *Education and the Transfer of Inequality*
                                   from Generation to Generation

ROBERT A. LEVINE   185 *Western Schools in Non-Western Societies:*
                                   Psychosocial Impact and Cultural Response

NICHOLAS HOBBS   192 *Families, Schools, and Communities:*
                                   An Ecosystem for Children

URIE BRONFENBRENNER   203 *Who Needs Parent Education?*

STEVEN SCHLOSSMAN   224 *The Parent Education Game: The Politics*
                                   of Child Psychology in the 1970s

                             245 CONTRIBUTORS

Foreword

HOPE JENSEN LEICHTER

This book is the outcome of two seminars jointly sponsored by the Smithsonian Institution in Washington, D. C., and the Center for the Study of the Family as Educator at Teachers College, Columbia University. The seminars were convened as part of a larger symposium on "Kin and Communities: The Peopling of America," organized by Wilton S. Dillon, director of Smithsonian symposia and seminars, and chaired by Margaret Mead. The first seminar met June 14-15, 1976; the second, June 15-16, 1977. The articles in this book were first published in the *Teachers College Record* of May, 1978.

The idea for the seminars was initially suggested by Wilton Dillon, who noted that the various scholars who had contributed to an earlier volume published under the title *The Family as Educator* (1974) had never actually met as a group to discuss their ideas. He was well aware that a good deal of research had gone forward since the appearance of that book, and he expressed the belief that the Smithsonian seminars, particularly in the context of the symposium on "Kin and Communities," would provide an ideal vehicle for such an interuniversity, interdisciplinary gathering. It was agreed, therefore, that the Center for the Study of the Family as Educator and the Smithsonian Institution would collaborate in sponsoring the seminars. We are grateful to the Spencer Foundation for its generous support of the research program of the center, and to the Smithsonian Institution for its initiative, hospitality, and assistance in making the seminars possible.

Most of the original contributors to *The Family as Educator* were present at the 1976 seminar, including Urie Bronfenbrenner, Lawrence A. Cremin, J. W. Getzels, Peter R. Moock, and myself. Robert A.

LeVine, who was conducting field work in Africa, was unable to attend, but remained in touch with the proceedings, as did Margaret Mead. In addition, a number of other individuals were invited because of the special relevance of their work to the issues of families and communities as educators, including Eliot D. Chapple, an anthropologist who has pioneered in research on human interaction; Philip W. Jackson of the University of Chicago, a psychologist who has imaginatively applied the techniques of ethnography to the classroom; Nicholas Hobbs of Vanderbilt University, a psychologist who has become a leading student of family policy; Dorothy Rich, the able director of the Home and School Institute in Washington, D.C.; and John Henry Martin, an experienced school administrator who has been especially interested in family-school relationships. I served as chairman of the seminar and Frank G. Jennings, editor of the *Teachers College Record* at the time, served as rapporteur.

The same group met again in 1977, along with Margaret Mead and Rhoda Métraux (who presided over another, closely related session at the symposium on "Kin and Communities," at which research on the question of kinship by choice was a significant topic of discussion). Urie Bronfenbrenner was unable to attend the 1977 session but kept in touch with the proceedings. I again served as chairman and Frank G. Jennings, as rapporteur.

Both the 1976 and the 1977 seminars were recorded and transcribed in full. As chairman I took responsibility for excerpting materials from the 1976 transcript and for preparing these in a form that would most effectively launch our 1977 discussion. In this task I had the able collaboration of Frank Jennings. At the end of the 1977 seminar it was agreed that we would produce a volume of articles on families and communities as educators that would complement the earlier volume *The Family as Educator*. For this purpose the transcripts of the second session were made available to participants, for use in the preparation of their prospectuses and eventually their contributions. The articles that have resulted reflect the discussions of the two seminars at a number of points, but each has been individually written and each in its own way goes beyond the seminar discussions. Although not all of the participants contributed to the present volume, I have endeavored to incorporate the principal themes of the seminar discussions into my own article. Finally, the present volume includes contributions from two individuals who were not actually present at the seminars but who stayed in touch with the proceedings via the transcripts: Steven Schlossman, with whom I was engaged on a parent education project at the time of the seminars, and Robert A. LeVine, a contributor to the original volume.

In *The Family as Educator* we examined a variety of ways in which education takes place within the family and suggested certain lines of inquiry into how this education proceeds. The essential thrust of that volume was to emphasize the wide range of activities on the part of members of the family that may usefully be regarded as educative and the variety of individuals—husbands, wives, siblings, grandparents, and other relatives—who engage in them. The goal of the volume was not only to deepen our insights into the educative process within the family but also to apply those insights to the improvement of education throughout the society. The several contributors wrote independently, from the perspective of their various disciplines and specialized concerns. Yet, a number of common emphases emerged. First, there was a fascinating subtlety about the concepts drawn from the various behavioral sciences to illuminate the processes of teaching and learning within the family: Robert LeVine used the concept of "encoding" to explicate the problem of cultural transmission across the generations; Peter Moock used the concept of "allocation of time" to explicate family relationships with respect to education; while J. W. Getzels juxtaposed the concepts of "socialization" and "education" in discussing teaching and learning in different settings. Second, there was a remarkable breadth about the various canvasses of the literature, as one contributor after another reached beyond the studies formally labeled "educational" to a much wider range of inquiries illuminating phenomena as varied as language interaction, the organization of activities in time and space, memory as an interactive process, and the processes of evaluation and labeling. Finally, there was the concern that ran throughout the volume, that while much of the research on the family's educational activities has stressed the consequences of these activities in other institutions, notably schools, far broader questions needed to be posed about the family's educational activities in their own right. Moreover, there was general agreement that many of those questions were best posed in the context of the family's relationships with other institutions. In effect, questions about education within the family were seen as frequently requiring attention to education beyond the family as well.

It was essentially these problems of relationship—among educative institutions and across generations—that marked the starting point of our seminars on families and communities as educators. Our initial agenda in 1976 included field mapping, or spelling out needs and opportunities for research; examining methods of research; reporting and discussing ongoing inquiries; spelling out new knowledge and rediscovering existing knowledge relevant to ongoing inquiries; and redefining the problems of the field of families and communities as educators. We were aware that we would need to scrutinize in a fundamental way concepts of family and community as they have been (and might be) applied to education, concepts of relationships among individuals and institutions, and the various methods for studying and applying these concepts. And we took it as an important concern to explore the policy implications of our inquiry—in this respect the participation of Dorothy Rich, John Henry Martin, Nicholas Hobbs, and Urie Bronfenbrenner was of special importance.

The present volume has emerged from these discussions. It focuses on issues of relationship between the family as educator and other institutions that educate, with the several articles illustrating a variety of approaches to the topic. J. W. Getzels examines concepts of community in terms of their implications for education. Lawrence A. Cremin examines family-community linkages as they are portrayed in the recent historiography. Margaret Mead considers the conservation of insights over time, focusing on an educational understanding of bilingualism. Eliot D. Chapple discusses the relationships among educative institutions in the American society as those relationships have been influenced by advancing technology. Peter R. Moock considers the transfer of inequality from generation to generation. Robert A. LeVine examines the relationship of schools to the community in non-Western societies where Western education has been adopted. Nicholas Hobbs proposes a system of ecological concepts for work with children that encompasses family, school, and community. Urie Bronfenbrenner discusses the special question of who needs parent education. And Steven Schlossman examines the assumptions and goals of recent parent education programs. My own paper introduces the volume by considering a variety of concepts from the institutional and individual perspectives that appear to have potential in studying families and communities as educators.

As in *The Family as Educator*, many areas have remained untouched by our discussions and our papers. Our goal has been to formulate problems for inquiry and to exemplify a variety of approaches and perspectives that seem promising in the consideration of families and communities as educators.

Families AND Communities AS Educators

Families and Communities as Educators: Some Concepts of Relationship

HOPE JENSEN LEICHTER
Teachers College, Columbia University

An essential paradox of research on education and the family inheres in the fact that the more one looks at the family, the more it isn't there.[1] And it is in contending with this paradox that the various approaches to research on the family diverge. It is also in finding a sophisticated and useful stance with respect to this paradox that the most fruitful opportunities lie for enhancing our understanding of the family's role as educator and its relation to other institutions that educate.

From the perspective of the practice called education, a basic question concerns the location of education in various settings within the society and the relationship of education in one setting to that in another. A process variously called education, socialization, acculturation, enculturation, development, and learning takes place in all societies. In order to improve educational practice, it is important to understand where and how this process proceeds. The question may be narrowed to manageable proportions by defining certain activities as education and certain situations as its locale. Indeed, it is only by some form of selection that one can avoid the boundless study of all life. Yet the problem is far from simple. If one arbitrarily narrows the domain that one regards as education and the domain that one considers family, one creates

I wish to express my appreciation to the Spencer Foundation for its generous support of the work of the Elbenwood Center for the Study of the Family as Educator, and of my own research within the Center.

1 A classic description of this experience is given by Milne, "The more he [Pooh] looked ... the more Piglet wasn't there," A.A. Milne, *The House at Pooh Corner* (New York: E.P. Dutton & Co., 1928), p. 1.

blinders at the very point where a more flexible paradigm would facilitate a deeper insight into the changes going on and the resources for further evolution.

In our book *The Family as Educator*, we argued that a fuller and richer understanding of education within social units termed families is essential for an adequate theory of education. In our meetings at the Smithsonian Institution to discuss the progress of research on the family as educator, the importance of examining the process of education within the family was again highlighted. Yet, as the discussions proceeded, the question of how the family relates to other institutions that educate emerged again and again, both as problematic and as profoundly important for our understanding of the family's role as educator, and for the development of a fundamental theory of education as it takes place in the full range of educative institutions.

Initially, it had been my intent (as well as that of the Smithsonian Seminars) to examine questions of the relationships among institutions that educate, with the family as figure and the other institutions that educate as ground. But the paradox of the elusive family makes it difficult to start consistently from the perspective of the family. When the individual learner is the focus, the selection of an institution from which to start one's investigation into education is less problematic. One starts with an individual and traces that individual's experience over time, and the selection of institutions for attention becomes in part an empirical matter. When a cultural, societal, or institutional perspective is employed, the selection of a starting point becomes more difficult. Conventionally, in much educational thinking and research, the starting point has been the school. But since my attempt has been to shed light on the family as educator and my concern has been to consider concepts that may be fruitful in advancing our understanding of connections among institutions, the point of reference, if not always the starting point, will be the family, even though it remains elusive and its definition problematic, and even though at some points I have examined relationships among institutions without specifically referring back to the family.

One may raise two different kinds of questions about the relationships among diverse institutions that educate. One set of questions takes an institutional perspective and examines the way in which one institution relates to another. Another set of questions focuses on the individual as learner and examines the way in which the individual engages in, moves through, and combines diverse educative experiences in different settings over a lifetime.[2] Examination of education from both these perspectives is vital for the development of a comprehensive theory of education.

Since a variety of behavioral science concepts have potential significance for our understanding of these basic questions of education, it should be useful to review certain of these concepts—whether or not they have been specifically applied to education—with an eye to their possible value in the further development of a theory of education as it takes place in a variety of settings and across the individual's life. I shall not attempt a comprehensive review of all possibly relevant behavioral science concepts, nor shall I attempt a comprehensive review of all of the instances in which the concepts I discuss have been used with a specific focus on education. Rather my attempt will be to select and analyze concepts that I regard as particularly meaningful for a framework of inquiry into education as it takes place across settings—concepts that should help to raise our understanding of education to more complex and sophisticated levels.

PRELIMINARY OBSERVATIONS

Some Assumptions about Education   Before proceeding with the analysis of the relationships of education in diverse settings, it may be useful to set forth a few assumptions about education. Education has been defined as "the deliberate, systematic, and sustained effort to transmit, evoke, or acquire knowledge, attitudes, values, skills, and sensibilities, and any learning that results from the effort, direct or indirect, intended or unintended."[3] While this definition offers one useful guide, it will be assumed, for present purposes, that an understanding of education must include not only deliberate processes but also those processes that are at the margins of awareness. Moreover, it has been made clear that education and socialization both go forward in a variety of settings;[4] it is not sufficient to regard socialization as taking place in the family and education as taking place in the school. It is, therefore, important not to overlook the literatures on socialization, acculturation,

2   Hope Jensen Leichter, "The Concept of Educative Style," *Teachers College Record* 75 (December 1973): 239-50.

3   Lawrence A. Cremin, "Family-Community Linkages in American Education: Some Comments on the Recent Historiography," *Teachers College Record* 79 (May 1978): 701.

4   J.W. Getzels, "Socialization and Education: A Note on Discontinuities," in *The Family as Educator*, ed. Hope Jensen Leichter (New York: Teachers College Press, 1975), pp. 44-51.

enculturation, development, and learning in formulating a theory of education across settings.

It is thus assumed that education takes place in a wide range of institutions, among them, families, schools, museums, religious institutions, places of work, hospitals, community centers. Beyond this, it is assumed that it is important to understand education in each of these settings in its own right, not merely in terms of its consequences for schooling. Education is thus conceived as a lifelong process that may take place in a variety of settings and that needs to be understood as it takes place in each of these settings.

Another assumption is that education takes place on multiple levels, often simultaneously. Both the content of learning and instruction and the processes of learning and instruction must be understood. Of particular importance are the processes of learning to learn, or what has been called deutero-learning or meta-learning.[5]

Still another assumption is that affective and cognitive learning are intertwined in each and every setting in which education takes place. One cannot presume, for example, that affective learning takes place at home and cognitive learning in the school. On the contrary, both aspects must be understood in both settings. This is not to presume that the character of affect in one setting is equivalent to that in another, nor that the relation between cognitive and affective learning is the same at all stages of life. However, it is assumed that the two components are present in all settings in which education takes place and must be understood as part and parcel of the same educational process.

Institutional Domains and the Understanding of Education   Recently, a host of assumptions has been made about the location of education in various institutions, and particularly the location of sources of educational failure and achievement. The basic point that many institutions educate, and that a comprehensive theory of education needs to cover not merely education in schools but in the entire range of institutional settings in which education takes place, has by now been widely discussed.[6] Yet, the underlying question of how education in one setting relates to education in another is only beginning to be understood. This issue has profound policy implications, since a variety of governmental

5   Gregory Bateson, *Steps to an Ecology of Mind* (New York: Ballantine Books, 1972).

6   Cf. Lawrence A. Cremin, *Public Education* (New York: Basic Books, 1976); also Lawrence A. Cremin, *Traditions of American Education* (New York: Basic Books, 1977); and Leichter, ed., *The Family as Educator.*

and other programs rest upon assumptions—implicit or explicit—about the locus of effective education and the way in which education in one setting influences education in another.

One instance is early intervention and parent education programs, from day care to homestart and Head Start,[7] where assumptions inhere about the extent to which the most significant educational influences on a child come from the family or the school, and about the sequential organization of the individual's educational experience, that is, the time during which deficits in the home can still be corrected by intervention, and the extent to which early patterns remain fixed throughout life.[8] Another instance is experimental programs such as the open classroom, where assumptions inhere about the locus of the most vivid educational experience inside or outside the classroom, and about the relation of experiential to abstract learning. These and related instances point to the importance of examining education as it takes place across a range of institutions and settings. But here the problem immediately becomes complex, since one must face the question of how to define institutions and how to draw boundaries among them.

Let us briefly examine the definition of the family, as a paradigm for considering the general question. Definitions of the family must contend with the fact that families vary from one society to another, and from one stage of the life cycle to another, and that significant historical changes are taking place in the family. In addition, the boundaries of the family are permeable, and even in traditional forms the family rarely, if ever, encompasses the totality of the individual's life.

It is commonly recognized today that the institution termed *the family* has a variety of forms in different societies. The nuclear family of husband, wife, and children may or may not be coterminous with the household unit; life-cycle changes in household units vary from one society to another, and the range of social relationships that are defined on the basis of kinship also varies. In our own society, the possibility of widespread social change and substantial variation in family forms is very much with us and is reflected in the enormous current concern

7   See Urie Bronfenbrenner, "Who Needs Parent Education?" *Teachers College Record* 79 (May 1978): 767-87; also Nicholas Hobbs, "Families, Schools and Communities: An Ecosystem for Children," *Teachers College Record* 79 (May 1978): 756-66; and Steven Schlossman, "The Parent Education Game: The Politics of Child Psychology in the 1970s," *Teachers College Record* 79 (May 1978): 788-808.

8   Urie Bronfenbrenner, "Is Early Intervention Effective?" in Leichter, ed., *The Family as Educator*, pp. 105-29; Benjamin S. Bloom, *Stability and Change in Human Characteristics* (New York: John Wiley and Sons, 1964); also Benjamin S. Bloom, *Human Characteristics and School Learning* (New York: McGraw-Hill, 1976).

with the family. Changes in forms of the family are related to basic demographic and social changes, including the increasing number of older individuals in the population, the increasing number of women working outside the home, the changing definition of sex roles, and the increasing divorce rate. A number of experimental forms of living are emerging, including adoption of children by unmarried parents and openly acknowledged homosexual marriages. Today, families may exist by conventional marriage or a variety of forms of choice and fiction. Kinship, once thought of as ties by blood and marriage, is now open to consideration as a matter of choice,[9] thus bringing a new distinction between ties of kinship and ties of friendship.

In considering these changes in the family, some sociological theorists have argued that the family has lost its traditional functions to other institutions during the process of industrialization and urbanization. Others argue that changes in the function of the family are continuing, and that, in fact, the direction of change is far from clear. Some changes —for example, widespread television viewing—are reintroducing educational activities into the family that had earlier moved outside it. As a result, the concept *family* has many variant meanings in everyday vocabulary.

Other institutions are also undergoing fundamental change. Schools are changing in form and function, shifting from locations for basic education of children and young adults to possible centers for lifelong education.[10] Television, in a span of a few years, has shifted from being largely recreational to including a series of explicitly educational programs.[11]

In a period of social transition in which institutions themselves are undergoing rapid change in form, function, and definition—and indeed the everyday meaning of institutional names is shifting—it is important for behavioral scientists concerned with understanding and enhancing education to step back momentarily from contemporary definitions and not be overly caught up in specific and time-bound institutional categories. Rather, the need is for flexibility on the part of educational

9   The question of kinship by choice was discussed by Dr. Rhoda Métraux at the Smithsonian Seminar on Families and Communities as Educators and also in another session of the Smithsonian Symposium on Kin and Communities in which "Future Research Opportunities" were considered.

10   Cf. R.H. Dave and N. Stiemerling, *Lifelong Education and The School: L'Education Permanente et L'Ecole* (Hamburg, Germany: UNESCO Institute for Education, 1973).

11   Among the explicitly educational programs are "Sesame Street," "Nova," Jacques Cousteau's productions, the National Geographic Society programs, and a variety of museum programs.

scholars in defining the family and thinking about the boundaries between the family and other institutions. At the same time, it is clear that something usefully referred to as the family exists in most societies and that it exists as a sufficiently definable social unit to be a meaningful point of entry in understanding education within the society.

The problem in analyzing institutional domains with respect to educational questions is thus one of balance. It is essential not to be caught in time-bound and rigid institutional definitions. Yet, if the whole world spins at once, even the vocabulary for describing it evaporates. The methodological problem is to find a balance between ever-changing concepts[12] and concepts sufficiently fixed to enable one to describe and analyze change.

The argument thus far is that for an effective understanding of the way in which education in one situation—family, school, neighborhood, peer group, museum, hospital, factory, corporation—is related to education in other situations, one must back off from rigid and fixed institutional definitions and start afresh with an open question of the location of education, and the way in which different spheres of education are related. In one sense, this means focusing attention in new ways on the learner.[13] Even in attempting to understand the individual's educational experience, however, the need to understand the organization of the institutions through which the individual moves is apparent. An emphasis on the growth of the individual as the ultimate goal of education may be a reflection of a deep-rooted individualism in American culture;[14] yet the goal of individual educational growth requires an understanding of the "moving and multiple associations" in the individual's life and the symbolic and cultural surround in which the individual's experience is framed and from which it derives meaning.[15]

Analytic Levels in Family Research The issue of defining the domains in which education takes place within a society is also complicated by the variety of levels of analysis that have been employed in studying

---

12   In the words of Ortega, "Whoever aspires to understand man—that eternal tramp, a thing essentially *on the road*—must throw overboard all immobile concepts and learn to think in ever-shifting terms." José Ortega y Gasset, *Concord and Liberty*, trans. Helene Weyl (New York: W.W. Norton & Co., 1964), p. 75.

13   Leichter, "The Concept of Educative Style."

14   The emphasis on individualism in American culture has recently been analyzed by Herve Varenne in *Americans Together: Structured Diversity in a Midwestern Town* (New York: Teachers College Press, 1977).

15   John Dewey, *Human Nature and Conduct* (New York: Henry Holt & Co., 1922), p. 16.

various institutions. Here, again, research on the family may be examined briefly as a paradigm for raising the question of levels of analysis in other institutions as well. Variations in research definitions of the family reflect, not merely social changes and the variety of family terms in everyday vocabulary, but also differences in methodological stance.

One pertinent distinction among methodologies is that between approaches that emphasize the participant's, or *emic*, view, as compared with those that emphasize the researcher's, or *etic*, view.[16] In an emic approach, where the meaning of the concept *family* to participants in the society being studied is emphasized, the term *family* may have many varied meanings, from a monogamous, nuclear family of husband, wife, and children, to an extended family with the wife's mother resident in the household and no husband present, to a polygamous marriage. The family may be defined not merely in terms of its membership but also in terms of its activities: for example, it may be regarded as a place where one keeps one's things or sleeps. Indeed, without careful specification of the question, it is impossible to arrive at the meaning of the term *family* for participants. The term *family* may, for example, refer to a household unit, or to those with whom one is emotionally close, or to relatives of a certain degree of genealogical connection, or to any or all of these depending on the context. In an etic approach, where researchers rely on their own theoretically oriented definitions, for example, distinguishing between family and household or between nuclear family, extended family, and modified extended family, the researcher's definitions are employed regardless of the meaning that may be attached to the terms by those being studied.

Yet another approach is to examine family concepts at the level of the underlying symbolic meaning of the term *family*.[17] Here, *family* ceases to refer to household units for any specific social grouping based on ties of kinship or marriage, but refers rather to the underlying symbolic construction and meaning of family terms.

At a still broader level, behavioral science research diverges in emphasizing the primacy of one explanatory level as compared with another as a determinant of a family's behavior. Some, represented by the be-

---

16 The distinction is useful, although in practice, it may be blurred by the fact that an emic view is generally obtained through a researcher and therefore represents a joint product of the participant and the researcher.

17 Cf. Varenne, *Americans Together*; also David M. Schneider, *American Kinship: A Cultural Account* (Englewood Cliffs, N.J.: Prentice-Hall, 1968); and David M. Schneider and Calvert B. Cottrell, *The American Kin Universe: A Genealogical Study* (Chicago: University of Chicago Press, 1975).

havioral biologists, would explain human as well as animal family forms in terms of underlying biological "substrata," propensities, or instincts. Human family forms are seen as a reflection of animal mating, territorial and dominance behaviors, and innate sexual differences. Similarly, personality and character traits, and even intelligence, are seen as derivative from innate biological propensities and inherent developmental sequences.[18] Others point to underlying psychological needs and propensities of the individual as the most critical determinants of human behavior.[19] Others, particularly those from symbolic interactionist traditions, tend to see the prime determinants of human behavior in the immediate interpersonal interactions of individuals with significant others in their environments, and in the meaning that is constructed through these interactions.[20] Still others point to cultural and symbolic forms as basic determinants of behavior, arguing that the behavior of the individual, and indeed the relationships among individuals, are essentially derivatives of underlying cultural beliefs and symbolic organization, and pointing to the diverse meanings that may be attached to similar biological phenomena in different cultures.[21] Yet others tend to see economic factors as the most critical determinants of human behavior.[22] All these forms of explanatory primacy can be found in different approaches to family research.

While acknowledgement is often made of the need for multiple levels, multiple determinants, and systematic connection of different levels, the tendency—often correlating with disciplinary training—is to place primacy on one level as compared with another. Thus, the new behavioral biologists look at human families as a reflection of instinctual imperatives; the psychoanalytically oriented psychologists examine the dy-

18 Stemming in part from the work of Edward O. Wilson, *Sociobiology* (Cambridge: The Belknap Press of Harvard University Press, 1975), this emphasis has also been reflected in specific discussions of the family, for example, at the meetings of American Anthropological Association, Washington, D.C., November 1976.

19 This emphasis is reflected in the work of Bruno Bettelheim, for example, his study of the kibbutz, *The Children of the Dream: Communal Child-Rearing and American Education* (New York: Macmillan, 1969); see also Melford E. Spiro, *Children of the Kibbutz* (New York: Schocken Books, 1958).

20 Cf. Peter L. Berger and Thomas Luckmann, *The Social Construction of Reality: A Treatise in The Sociology of Knowledge* (Garden City, N.Y.: Anchor Books, Doubleday and Co., Inc., 1967).

21 Cf. Schneider, *American Kinship*; and Varenne, *Americans Together.*

22 Cf. Peter R. Moock, "Education and the Transfer of Inequality from Generation to Generation," *Teachers College Record* 79 (May 1978): 737-48; also Kenneth Keniston and the Carnegie Council on Children, *All Our Children: The American Family Under Pressure* (New York: Harcourt Brace Jovanovich, 1977).

namics of the resolution of psychological needs and dependencies in the family; the interactionists look at the family as an arena of interpersonal encounters; the economists consider family behavior in relation to outside economic forces or as a determinant of outside opportunities for its members; and the cultural and symbolic analysts look to the symbolic organization of family behavior and the meaning of family terms as components of broader symbolic systems.

The existence of these diverse perspectives again highlights the point that the more one looks at the family (or any other institution), the more it isn't there; or, stated somewhat differently, the more one looks at the family (or any other institution), the more it takes on different meanings from the perspective of different frameworks. For this reason it is useful to examine a variety of concepts that may be used in defining institutions, in looking at relationships across institutions, and in tracing and understanding the organization of the individual's life experience.

The Concept of Institution   The same diversity of meaning that one finds in the various analytic approaches to the family is found if one examines the meaning of the term *institution*. On the one hand, *institution* has been defined as a "cluster of social usages," connoting a "way of thought or action of some prevalence and permanence, which is embedded in the habits of a group or the customs of a people." On the other hand, "any formal organization—the government, the church, the university, the corporation, the trade union"—may also be seen as an institution. With this diversity in meanings, it is not surprising that "the range of institutions is as wide as the interest of mankind."[23]

Not only the definition of the term *institution* but also the groupings of organizations to which the term is applied have varied enormously in the social science literature. A few examples will illustrate this diversity of usage. In Davis's *Human Society*, the section on major institutions includes economic institutions, political institutions, and religious institutions. Yet, marriage and the family, while dealt with fully, are placed in another section.[24] In Williams's *American Society*, the institutions

---

23   Walton H. Hamilton, "Institution," in *Encyclopaedia of the Social Sciences*, ed. Edwin R. A. Seligman and Alvin Johnson, 15 vols. (New York: The Macmillan Co., 1932), 7, pp. 84-89.

24   Kingsley Davis, *Human Society* (New York: The Macmillan Co., 1948). The reasons for treating marriage and the family in a separate section include the difficulty of examining a domain of intense moral importance with scientific objectivity—"It seems clear that the very qualities which have made family affairs a subject of extreme popular interest have also made them a subject of neglect in social science" (pp. 393-94).

discussed are kinship and the family, social stratification, economic institutions, political institutions, education as an institution, and religion.[25] Other clusterings can be found through examination of some of the classic community studies. For example, in *Small Town in Mass Society*, Vidich and Bensman include a section on major institutional realities that covers the dimensions of social and economic class and the relationships of the local community to "the mass society."[26] In the Lynds' classic study of *Middletown*, the divisions for examination of the life of the community are structured without the explicit use of the term *institution*, but include "getting a living," "making a home," "training the young," "using leisure," "engaging in religious practices," and "engaging in community activities."[27] In *Middletown in Transition*, the headings are similar, with the notable addition of "getting information: the press," "keeping healthy," and "the machinery of government."[28]

In *Democracy in Jonesville*, Warner and his associates focus on social stratification, and their discussion does not center specifically on formal organizations, but rather on questions of social stratification; whether there is "room at the top," and the relation between "status aspirations and the social club." The limited use of the term *institution* in this work refers to churches, lodges, secret societies, Rotary clubs, women's organizations and associations, the school, and the factory.[29] Similarly, in *American Life: Dream and Reality*, Warner analyzes social stratification and the "American melting pot," and again focuses specifically on the class system and its relation to the family, the factory, ethnic and sectarian groups, and associations and the mass media. Here, too, the term *institution* does not appear in the index but is used from time to time, for example, in the definition of voluntary associations as "institutions which, unlike age grades or social classes, do not cross-cut or encompass the whole society."[30]

25   Robin M. Williams, Jr., *American Society* (New York: Alfred A. Knopf, 1956).

26   Arthur J. Vidich and Joseph Bensman, *Small Town in Mass Society* (Princeton, N.J.: Princeton University Press, 1968, revised edition).

27   Robert S. Lynd and Helen Merrell Lynd, *Middletown* (New York: Harcourt Brace and Co., 1929).

28   Robert S. Lynd and Helen Merrell Lynd, *Middletown in Transition* (New York: Harcourt Brace and Co., 1937).

29   W. Lloyd Warner and associates, *Democracy in Jonesville: A Study in Quality and Inequality* (New York: Harper & Brothers, 1949), p. xviii.

30   W. Lloyd Warner, *American Life: Dream and Reality* (Chicago: University of Chicago Press, 1953). Here the term *associations* is used to refer to secret societies, fraternities, and civic organizations (p. 191-92).

In his study of Italian-Americans in the West End of Boston, *The Urban Villagers*, Gans, on the other hand, uses the term *institution* explicitly and clarifies its relation to the term *community*. *Community* is used to refer to the set of institutions through which basic functions are carried out and is not limited to the spatial community or the neighborhood. Two specific lists of institutions that constitute the community are given: first, those that are predominantly Italian—the church; the parochial schools; formal social, civic, and parochial organizations, some of them church-related; and some commercial establishments; and second, those that are seen as part of a larger, non-Italian society or the "outside world," including work, education, health services, welfare agencies, government, and the mass media of communication.[31] Here then is yet another list of institutions and a distinction among institutions in terms of their relation to the ethnic society.

As in the case of definitions of the family, a basic issue in defining other institutions is whether the definitions are arrived at through the social scientist's (etic) concept (e.g., units that exist for the purpose of carrying out basic societal functions) or the participant's (emic) views (e.g., names and clusterings of activities in everyday usage). The term *institution* itself has come and gone in sociological, anthropological, and related social science research, being widely used at some times, almost disappearing from the scene at others, and then reemerging. The purpose here is not to settle upon a particular definition as the most useful for the analysis of education, but rather to alert scholars of education to the variety of possible meanings that the term may have and, more important still, to the variety of possible clusterings of organizations and activities that may arise depending on one's perspective and purpose. In one sense, the diversity of possible definitions of institutions and institutional clusterings compounds the problem. Yet, in another sense, it is precisely the issue at hand.

IMAGES OF INSTITUTIONAL INTERRELATIONSHIP

Assuming that one selects, for particular purposes, a definition of institution and an analytic level through which to carry out analysis, one may then return to the central educational question under consideration, that of the concepts through which one may examine the relationships among the diverse institutions that educate. For this purpose, a variety of concepts have potential value. Since these concepts vary in

31   Herbert J. Gans, *The Urban Villagers: Group and Class in the Life of Italian-Americans.* (Glencoe, Ill.: The Free Press, 1962), pp. 105-06.

the images that they suggest of institutional interrelationships, they offer a variety of possible angles of vision.

THE CONCEPT OF COMMUNITY

In considering the possible images of the relationships among institutions that educate, the concept of community itself is significant, since the manner in which the community is defined has important consequences for the clusterings of institutions that one includes within one's examination. The issue of the definition of the community is at least as complex as that of the definitions of the family or of other institutions. Here, too, differences in methodological stance and theoretical perspective influence the nature of the definition.

The *community* has been defined in a great variety of ways, depending on the perspective and purpose. A few illustrations will make clear the extent of the variety. Community has been defined as physical place, for example, the space within a geographic boundary such as a school district or a city limit constitutes a community. Community has been defined in terms of functional relationships among institutions, for example, the institutions that carry out certain economic functions are a community. Community has been defined in terms of communication, for example, those who communicate directly on a face-to-face basis constitute a community, or those who share information and ideas across geographical space constitute a community. Community has been defined in terms of sentiment, for example, those who have a sense of belonging or a sense of common heritage constitute a community. Community has been defined in terms of time dimensions, for example, those who have a common history of interactions and memories constitute a community. Indeed, one might cite an almost endless number of definitions of community.[32]

Definitions of the community also vary in terms of the theoretical perspectives of those studying the community. Here one may note the differences between the Chicago school of community studies, which rested heavily on ecological and spatial definitions of community,[33] and the more recent school of culturally and symbolically oriented anthropologists, who examine the community in terms of the "core"

32 J.W. Getzels, "The Communities of Education," *Teachers College Record* 79 (May 1978): 659-82.

33 A useful review is contained in Colin Bell and Howard Newby, *Community Studies* (New York: Praeger Publishers, 1972).

symbols (e.g., love) around which the interactions of individuals are organized.[34]

Like concepts of family and institution, the concept of community varies depending on whether the researcher's (etic) or the participant's (emic) definition is employed, and indeed with the extent to which this distinction is explicitly recognized. Herbert Gans's distinction in his study of Italian-Americans in the West End of Boston between those institutions that are part of the ethnic community and those that are part of the "outside world" illustrates the potential difference between an emic and an etic view.[35] If Gans had examined only those institutions that were part of the Italian-American ethnic community as distinct from the outside world in his analysis of social life in the West End, his understanding would clearly have been limited.

A number of examples can readily be found in the literature of community studies in which the boundaries of the community, defined in terms of communication, sentiment, or obligation, do not correspond with geographic boundaries. The analysis of space and spatial organization, both as a factor conditioning other aspects of interaction and as a reflection of other areas of social life, has received considerable attention. From the early community studies of the Chicago school, with their concept of zones and physical boundaries, to the more recent analyses of space in the work of community planners,[36] an understanding of the nature of spatial organization and geographic boundaries has been of great importance. Here the particular issue of locality in relation to instant worldwide communication also arises.[37] But even the definition of spatial boundaries is complex and cannot rest on physical definitions alone, because physical boundaries or territories are defined on the basis of other aspects of interaction as well.[38] Beyond this, the unit that is encompassed varies substantially if one shifts from a geographic to a communicational, obligational, or exchange definition of the community. Here again, the example of Gans's analysis of the Italian-Americans in the West End is illustrative, since, although the outside

34 Varenne, *Americans Together*.

35 Gans, *The Urban Villagers*, p. 106.

36 A particularly interesting example of the analysis of space in community planning is represented by the ekistics movement, cf. Constantinos A. Doxiadis, *Ekistics: An Introduction to the Science of Human Settlements* (New York: Oxford University Press, 1968).

37 One discussion of the role of media in creating instant worldwide communication is given by Tony Schwartz, *The Responsive Chord* (Garden City, N.Y.: Anchor Press, Doubleday, 1974). This analysis draws heavily on the earlier work of Marshall McLuhan.

38 Norman Ashcraft and Albert E. Scheflen, *People Space: The Making and Breaking of Human Boundaries* (Garden City, N.Y.: Anchor Press, Doubleday, 1976).

world was outside of the local geographic community, it was within the community defined in terms of economic exchange and communication. Arensberg and Kimball give another example, familiar in the literature on immigration, of the wide geographic spread over which ties of community defined in terms of kinship obligation and sentiment may extend. They vividly describe the fact that the dispersal of the members of the farm family—even emigration to America—did not destroy family ties, as demonstrated, for example, by remittances of money and gifts from America to Ireland.[39]

Indeed, like the family, the more one looks at definitions of the community, the more diverse they appear, until the whole idea of community virtually dissolves under scrutiny. Yet, the image of community is of vital importance in understanding the social world through which the individual moves, and is therefore of significance in framing educational questions about the relationships among institutions that educate. A particularly important issue, where the sophistication of one's perspective in defining the community is consequential, is that of the structuring of coherence and diversity within the world of an individual or family. If one is attempting to understand the character of education in a society, it is important to be able to make shifts in perspective in defining community for different purposes of inquiry, so that one does not miss important sources of education. It is clear that even in small geographically bounded communities, influences outside the community may have a vital role in molding the character of the community, for example, its class structure and its interpersonal relationships.[40] This is not to argue that the geographic locale may not represent one important level of analysis, particularly in relation to the allocation of time,[41] but rather that it represents only one level. A clear understanding of the variety of different units that may be encompassed by different definitions of community is important for understanding the full range of the sources of education.

THE CONCEPT OF SYSTEM

The concept of *system* is useful in attempting to understand relationships among institutions that educate, since it offers a perspective on the way in which one area of social life is related to another. A number

---

39   Conrad M. Arensberg and Solon T. Kimball, *Family and Community in Ireland* (Gloucester, Mass.: Peter Smith, 1961 [1940 copyright]), p. 148.
40   Vidich and Bensman, *Small Town in Mass Society*.
41   Doxiadis, *Ekistics*.

of sophisticated and highly technical discussions of system may be found in the literature, among them Bateson's discussion in *Steps Toward an Ecology of Mind*,[42] Bateson's analysis in *Naven*, particularly in the epilogue,[43] and Buckley's review in *Sociology and Modern Systems Theory*.[44] For present purposes, it will suffice to note three points where systems concepts diverge. First, systems concepts vary in the extent to which a system is seen as a closed and bounded unit, as compared with an open and permeable one. Second, systems concepts vary in the extent to which all areas within a system are seen as equally interconnected. Third, systems concepts vary in the extent to which they deal explicitly with corrective processes and change.

The basic thrust of the concept is contained in the idea that "in a system of interdependent parts, a change in any relationship will have an effect on all other relationships."[45] With this concept wide scanning in search of connections among institutions that educate within a community becomes necessary.[46] A number of classic community studies have been based in one way or another on the idea that the community can be viewed as a system. Arensberg and Kimball's study of family and community in Ireland offers one example, deriving as it does from earlier work on the Yankee City project with Warner and his associates. The image of the community that Arensberg and Kimball employ is that of "an integrated system of mutually interrelated and functionally dependent parts."[47] This image suggests the need for broad coverage of the different realms of life within the community as well as a determination of the way in which a change in one area will have ramifications in other areas.

With respect to the question of whether the boundaries of the system are conceived of as closed or permeable, we may assume, for present purposes, that a system can most usefully be understood as having permeable rather than closed boundaries.[48] With this assumption, the need

42   Bateson, *Steps to an Ecology of Mind*.

43   Gregory Bateson, *Naven*, 2nd ed. (Stanford: University Press, 1958).

44   Walter Buckley, *Sociology and Modern Systems Theory* (Englewood Cliffs, N.J.: Prentice-Hall, 1967).

45   Neal Gross, Ward S. Mason, and Alexander W. McEachern, *Explorations in Role Analysis: Studies of the School Superintendency Role* (New York: John Wiley & Sons, 1958), p. 53.

46   This point is discussed in Eliot D. Chapple, "New Directions in Education in Advanced Technological Societies," *Teachers College Record* 79 (May 1978): 722-36.

47   Arensberg and Kimball, *Family and Community in Ireland*, p. xxvi.

48   Leichter and Mitchell discuss this issue with respect to boundaries between nuclear family and kin in Hope Jensen Leichter and William E. Mitchell, *Kinship and Casework* (New York: Russell Sage Foundation, 1967).

for wide scanning for influence, for example, outside the geographic community, becomes even more evident. As we have seen, the economics of the Irish farm family cannot be understood without looking at remittances and gifts from America, and presumably any change that affected those remittances and gifts from America would produce a change within the farm family and the local farm community as well.

With respect to the question of the tightness of fit of the interrelationships within the whole, we may assume, for present purposes, that even in an "integrated" system of "interdependent" parts, the nature of the integration or the degree of interrelationship of one area to another is not necessarily the same throughout the system. Here the Arensberg and Kimball study again offers a useful example. While the authors assume that the society constitutes an interrelated system, the way in which the different parts of the societal system fit together is by no means similar in all areas of life. On the one hand, the family's involvement with neighbors appears to reinforce its educational function—children see the neighbors' respect for their parents' skill and thereby are influenced in valuing this skill. On the other hand, the family's ties with the school appear almost tangential to the family's main activities —school is described largely in terms of the way in which the children's departure for and return from school fits in with and influences family routines. Yet in still another area, the family's relation to the economy, the connection is seen as so tight that indeed the "spheres are one"— the son is almost totally subordinate to his parents, particularly his father, in these combined realms of family life and economic activity.[49] Thus, even with a functionally oriented systems approach, the nature of the integration within the system varies considerably from one realm to another. An image from topological psychology, that within a whole there may be stronger and weaker *Gestalten*, helps point to this variation in the nature of interrelationships within a system.[50] This implies, for example, that a change in television programming or child-rearing techniques may affect the school, but that the concept of the entire society or some specified community within the society as a system is insufficient to understand the extent to which a change in one area will produce a change in another, apart from further specification.

The augmented perspective to be derived from a systems analysis, as well as the issue of the extent of integration of different parts of the

49   Arensberg and Kimball, *Family and Community in Ireland*, p. 54.
50   Kurt Lewin, *Principles of Topological Psychology* (New York: McGraw-Hill Book Company, 1936), pp. 173-74.

system, is illustrated in the study of the school superintendency role by Gross, Mason, and McEachern, in which systems analysis is specifically applied to the relation of the school to the community. In this analysis, it is argued that a "systems model" as compared with a "position centered model" offers a more meaningful interpretation of the school superintendent's role. In the position-centered model, the school superintendent's role is analyzed in terms of its relationship to a series of other positions. In the systems model, the analysis of the school superintendent's role is augmented by examining the relationship among these several other roles, that is, school board members, teachers, and parents, with the "interrelationships among counter-positions" becoming a central feature of the analysis.[51] In other words, the relationship between parents and teachers influences the behavior of the school superintendent, as does the relationship of either one of them to the superintendent himself. If this concept is applied to the family's relationship to the school, it suggests that it is necessary to understand the family's relationship with relatives, neighbors, and others that impinge upon the family, as well as the relationship of relatives and neighbors to one another, in understanding the family and its relation to the school.

Yet, here again, the problem of the degree of integration of different parts of the system arises. It is necessary to determine those relationships that are most critical for a particular aspect of the family's connection with the school—this cannot automatically be assumed. Nor can it be assumed that all realms of the family's environment are equally salient for its relationship to the school. This point has been made clear in critiques of holistic thinking.[52] Yet, granted these qualifications, the advantage to be derived from the search for sources of education and educational influence that the systems concepts suggest is considerable.

With respect to the question of corrective processes and change, those systems concepts that deal explicitly with these processes offer yet another set of images for consideration. In systems theories that have drawn upon cybernetics, the image of self-corrective mechanisms or feedback within the system itself suggests that the system as a whole is not so tightly knit as to make change impossible. In this perspective, timing becomes critical. As Bateson states, "The characteristics of any

51   Gross, Mason, and McEachern, *Explorations in Role Analysis*, pp. 52-53; for another example of the extensive use of systems perspectives in analyzing schools see Rachel Elboim-Dror, "Some Characteristics of the Educational Policy Formulation System," *Policy Sciences* 1 (Summer 1970): 231-53.

52   D.C. Phillips, *Holistic Thought in Social Science* (Stanford: Stanford University Press, 1976).

system will depend upon timing. Will the corrective event or message reach the point at which it is effective at an appropriate moment ar d will the effect be sufficient? Or will the corrective action be excessive? Or too little? Or too late?"[53] If one applies this image to thinking about the family's relationship to other institutions that educate, it suggests that it is not sufficient merely to look at the family's values as compared with the school's values at a given moment in time; one might look rather at the way in which communication between family and school serves to modify the values and perspectives of each.

Anything approaching a full systems analysis of the family as educator or the family's relation to the school has yet to be undertaken. However, the systems perspective, when it emphasizes corrective processes and change, does suggest a special image of interconnections among institutions, and indeed a special definition of institution itself. When one looks seriously at feedback processes the formal structure becomes less a matter of fixed positions and fixed "rules" than of continuous interaction in which positions and "rules" are negotiated and renegotiated.[54] From this perspective one may see the school, for example, not merely as a hierarchy of statuses, rules, and organizational goals, but also as a complex of transactions among different types of actors: administrators, teachers, guidance counselors, school community workers, teachers, children, and parents. The use of a systems concept implies that the relationship of the family to the school (or to any other institution that educates) cannot be adequately understood merely by looking at the contacts between the family and the school; one must also inquire into other influences that impinge upon the family, the school, or the other institution. It also implies that the relation of the family to the school (or other institution) may change considerably over time and that the process of negotiation between the family and the school must be understood.

THE CONCEPT OF CONFIGURATION

Yet another way of looking at the interrelationships among institutions that educate is suggested by the concept of *configuration*, or the idea that within a society education takes place through certain institutional clusterings. The concept of educational configuration has

53 Bateson, *Naven*, p. 289.

54 For one useful discussion of an institution from this perspective see Anselm Strauss et al., "The Hospital and Its Negotiated Order," in *The Hospital and Modern Society*, ed. Eliot Freidson (London: The Free Press of Glencoe, 1963), pp. 147-69; also Anselm Strauss et al., *Psychiatric Ideologies and Institutions* (London: The Free Press of Glencoe, 1964).

been employed by Cremin to refer to the constellations of institutions that educate in a particular society and the ways in which the various institutions relate to one another and to the society.[55] The institutions that make up the educational configuration or configurations of a particular community vary from one time and place to another. In colonial America, for example, families and churches constituted the most vital elements within the educational configuration, whereas today it is impossible to think of education without considering the media of mass communication, particularly television. The number as well as the kinds of institutions within the configuration of a society may be different from society to society. If one is to understand how the family relates to other institutions that educate, it is important to have some idea of which other institutions are educationally important for the family in a particular time and place. This again suggests the need for flexibility and for a systematic use of varying concepts of community in searching for institutions that fit within a given educational configuration, as well as the need to search beyond the boundaries of a geographic community for educational influence. The classic description by Thomas and Znaniecki of the Polish peasant in Europe and America contains a series of letters between immigrants in the United States and kin in their homeland, which serves to "manifest the persistence of familial solidarity in spite of separation." This again illustrates the fact that an educational configuration may extend beyond a geographic locale.[56]

Within a complex urban industrial society, the variety of institutions that may form an educational configuration is considerable. For a meaningful understanding, one cannot merely look at those institutions that have most educational influence on most people and from this construct a composite picture for an entire society; rather, it is important to look for different clusters for different subgroups within the society.[57] In this respect, some of the community studies of Chicago offer a useful reminder of the extent to which families and individuals in one segment of the larger society may confine their activities to particular, narrow paths within particular communities. The description of the distinction between the Gold Coast and the slum in the classic investigation of Zorbaugh is one illustration.[58]

55 Cremin, *Public Education*, pp. 30-37.

56 William I. Thomas and Florian Znaniecki, *The Polish Peasant in Europe and America*, 2 vols. (1918-20; New York: Dover Publiscations, 1958), p. 303.

57 Cremin, *Traditions of American Education*, pp. 117-19.

58 Harvey Zorbaugh, *The Gold Coast and the Slum* (Chicago: University of Chicago Press, 1929).

Thus, the concept of configuration adds yet another image to the idea of relationships among institutions that educate, suggesting the importance of looking for particular combinations or clusters of institutions and situations at particular times and places.[59] Moreover, it is important to recognize that relationships among institutions within a configuration may take a variety of forms. As Cremin indicates, the relationships among institutions that constitute a configuration may be "political, pedagogical or personal."[60] His observation sets the stage for considering the nature of such relationships.

THE CONCEPT OF LINKAGE

The concept of *linkage* may suggest a specific physical link, as in a chain; it may also be used in a broader sense to refer to the nature of the connections among institutions that educate. A great variety of forms of linkage may be detected. Here Cremin's analysis of historical materials for what they reveal concerning different forms of linkage is useful.[61] The concept of linkage offers yet another way of coming to grips with the question of the degree of integration among institutions within a system.

One important form of linkage among institutions occurs when there is overlapping membership. This is a basic feature of the organization of relationships among kin. Those in a nuclear family of husband, wife, and children are linked to the families of origin of both the husband and the wife, because the husband is simultaneously (during much of the life cycle) a member of both his family of origin and his family of marriage and in the same way the wife is simultaneously a member of both her family of origin and her family of marriage. Similarly, the family is linked to the school because the child goes daily from family to school and back. The child is at the same time a family member and a student in the school. The family is linked to the factory or corporation because the adults in the family are simultaneously members of the family and employees of the factory or corporation and also go daily back and forth between the family and work. Moreover, when individuals hold multiple memberships in several institutions at the same time, the organization of activity—the scheduling and allocation of time—in one area affects the scheduling and organization of activity

59 Since Ruth Benedict's concept of configuration will be discussed below, it is important to note the difference between her concept and the concept cited here.

60 Cremin, *Public Education*, p. 30.

61 Cremin, "Family-Community Linkages in American Education."

in another area.[62] Similarly, the scheduling of activities in the school, and particularly extracurricular activities and homework, may affect the activities that can be carried out in the home.

Another form of linkage arises through communication and exchange among institutions. The concept of linkage has been employed in analyzing the connections between schools and their environment, and here the notion of linkage or linking mechanism often refers to various forms of communication and exchange. The work of Litwak and Meyer offers one example of an instance in which the concept of linkage has been extensively developed in examining school-community relationships. Their analysis largely takes the perspective of school personnel looking toward the community, but it also examines linkages from the perspective of the family, although in less detail. Basic to their analysis is the idea that it is possible to determine an optimal extent of communication, involvement, or social distance between the school and the community and that school-community relations can be improved by working toward this ideal "balance" in the extent of communication. The balance is seen to lie between the extremes of "intimacy" and "isolation"; between the extremes of a "closed door" position, whereby community involvement is seen as extraneous, if not injurious, to the education of a child, and an "open door" position, in which it is assumed that basic educational processes take place outside the school—in the family, peer group, and neighborhood—so that close school-community contacts are necessary. Specific linking strategies are discussed, and particular strategies are recommended for particular situations in accordance with diagnostic schema for classifying families and neighborhoods as well as administrative styles within the school. The mechanisms that are examined for linking the school to the community include the detached worker, the opinion leader, the settlement house, the auxiliary voluntary association and the voluntary association, the mass media, the common messenger, and formal authority.[63]

Although the discussion of the community's use of linking mechanisms for influencing the school is less elaborate than the discussion of the school's use of linking mechanisms in reaching families—since Litwak and Meyer's analysis is addressed to professionals—some consideration is given to linking mechanisms that may be employed by the community,

62 Cf. Rosabeth Moss Kanter, *Men and Women of the Corporation* (New York: Basic Books, 1977).

63 Eugene Litwak and Henry J. Meyer, *School, Family, and Neighborhood: The Theory and Practice of School-Community Relations* (New York: Columbia University Press, 1974), pp. 6-7 and *passim*.

for example, advocate bureaucracy, voluntary associations, the mass media, *ad hoc* demonstrations, sustained collective action, and messengers. In this area, the essential focus is on the way in which community groups may exert political influence over the school. Comparatively little attention is devoted to the daily contacts between parents and teachers, or to the fact that the child is a simultaneous member of both the family and the school and is indeed a "common messenger" between family and school. Where the child is mentioned, for example, as one type of common messenger between the family and the school, it is with the note that "unpaid indigenous participants may, like paid workers, be *low-powered (school children)* or *high-powered (members of the local board of education)* [italics mine]."[64]

Litwak and Meyer's analysis therefore focuses on particular forms of communication between school and community and particular roles and procedures that may be used to enhance this communication. Certain general principles of communication that school personnel may use in analyzing their efforts to create linking mechanisms are reviewed, for example, "the principle of initiative to overcome selective listening" and "intensity to overcome selective retention."[65] Specific suggestions are also made with respect to the kinds of communication strategies that should be employed with particular kinds of families and communities.

While the concept of linkage as used by Litwak and Meyer concentrates on particular procedures of communication between school and community and does not attempt a full tracing of all the influences within the community that may have a bearing on a particular family's relation to the school, the analysis does include a discussion of the organization of the neighborhood. It is interesting to note that the community to which the analysis refers is the "local community" of any particular school, and this is assumed to consist of "families of children who attend it and their immediate neighbors."[66] It is not necessarily a geographically bounded community, since particularly specialized schools may draw their children from widely dispersed geographic areas. Nonetheless, the organization of the local neighborhood is considered to have special importance for the nature of school-community linkages. The authors argue that even in urban industrial societies, the neighborhood can, and often does, provide primary groups

64   Ibid., p. 39.
65   Ibid., pp. 20, 21.
66   Ibid., p. 1.

with assistance in special circumstances such as unanticipated emergencies, but neighborhoods vary considerably in their organization. Whether the neighborhood is heterogeneous, with multiple groups each having a different relationship to the school, as well as the extent of mobility within the neighborhood, are considered of special importance.[67]

The issue of change also arises in connection with the concept of linkage. In the Litwak and Meyer work, there is some discussion of "sequencing" of the various linking mechansims, but theirs is essentially a synchronic model of organizational characteristics, that is, of the administrative style of the school and the organization of primary groups within the neighborhood, and their influence on communication between the school and the community. Yet the issue of change over time is vital to a full conception of linkages among institutions that educate. A family's relation to the school, for example, may change substantially from the period when only one child is in attendance to the period when a second and third child are in attendance, and the family has had more experience relating to the school. The family's relation to the school may also vary significantly as the children's involvement with peers changes with age. The notion of feedback is also relevant to the analysis of linkages, although feedback processes have not been extensively examined in connection with linkages. The notion that communication is at least a two-way process is also important in thinking about the nature of linkages among institutions that educate. Again, Gans offers a useful example in his study of the Italian-Americans of the West End of Boston. The values of the local peer-group society—emphasizing "action-seeking" in contrast to "routine-seeking"—clearly influenced the West Enders' views of the school and other institutions in the outside world. And these attitudes in turn influenced the expectations of school personnel and personnel in other institutions, for example, hospitals and factories, toward members of the local community.[68] This suggests the need to search broadly for a variety of ways in which linkages among institutions may occur and to develop concepts that will make it possible to look at processes of communication over time and not merely at particular linking roles and strategies at a given moment.

Some useful examples of the possibility of extending our concept of linkages are suggested by examination of Arensberg and Kimball's analysis of the relation between the family and other aspects of the community in Ireland. Here, the issue of the visibility of different areas

67   Ibid., chap. 4.
68   Gans, The Urban Villagers.

of life becomes important. In their analysis, the rivalry of adult males in the neighborhood is visible to the young and reinforces their idea of the value of particular skills, so that "the son cannot fail to hear and value the techniques which he acquires."[69] The son not only sees the father in the full range of his daily tasks, but the performance of the father in these tasks is also visible, so that if his performance is wanting, "the criticism of his wife and neighbors soon establishes the value of careful husbandry in the son's mind."[70] A rather different kind of linkage is described between the family and the school, where evidently many of the children's activities in school are not visible to the parents, but interestingly (particularly in contrast to the analysis of Litwak and Meyer) "children are important purveyors of news."[71] Another kind of linkage between family and school is seen in the coordination of activities between family and school in the agricultural community, where priority is often given to the work, even to the extent of keeping children home from school when essential work must be done. "By the time he is ten or eleven he will be brought home from school, if needed, to take his part in the important agricultural work of the year, particularly at spring sowing and hay harvest."[72]

Thus, a variety of kinds of connections may be analyzed between the family and other educative institutions through the concept of linkage. While it may connote wooden, fixed, and mechanical connections, it need not do so if it is employed with sufficiently sophisticated and subtle ideas of communication and of change over time.

THE CONCEPT OF RESONANCE

The concept of *resonance* is useful in suggesting another, very different, level in which connections across diverse educative institutions and settings may be analyzed. The idea of resonance, developed by Métraux in connection with the analysis of cultural imagery, provides one approach to the study of configurations, patterning, ethos, idios, or what has been termed the "integration of culture." The approach is "based on the assumption that the details are consistent and form a coherent whole." The aim of the analysis of cultural imagery is "to organize the details—images—in such a way that the final delineation is an accurate statement of the configuration of a given culture." For this purpose,

---

69 Arensberg and Kimball, *Family and Community in Ireland*, p. 52.
70 Ibid.
71 Ibid., pp. 38-39.
72 Ibid., p. 53.

imagery is seen as "an expression of the perceptual system shared by the members of a society."[73]

The analysis of resonance in imagery is a technique for arriving at an understanding of the interconnections within a culture. It is a particularly helpful concept for present purposes because it actively evokes the idea of connections across domains of experience. As Métraux explains, "To understand and to describe how the world is perceived and what the people are like who so perceive it through imagery, it is necessary to learn to know the cultural models on which imagery is based and through this to work out how one image *echoes* and *reinforces* and *counterpoints* another [italics mine]."[74] For this echoing relationship of images, the term *resonance* is used.

The concept of echoes that reinforce and counterpoint one another offers an approach to the examination of education across different institutions and situations at a level very different from starting with institutional domains commonly named by participants in a culture, for example, family, school, museum, church. Analysts who have been concerned with cultural patterning may tend to emphasize similarities rather than differences across domains, but this approach is helpful in suggesting how that which appears dissimilar at one level of analysis may become similar at another level, and therefore in indicating the need for examination at many levels.

The search for resonance in imagery is similar in this respect to other forms of cultural and symbolic analysis in which the domains are different from common, everyday labels of domains. Benedict's concept of configuration is one classic illustration. In her usage, configuration refers essentially to the dominant themes in a culture, rather than to a particular set of institutional arrangements through which the individual is educated in a particular society, as in the usage of Cremin. In the search for cultural configurations, the need to shift levels is clear. As Franz Boas writes in his introduction to *Patterns of Culture*, "The desire to grasp the meaning of a culture as a whole compels us to consider descriptions of standardized behaviour merely as a stepping-stone leading to other problems." In the search for an appreciation of the inter-relationships between various aspects of a culture and an understanding of the integration or lack of integration of that culture, a "deep penetration into the genius of the culture" is required. Benedict calls this

73   Rhoda Métraux, "Resonance in Imagery," in *The Study of Culture at a Distance*, ed. Margaret Mead and Rhoda Métraux (Chicago: University of Chicago Press, 1953), pp. 343, 350.
74   Ibid., p. 343.

"genius of culture" its "configuration" or its "dominating idea."[75] Thus, particularly if one is interested in understanding the relationship between the individual and the culture, the behaviors become a stepping-stone in the search for the configurations or dominating ideas of the culture.

How the definition of a domain may shift with the level of analysis is further illustrated by Bateson in the discussion of what he calls "common motifs" of relationships among individuals in a society. The issue takes on special significance in heterogeneous cultures. Bateson argues that even in extremely heterogeneous cultures, it is "inconceivable that two differing groups could exist side by side in a community without some sort of mutual relevance between the special characteristics of one group and those of the other."[76] In situations in which the social differentiation within a community is stable, such "mutual relevance" between the special characteristics of one group and those of another is basic. Where one finds extremes of heterogeneity, however, such as in modern "melting pot" communities, the search for common motifs in the relationships among individuals becomes more complex. The analysis of cultural heterogeneity is, of course, essential in examining education across institutions and settings in a complex society, so that Bateson's discussion has particular relevance.

Interestingly, in the attempt to find common motifs or themes that cut across heterogeneity, the solution posed by Bateson entails a shift of the *level* of analyis. His statement is intriguing to anyone who has attempted to wrestle with the complexities of tracing relationships within a complex society. "Suppose we attempt to analyze out all the motifs of relationship between individuals and groups in such a community as New York City; if we did not end up in the madhouse long before we had completed our study, we should arrive at a picture of common character that would be almost infinitely complex—certainly that would contain more fine differentiations than the human psyche is capable of resolving within itself." His picture calls to mind some social science descriptions, but then comes a shift of level; "at this point, then, we and the individuals whom we are studying are forced to take a shortcut: to treat heterogeneity as a positive characteristic of the common environment."[77] The example is striking for anyone attempting to analyze

75   Franz Boas, "Introduction," in *Patterns of Culture*, by Ruth Benedict (1934; Boston: Houghton Mifflin, 1959), pp. xvi, xvii.

76   Gregory Bateson, "Formulation of End Linkage," in *The Study of Culture at a Distance*, ed. Mead and Métraux, p. 369.

77   Ibid.

education in complex communities, but the general point it raises is of particular importance: That which is dissimilar at one level of examination may become similar at another level.

Thus, to apply the concept of resonance and the importance of being able to make shifts in the level of analysis to the relationship between the family and the school, the "dominating idea," the "motif," the "image" of the individual that is expressed in the school may be different from that which is expressed in the family at one level of analysis—leading to an assumption of cultural discontinuity between family and school; yet, at another level of analysis, the same set of ideas may be seen as having underlying similarities. The family, for example, may have a concept of learning that is based on the acquisition of basic skills—reading, writing, and arithmetic—and a style of discipline that is strict and demanding, whereas the school, carrying forward certain notions from the "progressive" era, may have a concept of learning by doing and a more child-centered and "permissive" approach to discipline, therefore appearing very different from the family. Yet, at another level the family and the school may be similar in basing their assumptions about discipline and learning on certain underlying cultural images of individualism and individual responsibility.

The significance of shifting levels for those who have worked with concepts such as *resonance, configuration, ethos, idios, theme*, is related to the distinction between "surface structures" and "deep structures" made by some structuralists today. In a symbolic analysis, too, a shift of institutional domains may take place; two domains may be distinguished at one level but may merge at another level. And here, too, images in one sphere may "echo," "reinforce," and "counterpoint" those in another sphere. An illustration of this shift of domains with the level of scrutiny can be seen in Schneider's analysis of the underlying symbols of American kinship in which he argues that "at the level of 'pure' domain, religion, nationality, and kinship are all the same thing (culturally)."[78] In other words, at the level of cultural symbols, similarities can be found between kinship, nationality, and religion.

This point is often missed in analyses that fail to take sufficient account of the multiple levels in terms of which comparisons across institutions can be made. Symbolic analysis offers a very different perspective from one that takes an institution as an a priori domain, based

---

78   Janet L. Dolgin, David S. Kemnitzer, and David M. Schneider, eds., *Symbolic Anthropology: A Reader in the Study of Symbols and Meanings* (New York: Columbia University Press, 1977), p. 71.

on certain functional requirements of the society, for example, econom-ic, reproductive. Indeed, some symbolic anthropologists argue more abstractly that reification of domains is problematic, resulting in a significant difference between "a social science which relies on *a priori* definitions of what *is*, reified as the categories of analysis, and a social science potentially able to study forms of action-in-process, such as *how* meanings become reified for and by actors." Carrying the argument still further, it is claimed that "the human being, acting, can put new life into old meanings."[79] Thus, the distinction among institutional domains may vanish if one approaches the analysis through symbols of action, and, in attempting to understand the various sources of education for individuals in a society, a narrow definition of institutional domains may obscure the process by which the individual creates meaning as he or she moves through various experiences. Recent work in cognitive anthropology and ethno-science also indicates how a given domain may be defined differently by those within a culture and by observers, that is, how the emic and etic definitions differ. By extension, institutional domains may take on different meanings from different perspectives.[80]

When resonance in imagery is seen as a technique of uncovering rela-tionships that transcend specific domains or areas of experience, a further point arises. To uncover echoing relationships in imagery, the analyst "must continually shift back and forth between intended literal statements and analogy." In this way, it is possible to uncover image clusters or complexes of images that evoke and echo other related images. Moreover, there may be a systematic relationship between images within and among different modalities—"visual, auditory, kines-thetic, tactile, and so on."[81] The ability to shift between literal state-ments and analogy is vital. Here one may draw upon the complex and formal discussions of analogy, metaphor, and metanym in symbolic anthropology and linguistics. The concept of resonance is a useful reminder, too, of the importance of examining relationships across different domains of educational experience in ways that take into account shifts of level and multiple meanings. This is not to suggest

79   Ibid., pp. 27, 31; Dolgin et al. direct their analysis to the process of reification be-cause, in their view, "such reification is the practical key and ontological root of domination" (p. 37). In this respect, some critical perspectives diverge sharply from those of ethnomethod-ology and symbolic interactionism. Understanding the ways in which meaning is created in action may be directed toward uncovering "false consciousness" but this need not necessarily be the aim of such analysis.

80   Getzels's discussion of the variety of definitions of the community is useful in this respect, cf. Getzels, "The Communities of Education."

81   Métraux, "Resonance in Imagery," p. 351.

that one should abandon the analysis of institutions that educate in terms of definitions based on participants' concepts or some analytic schema for defining domains; it is rather to suggest that an institutional analysis is incomplete unless it is placed beside a cultural and symbolic analysis that is sufficiently subtle to search actively for a variety of ways in which similarity and dissimilarity may occur. The need for multiple levels and complex analyses of cultures is clear in the work of those who have sought to find configurations or themes that carry over from one area of a culture to another. As Benedict indicates, "There is no 'law,' but several different characteristic courses which a dominant attitude may take," even dominant themes take on different meaning in different settings. The dominant motifs may be applied in some situations and curtailed in others, with the result that there is "unevenness in the extent to which behaviour is coloured by the dye of the cultural pattern."[82] Thus, the need to combine different levels of analysis is again highlighted.

THE CONCEPT OF MEDIATION

Yet another concept that directs attention to very different aspects of the relationship among educative institutions is the concept of *mediation*. For our purposes the concept of mediation will be used to refer to those processes by which the family (or other institution) filters educational influences—the processes by which it screens, interprets, criticizes, reinforces, complements, counteracts, refracts, and transforms. While the term *mediation* is sometimes used to refer to processes of negotiation in situations of conflict, for example, mediation in labor union-employer negotiations, the use intended here is not restricted to situations of conflict. A preliminary discussion of the way in which the family mediates the educational experiences of its members in other spheres is discussed in *The Family as Educator*.[83] As applied to the family, the concept refers to the ways in which the family negotiates and creates meaning in the educational experiences of its members, both adults and children. The family mediates not only with respect to school but with respect to other institutions, particularly television.[84]

The concept of mediation may be further spelled out with reference to terms related to those used in the definition. The term *screen* implies

82   Benedict, *Patterns of Culture*, pp. 238, 239.
83   Leichter, "Some Perspectives on the Family as Educator."
84   The mediation of television by the family is currently being studied in one of the projects in the Center for the Study of the Family as Educator.

a selective process and may also be expressed in words such as pick out, lay over, sort, divide, separate, segregate, keep apart, or in a somewhat different meaning, hide, conceal, or mask. The term *interpret* may be taken to mean construe, infer, explain, explicate, diagnose, analyze. The term *criticize* may be taken to mean judge, comment upon, remark upon, censure. The term *reinforce* may be taken to mean intensify, exaggerate, magnify, sharpen, consolidate. The term *complement* may mean supplement, fill in, round out. The term *counteract* may be taken to mean go contrary to, contradict, oppose, contrast, offset, take issue with, take a stand against, counterbalance. The term *refract* may be taken to mean divert, diverge, turn, bend, twist, diffuse, disperse. The term *transform* may be taken to mean transfigure, transmute, convert, revamp, or, in a slightly different sense, metabolize. This variety of terms related to the definition of educational mediation is presented in order to direct attention to everyday acts of filtering and interpretation. Mediation is thus the moment-to-moment process of interpretation and reinterpretation or the creation of educational reality on the part of those in a particular setting, such as the family. If refers to processes within an institution that affect the definition of reality vis-à-vis other settings.

The concept of mediation has been most fully explored with reference to the family, for example, in the work of Berger and Luckmann, who discuss the fact that "significant others" in the family mediate the world of the child and "modify it in the course of mediating."[85] This modification is a form of filtering and selecting. The term *mediation* has also been used with reference to other institutions, for example, in the discussion by Berger of "mediating structures," in which he refers broadly to primary groups.[86] The concept of mediation, however, may also be applied to related processes within other institutions, particularly schools. The school, for example, mediates the child's experience in the family in a variety of ways, some subtle, some not so subtle, by criticizing, evaluating, and appraising aspects of the child's family life. The classic example of the treatment of Sioux Indian children in government schools discussed by Erik Erikson is perhaps an extreme instance of deliberate attempts to filter out the influence of the family, but it suggests processes that may go on in subtler forms in other situations.

85 Berger and Luckmann, *The Social Construction of Reality*, p. 131.
86 Peter L. Berger, "In Praise of Particularity: The Concept of Mediating Structures," *The Review of Politics* 38 (1976): 399-410; also Peter L. Berger and Richard Neuhaus, *To Empower People: The Role of Mediating Structures in Public Policy* (Washington, D.C.: American Enterprise Institute, 1977).

According to one source cited by Erikson: "Children were virtually kidnapped to force them into government schools, their hair was cut and their Indian clothes were torn away. They were forbidden to speak in their own language . . . those who persisted in clinging to their old ways and those who ran away and were recaptured were thrown into jail. Parents who objected were also jailed. Where possible, children were kept in school year after year to avoid the influence of their families . . . ."[87] In more general terms, Waller describes the way in which "the school serves as a point from which the cultural standards of the larger group are mediated . . . sifted and selected."[88] Thus, the concept of mediation may be usefully employed to examine processes within a broad range of institutions.

It is especially important to examine mediation within the family, however, because of the fact that family membership goes on over time and the return to the family on a daily basis makes the family a critical locale for the discussion and interpretation of experiences that take place elsewhere. Mediation within the family may be examined not only with respect to school but to the range of other institutions with which family members are in contact, for example, hospitals, clinics, museums, parks, and, of course, television.

Several important points about the process of mediation within the family may be noted. First, since mediation refers to the day-to-day process of interpretation of events, consistency does not necessarily exist among the various members of a family. Indeed, the differences in points of view within a family may be a vital stimulus for discussion, criticism, appraisal, and interpretation. The point may be obvious in terms of one's own daily experience, but analyses of the family's relation to the school often overlook the variety of perspectives that may exist within a family ("the family" is treated as a monolithic unit), especially in discussions of value differences between the school and particular ethnic groups. Since all families bring together individuals of somewhat different backgrounds, ages, and experiences, differences of perspective must be expected as a basic feature of the family, and these differences set the stage for mediation and interpretation of events.

Another important consideration is that families exhibit different styles of mediation. In dealing with schools, for instance, some families are assertive, assuming that the school will not take care of the educa-

87 Erik H. Erikson, *Childhood and Society* (New York: W.W. Norton Co., Inc., 1950), pp. 117-18.

88 Willard Waller, *The Sociology of Teaching* (New York: John Wiley & Sons, Inc., 1932), pp. 103, 107.

tional needs of the child unless pushed to do so, whereas others are more passive, defining the school as an unavoidable part in the child's life, but not the basic source of the child's education, which must be undertaken at home. Beyond this, different members of the family may mediate particular educational experiences in different ways. And the same family may mediate differently with respect to different institutions. For example, a family may accept a medical diagnosis without critical appraisal but take a strong adversary stand with respect to a school issue.

Yet another point about the process of mediation is that it may be either direct or indirect. Mediation vis-à-vis another institution may go on indirectly through discussions within the family about experiences in that institution, or directly through contact and discussions with representatives of the institution. A visit to the principal's office at the time of a particular crisis, such as a decision about a child's school placement, may stand out in memory as an event of special significance, yet by sheer repetition, the day-to-day discussions of educational experiences in other institutions have a cumulative effect that must not be ignored.[89] And mediation may take place through subtle, even elliptic, modes of communication. Thus, even for the child who responds to the parent's query, "What happened in school today?" with "Nothing," the school experience is nonetheless remembered, reenacted, and reinterpreted in the setting of the home.

Since most television viewing takes place within the home, the question of how the family mediates television is of particular importance. An examination of mediation of television by the family also illustrates the potential value of the concept of mediation. Much of the literature on the impact of television assumes, at least implicitly, that television viewing takes place in a vacuum. Yet it is clear most television viewing takes place in a social context and that families exert a variety of different kinds of efforts to influence the television experience of their members.

While much of the current literature on television is alarmist in flavor,[90] this literature also points to the great differences that may exist among families in their handling of television, and these differences in the handling of television suggest basic features of the process of educational mediation by the family. The process by which the family

89   This point is made vividly in Philip Jackson's *Life in Classrooms* (New York: Holt, Rinehart & Winston, 1968).

90   The character of some recent criticism of television is reflected in Marie Winn, *The Plug-In Drug: Television, Children, and the Family* (New York: Viking Press, 1977).

selects its television viewing is one aspect of mediation. Some families exert little or no effort to select and control the television viewing of their children, although they may differ among themselves in the selection of programs. Other families engage in rigorous planning of television viewing, setting specific schedules and criteria for watching programs and elaborate rules with regard to the number of hours watched and the times during which television may be seen. Still other families are totally opposed to television and simply do not have television sets in their homes, thus presumably blocking out the influence of television (although one may wonder in such cases whether the children have access to television in the homes of others). The process of selection with respect to television is undoubtedly connected with the way in which television is integrated into the family's habits of living, and particularly the organization of time. In some families television is a dominant clock around which other family routines (and even meals) are scheduled, whereas in other families the scheduling of other activities (and even meals) takes priority, interrupting programs of considerable interest that are generally regarded by the family as acceptable or desirable. Some families deal with television viewing in a regularized and routine manner, while others fluctuate over time in their efforts to select from and control television.

The process of criticism and appraisal of television represents another feature of the family's mediation. Here again, families differ in the extent to which they make deliberate attempts to interpret, counteract, and criticize the materials that are seen on television. In this respect, it is important to recognize that the processes of criticism and appraisal occur on a moment-to-moment basis even in families that are not deliberate and systematic in their critical efforts. From the perspective of research strategies, it is difficult to determine when such interpretations of television take place; the salient discussions and negotiations do not necessarily go on during actual television viewing; indeed, it is possible that there may be less discussion at that time. By contrast, such discussions may take place during meals or, if the family does not eat regularly together, during fleeting encounters at other times. This means that the understanding of the family's criticism and interpretation of television requires an almost round-the-clock examination of moment-to-moment encounters. A passing joke about an ad may, for example, contain the premises upon which a more embellished "literary criticism" of artistic style could be based. In fact, the criticism and appraisal of television may be so interwoven with other aspects of family discussion that television programs may become a basis for common experience of family members and become part of their repertoire of personal history, with television events being referred to with terms such as "Do you remember?" or "That is like the time we . . . ." In this sense, criticism is not necessarily negative judgment but includes commenting upon.

The processes by which the family attempts to counteract the influence of television represent another form of educational mediation. Once again, families undoubtedly differ in their strategies, as well as in the content of the issues where they feel it is necessary to take a stand on materials presented on television. Some families attempt to counteract violent scenes in television dramas, for example, by suggesting that this is imaginary. Other families attempt to counteract interpretations of the news commentators, for example, by suggesting that the presentation and selection of news materials are biased or one-sided. Still other families take a laissez-faire approach with respect to contradicting materials on television. And others, particularly when the objectional material is unanticipated, attempt to misdirect or momentarily divert attention, for example, during an unexpectedly frank love scene, suggesting to the child that the cat needs to be fed.

Yet another feature of the family's mediation of television is the process by which the family attempts to complement or supplement materials seen on television, for example, by suggesting additional readings following a program of interest on animals or a trip to a museum in a deliberate effort to further an interest stimulated by television. Again, families doubtless differ in their independence with respect to the directions suggested by television, particularly through commercials. Some families rush to purchase an educational toy advertised on television, whereas others reject it out of hand because it was advertised.

These examples are intended to show the variety of ways in which the process of mediation can take place in the family and to suggest some parameters along which families vary. Undoubtedly, the mediation of television varies significantly with the family's values, its economic resources, the organization of time and space in the home, the number of television sets, the number of members of the family, the relationship across generations, and a host of other factors. As yet, however, little is known about the process of mediation itself, let alone the way in which variations are related to other aspects of the family's life.

In addition to the fact that mediation is an ongoing, moment-to-moment process, certain other generic features of mediation are worth noting. As with other aspects of family interaction, the processes of mediation of television take place on multiple levels. Often the gap between ideal and actuality is sharp. Perhaps in part as a reflection of recent criticisms of television, parents sometimes voice considerable guilt for their failure to monitor their children's television viewing sufficiently and apprehension lest the television viewing of their children interfere with their children's school achievement. Indeed, an underlying question about this gap between intent and actuality concerns why some families find it so difficult to turn the television off, even when they disapprove of its content. This is particularly interesting since television, in contrast to schooling, takes place largely within the privacy of the home, and the family therefore has the right and the final decision with respect to whether, when, and how much to watch.

Another general feature of the mediation of television is that it is intertwined with and reflects other aspects of the interpersonal relationships within the family. Television may be the focus of differences and resentments that arise in other areas, for example, when wives criticize their husbands for too much television watching and not taking their share of household responsibilities, in keeping with newly emerging conceptions of men's and women's roles. Alliances within a family may be expressed in negotiations with respect to television viewing or may evolve in working out or contending with differences regarding television. Siblings may dispute over program preferences. One sibling may take sides with a parent on rules regarding television viewing during mealtime, while siblings may align with each other in pleading with a parent to delay a meal in order to see the conclusion of a favorite show. Differences between parents in basic values and concepts of education may arise and be triggered in negotiations concerning which programs to watch and how to monitor the children's television habits. One child may make fun of another child's interest in a particular show and even report a teacher's criticism of that show. While such differences may become a matter of heated argument, the fact of different perspectives within the family does indeed set the stage for the process of mediation.

These examples of the family's mediation with respect to television are intended to illustrate the concept of mediation generally. However, in view of the vast amount of television viewing that takes place today, the issue of the family's handling of television is likely to receive increased attention in years to come.[91] The family's handling of television is important in its own right and also in terms of the way in which television viewing fits into other activities of family members. Hope-

91   In 1953, 10 percent of American homes had television. In 1976, 97 percent of homes had television, with at least one member looking at television on the average of six out of every twenty-four hours. Cf. Cremin, *Public Education*, pp. ix-x: the extent of television watching today is also discussed in Winn, *The Plug-in Drug*.

fully, as research on television and the family progresses, it will be framed in terms that enable an understanding not merely of television and the family, but also of the broader educational processes within the family and the family's relation to other institutions that educate.[92]

The processes by which the family mediates the educational experiences of its members in other institutions may usefully be examined not merely with respect to television and the schools, but with respect to the whole range of institutions in which family members have educational experiences. Museums offer another interesting example where one may examine the ways in which the family selects, criticizes, appraises, complements, and transforms the museum experiences of its members, both during a museum visit and through discussions in the home before and after such a visit.[93] Experiences with hospitals and other health-care agencies are undoubtedly another realm where one can clearly see the processes by which the family mediates the experiences of its members. The essential point about mediation is that the experience of education in one sphere is reinterpreted through experiences in another sphere.

One example of a broader use of the concept of mediation is the analysis of Berger in which "mediating structures" are seen as part of the relationship among institutions within the society. Mediating structures for Berger are "those institutions which stand between the individual in his private sphere and the larger institutions of the public sphere." Berger argues that a dichotomy exists between two realms of life in modern societies, that is, the megastructures and private life. "These two spheres of modern society are experienced by the individual in very different ways. The megastructures are remote, often hard to understand or downright unreal, impersonal, and *ipso facto* unsatisfactory as sources of individual meaning and identity." By contrast, "private life is experienced as the single most important area for the discovery and the actualization of meaning and identity." Thus, certain institutions function as "mediating structures" with respect to other areas of life. The mediating institutions are the family, church, voluntary association, neighborhood, and subculture. In Berger's analysis these mediating structures are essential if private life is to remain "home," although this does not necessarily mean that they must continue in traditional forms, but rather that "the institutional anchorage

92   This discussion has drawn upon interviews conducted through the Center for the Study of the Family as Educator on the mediation of television by the family.

93   This process is examined in Deborah Parr Benton's "Intergenerational Interaction in Museums" (Ed.D. diss., Teachers College, Columbia University).

for individual need and identity" is derived from the mediating structures. Berger thus argues that the family and other private spheres serve
to provide the individual with meaning and thereby with a basis for
interpreting experience in other spheres. The mediating structures create
not merely a sense of meaning that is lost in the larger structures, but,
more important, a general sense of morality or "collective conscience."[94]
This line of argument suggests another reason why it is vital to understand the processes by which meaning is re-created within the family
and other mediating structures.

While it may be that the "mediating structures" create meaning in
ways that are different from the megastructures, broadly speaking, as
here defined, mediation can be examined in any institution vis-à-vis
other institutions; even if the processes of mediation are different in
different kinds of institutions, the same general questions about filtering, transformation, and screening may usefully be asked across institutions, since they represent the processes by which experience in
one sphere is reinterpreted through experience in another sphere. And,
to return briefly to the various meanings of mediation, perhaps the
most essential thrust is contained in the term *transformation*. Through
criticism, interpretation, and even reenactment, the meaning of experience is reinterpreted. The concept of mediation, therefore, represents
yet another approach to the examination of ways in which education
in one institution is related to education in another.

COMPARISONS ACROSS INSTITUTIONS AND SETTINGS

Yet another, somewhat different, approach to the examination of relationships among educative institutions and settings is the comparison of
one institution with another in terms of its structure and the ways in
which teaching and learning are organized. This approach does not deal
directly with the connections among institutions, either in terms of
particular roles that are set up to link one institution with another or
with the processes by which experience in one institution is reinterpreted
in another. Rather, it offers a different, but complementary, perspective
on relationships across institutions. Such comparisons have special sali-
ence in light of the recurrent assumptions and questions in educational
and social science theory about the consequences of similarity and dissimilarity, continuity and discontinuity, in the individual's experience in
different settings.[95] Assuming that one can settle on a sufficiently

94 Berger, "In Praise of Particularity," pp. 401, 402, 403.
95 Getzels, "The Communities of Education."

definitive, although provisional, definition of an institution or setting (whether from the analyst's or the participant's point of view), such an approach offers much of potential value.

Two sets of questions arise in comparing institutions that educate: first, how to select from among the many institutions and situations those in which significant education takes place, and second, what dimensions to use in making comparisons.

Assuming that a wide range of institutions do indeed educate in one way or another, whether or not education is their formal mandate or their primary task, one may search broadly for sources of education. And, given a definition of institution that is broad enough to include a range of settings and situations—not merely those bounded by a particular organizational structure, time duration, or geographic location—the possible list of institutions that educate becomes almost infinitely long, particularly in a complex urban industrial society. Such a list could include kin, neighbors, friends and peers, work places—corporations, businesses, industries, factories; religious institutions—churches, synagogues, Sunday schools; law enforcement agencies—police, courts, juries; military institutions, custodial institutions, hospitals and health-care institutions, libraries, museums, parks, recreational programs, clubs, associations, theaters, concert halls, service and welfare agencies, television programs, films, radio, newspapers, periodicals and other media. When one adds not only schools, colleges, universities, and other formal educational institutions but the host of lessons that can be obtained in many areas, such as sewing, cooking, hairstyling, writing, grooming, reading, music, sports, photography, arts and crafts, typing, driving, baby care, and drama, the possible list of institutions and settings in which education takes place becomes still longer.[96] This already lengthy list suggests an even longer list that could readily be compiled by examining the range of associations, clubs, and health, welfare, and recreational institutions that educate, even though education is not their primary formal task.

Whatever regional differences may exist, the variety of sources of education is so great and the potential list so long that the issue of leverage, primacy, or significance becomes important, that is, the issue of how to determine which of the numerous institutions have maximum educational importance. Clearly, as will be seen below, the diversity

96 An interesting list of educative institutions is contained in Richard Saul Wurman, ed., *Yellow Pages of Learning Resources* (Cambridge: MIT Press, 1972). A brief examination of the yellow pages of the New York City phone directory under schools also immediately suggests this great variety. This section includes twenty-five pages of listings of schools and lesson-givers.

of institutions through which particular individuals move is considerable. From a societal perspective, it is necessary to find criteria for determining which institutions exert major educational influence and therefore warrant special examination in considering the educational issues of a particular time and place. It has been shown that the clustering of institutions and the weight of one institution as compared with another can vary substantially from one society and one era to another.[97] If one considers which institutions are encountered by the largest number of individuals within the society, one criterion for evaluating impact is offered. In these terms, the families, the media, schools, places of work, and possibly religious institutions are clearly important today, as are clusterings of individuals such as kin and neighbors. However, in an effort to simplify the task of examining institutions, it is not necessarily helpful to limit one's examination to those that influence the largest number of individuals. If, for example, one shifts to an examination of the time spent in various locations, some surprises may emerge.[98] Moreover, for some purposes, the search for diversity of clusters may be of particular importance, for example, in comparing rural and metropolitan areas.

Yet the issue of leverage or significance remains vital for policy and practice, for it becomes important to know which institutions the society can rely on for what kinds of tasks. Assuming that it is possible to formulate a meaningful list of institutions and situations in which education takes place, one may move on to the second question, namely, which dimensions to use in comparing institutions. Here again, one faces a long list of possibilities, and different dimensions emerge, depending on whether one examines the institution from the perspective of the learner or from the perspective of those working in the institution, that is, the teachers. A variety of organizational dimensions, such as administrative style, have been considered to have a bearing on the relationship between institutions that educate and their surrounding environment. Such analyses, however, often focus on the relationship of educators in the institution to their clients outside it, rather than on the comparison of education as it takes place inside and outside the institution. Most comparisons to date have contrasted the family

---

97   Cremin, *Traditions of American Education.*

98   Here Barker and Wright's analysis of the "occupancy times" in various community settings is instructive, particularly in indicating the extensive time spent in "trafficways"; Roger G. Barker and Herbert F. Wright, *Midwest and its Children: The Psychological Ecology of an American Town* (Hamden, Conn.: Archon Books, 1971) (First published, 1955), especially pages 108-09.

and the school, particularly where a cultural gap or discontinuity is assumed to exist between family and school. Here it is worth noting that not merely the modes of instruction but also, as suggested by LeVine,[99] the modes of evaluating may be significant dimensions of comparison.

In examining educative institutions from the perspective of those working in them, the organizational literature suggests a wide range of dimensions for consideration. If one's purpose is to consider possible roles of educators—either those that exist or those that might exist— a number of dimensions may be examined, such as the way in which coordination of roles in one area of the institution with those in another area is worked out and the extent to which the institution is formally or informally organized.[100]

In examining institutions that educate from the perspective of the learner, a somewhat different set of concerns emerges. Here one may raise such questions as who educates, how the person being educated participates, what the attitude of the participant is, how those being educated are grouped or separated, and the differences in education for those of various backgrounds or different sexes. An interesting list of dimensions from both the institutional and the learner's perspective is offered in Jules Henry's outline for a cross-cultural comparison of education. This outline, while intended for a somewhat different purpose, nevertheless raises useful questions that may be included in comparisons across institutions and settings within a society, and applied to the education of adults as well as to the education of children. His outline contains considerable detail within each heading and covers the following basic points: (1) On what does the educational process focus, for example, environment, values, use of mind? (2) How is the information communicated (teaching methods)? (3) Who educates, for example, males, females, relatives, older children? (4) How does the person being educated participate (what is his attitude), for example, accepting, rejecting, resisting, defiant, eager? (5) How does the educator participate (what is his attitude), for example, eager, bored, embarrassed, insecure? (6) Are some things taught to some and not to others, for

99   Robert A. LeVine, "Western Schools in Non-Western Societies: Psychological Impact and Cultural Response," *Teachers College Record* 79 (May 1978): 749-55.

100   Some of these issues of the educative roles that exist in a variety of institutions and settings are being discussed in a seminar at the Center for the Study of the Family as Educator, focusing on education in community settings. The participants in the seminar are Vera Hamid, Hope Jensen Leichter, David Thornton Moore, Hervé Varenne, Sloan Wayland, and Ruth Westheimer.

example, differences by age, sex? (7) What are the discontinuities in the educational process, for example, in values and techniques, and between age groups and sexes? (8) What limits the quantity and quality of the information a child receives from a teacher, for example, methods of teaching, available time? (9) What forms of conduct control (discipline) are used? (10) What is the relation between the intent and the result of education? (11) What self-conceptions seem reinforced? (12) How long does the process of formal education last?[101]

A few of the many basic dimensions derived from the outline and elsewhere may be examined to indicate the possibility of comparisons across institutions and settings.

Who Teaches and Learns with and from Whom? Institutions and settings that educate vary considerably with respect to those who participate as teachers and learners. For the social composition of those involved, the term co-presence may be used.[102] Institutions that educate vary in the age and sex composition of their participants and in the range of the life cycle that is covered, that is, the ages and stages of life of those who are educated together. Here an interesting contrast may be seen between churches, where the entire family attends together, television programs that are watched by all members of the family, and regular school classes that are specifically separated by age.

Institutions that educate also vary in their implicit and explicit concepts about the learning that is appropriate at different stages of development, the time during which a particular skill, for example, sports, music, or math, can most readily be acquired, and the age at which it is too late to learn this skill. While experiments in modifying age-grading within schools have been made, for example, nongraded classes and variation in the age of kindergarten entry, by and large, rather specific age-grading inheres in much curriculum thinking, for example, particular kinds of learning are deemed appropriate for particular ages. This implies that a different set of premises must be worked out in institutions that seek to educate more than one generation at the same time. Some institutions that seek to educate more than one age group, wittingly or not, gear their instructional procedures and levels to those of a particular age, for example, museums may direct the eye

---

101   Jules Henry, *On Education* (New York: Vintage Books, 1972), especially chap. 5, "A Cross-Cultural Outline of Education," pp. 76-88.

102   This term arose in a Conference on Multi-Generational Education at the Center for the Study of the Family as Educator, Teachers College, Columbia University, Spring 1977.

level of their displays and the explanatory level of their texts to upper elementary-age boys.

Variations also exist in assumptions about whether older members learn from younger, or younger from older, and whether teachers are specifically designated or include peers or other participants. Some interesting special issues arise where families are educated together, for example, the difficulty that parents sometimes experience when children go to a museum with prior knowledge that exceeds that of their parents. These difficulties have been recognized by museum educators, and special procedures for instructing parents prior to their tour of a museum with their children have actually been tried out.[103]

The question of who teaches and learns from whom also relates to the criteria that are used for entry into an educative institution or setting, both for full participants and "permitted intruders."[104] Criteria for inclusion in an institution may range from highly exclusive and specific, for example, only those that pass certain tests or have certain prior credentials, to more open criteria or those based on ascription, for example, being a member of a particular family or community.

The nature of co-presence in an educational institution or setting also varies depending on the procedures that are use to organize groupings within the insitition, for example, the placement procedures. Here criteria may vary from special examination for placement purposes to duration of time in the institution (e.g., in an in-service training program in industry), to special needs (e.g., personal growth courses for industrial executives), to fixed ascriptive criteria (e.g., those whose birthdays are prior to September 1).

The examination of who teaches and learns with and from whom suggests that when one moves outside of formal educational institutions such as schools, the structure of co-presence may vary considerably, particularly in terms of age and generation, with related differences in assumptions about the nature and processes of education, making co-presence an important dimension for comparison.

Outcome Measures and Markings Educational institutions and settings also vary in the procedures that are used to evaluate and mark

103   An interesting program for instructing parents was discussed at the Conference on Multi-Generational Education by Karen Hensel, Curator of Education at the New York Aquarium.

104   This term was suggested by Rhoda Métraux at the Smithsonian Conference. Willard Waller's discussion of school-community relations is also instructive in this respect, Waller, *The Sociology of Teaching.*

their outcomes. The differences that may arise in evaluation are vividly described in the article of LeVine.[105] Procedures of evaluation range from formal examination—inside or outside the institution—to informal comments of approval for something learned well, to no comment at all. The schools clearly vary in the extent to which they make public differences of achievement on the part of students, from publicly posting grades to privately discussing evaluative comments. Families, too, vary in their procedures of evaluating educational attainment, from openly acknowledged—even monetary—rewards for grades attained in school to private, circumspect discussions of report cards. Families vary, too, in their handling of differences among siblings, from open comparison of the achievements of one sibling with another to attempts to downplay competition and build up different areas of achievement in different children. Here an interesting point is whether and how the standards of evaluation differ for boys and girls.

In comparing educative institutions in their procedures for evaluation and measurement of achievement, it is important not to lose sight of the distinction between the acquisition of knowledge and the acquisition of credentials. In a society in which a great variety of institutions offer some sort of credential (and recently even "life experience" has been considered a basis for academic credit), it becomes particularly important to examine the way in which credentials from one institution pertain to other institutions and influence life-chance opportunities. No matter how important the family may be as the basic educational institution of society, even the family with the highest level of technical skills and knowledge cannot give a Ph.D, M.D., B.A., or any other degree.

Other kinds of markings, in addition to credentials, may also indicate the outcome of education. A wide range of rituals serve to mark successful conclusion of educational undertakings. Often these rituals are modeled on procedures used in schools, even in other kinds of institutions, for example, graduation ceremonies with cap, gown, recitation, and diplomas to mark the successful conclusion of a Sunday school program. Sometimes, by contrast, the completion of a sequence of learning is barely marked, as when one walks through a museum display and simply leaves at the end. Most television programs contain little marking at the completion of a sequence, even when they are explicitly educational, although some special educational programs do include related home-study sequences with formal indicators of satisfactory completion of units.[106]

---

105   LeVine, "Western Schools in Non-Western Societies."
106   Some work of the Open University in England is interesting in this respect.

While the procedures of measuring and marking the outcomes of education have not as yet received extensive comparative examination either across societies or across institutions within a society, the issue of similarity or difference in these procedures is clearly one that warrants consideration.

The Organization of Space Spatial organization is yet another dimension in terms of which educative institutions may usefully be compared.[107] Spatial organization must necessarily occur, and this organization varies from one institution and setting to another. The organization of space both reflects and influences other spheres of human interaction.

Explicit attention has been devoted to the relationship between spatial organization and learning, for example, in school architecture and city planning.[108] Some curricular innovations, for example, the open classroom, assume that varying the spatial organization of activities will modify and improve learning. Spatial organization may be deliberately used to enhance learning both in obvious and in more subtle ways. Turner's description of the use of disproportion in initiation ceremonies points to a fascinating manner in which modification of the size of a cultural object is used to foster learning. When some cultural objects are represented as disproportionately large or small, huge or tiny, by comparison with their normal size, this, in Turner's analysis, serves to foster "a primordial mode of abstraction."[109] This suggests a possible connection between the scale of spatial organization in a setting or cultural object, particularly whether it is on a "human scale," and the nature of learning that takes place. For example, television viewing with a large screen—particularly a life-size or super life-size screen—may be different from television viewing with a small screen, and viewing a movie where the image is blown up beyond life size may be different from viewing television on a small screen where the image is miniaturized.[110]

Spatial organization is also an important dimension in comparing educative institutions because it influences the character of interactions that take place within an educational setting. For example, the number and placement of television sets within the home is undoubtedly related

107 The importance of space in the family's educative functions was discussed in Leichter, "Some Perspectives on the Family as Educator."

108 Cf. the interesting discussion of the organization of space and distances between the home and other institutions in Doxiadis, *Ekistics*.

109 Victor Turner, *The Forest of Symbols: Aspects of Ndemdu Ritual* (Ithaca and London: Cornell University Press, 1967), p. 103.

110 This issue was raised in the Smithsonian seminar by Margaret Mead.

to the amount, timing, and organization of viewing on the part of family members, as well as the way in which television is combined with other activities; for example, in some homes the television set may be placed where it is visible from a meal table, while in others it may be placed in a far corner of the room out of the range of other activities and even covered over when not in use.

While the educational implications of certain aspects of spatial organization have been explicitly examined in educational architecture and planning, some of the less explicit ways in which the organization of space may vary from one institution to another are worth considering, particularly since spatial organization is often at the margins of awareness.[111]

The boundaries that mark different activities and the space that is considered appropriate for an activity varies from one setting to another. In some institutions, particular spaces may be set aside for particular activities, for example, art rooms within a school, whereas in other institutions the same space may be used for a variety of activities, for example, the kitchen table, which may be used for cooking, eating, or studying. Definitions of the spatial boundaries of institutions also vary. In some institutions the boundaries may be conceived of as extending out in widening circles, for example, the school building, the school yard, the school district, or the health-care building and the health-care district, whereas in others the boundaries are more circumscribed, for example, the family's home or yard.

Spatial organization also varies with respect to the boundaries or territories that separate or relate different participants. The issue of personal space or privacy clearly arises in a range of settings. Philip Jackson's vivid description of crowding in elementary school classrooms provides an instance in which minimal recognition is given to the individual's need for personal space.[112] At the same time, most classrooms do have individually assigned territories, whether desks or lockers. By contrast, the individual moving through a museum rarely has any personal territory within the institution, while the individual in a hospital may be assigned to a particular bed, yet have personal possessions removed—for safekeeping—to another area, thus at least partially stripping him of personal "identity equipment." And in prisons the inmate may lose even more control over personal space and identity equipment.[113]

---

111   Edward T. Hall, *The Hidden Dimension* (Garden City, N.Y.: Doubleday and Co., 1966).

112   Jackson, *Life in Classrooms.*

113   Cf. Erving Goffman, *Asylums: Essays on the Social Situations of Mental Patients and Other Inmates* (Chicago: Aldine Publishing Co., 1961); also David J. Rothman, *The Discovery*

The scale of spatial organization represents yet another way in which institutions may vary. As Turner has suggested, unusual handling of scale may be a deliberate procedure for fostering learning and abstraction, but scale may also exist and influence education in less explicit ways. The contrast in scale may be of special importance in the transition from home to school for young children, since even where there is crowding within a classroom, the size of the spaces in the school may be very different from the size of spaces in the home. In some instances, deliberate efforts may be made to change the scale of the space for particular activities.[114]

In considering the similarity or dissimilarity in the organization of space across institutions, it is important to recognize that physical space and definitional space are interrelated. Thus, that which is defined as crowded for some individuals or subcultures may be defined as spacious by others.[115] And here, as elsewhere, one faces the complex yet important problem of examining institutions both in terms of the views of participants and from the perspective of the outside analyst.

The Organization of Time   The organization of behavior in time represents another dimension that is useful in understanding education within particular institutions and in comparing one institution or setting with another. Some ways in which time may be viewed in considering the family as educator have been discussed in *The Family as Educator*.[116] The organization of activities in time is fundamental in any area of social life, since "all forms of coordination involve problems of time, synchronization, and sequence."[117] And the organization of time in one institution is not only important in its own right but may also have consequences for the organization of time in other institutions. Many examples may be given of the way in which the time organization in one institution affects that in another. In France, for instance, where

---

of the Asylum: Social Order and Disorder in the New Republic (Boston: Little, Brown, and Co., 1971); also Michel Foucault, *Discipline and Punish: The Birth of the Prison* (New York: Pantheon, 1977).

114   The People Center and the Discovery Room at the American Museum of Natural History represent interesting examples of efforts to create more intimate space within the museum's large-scale architecture. For a description see Malcomb Arth, "The People Center—Anthropology for the Layman," *Curator* 18 (1975): 315-25.

115   Hall, *Hidden Dimension*; also Ashcraft and Schleflen, *People Space*; also Robert Somer, *Personal Space: The Behavioral Basis of Design* (Englewood Cliffs, N.J.: Prentice-Hall, Inc., 1969).

116   Leichter, "Some Perspectives on the Family as Educator."

117   Wilbert E. Moore, *Man, Time and Society* (New York: John Wiley & Sons, Inc., 1963), p. 136.

children had a midweek holiday and attended classes on Saturday, the school schedule did not affect the family's activities as long as fathers had a six-day week; but when fathers were increasingly given two-day weekends, the school schedule began to interfere with the family's recreational activities.[118]

The organization of time is of clear educational significance, and here, too, assumptions about time inhere in concepts of curriculum. Assumptions are made, for example, about how long it takes to learn a given unit of material, about whether spaced or repeated practice is better, or about the optimal duration of learning at different age levels. Timing is also important in the measurement and evaluation of performance, as, for example, in timed tests where both speed of response and ability to organize one's activities in terms of the time frame of the examination become vital. Some educational innovations, in fact, make a point of reorganizing the timing of activities.[119] Such modifications as altering the nature of the external time requirements to enable self-timing on the part of the learner, regrouping lessons in order to allow more intense concentration over shorter periods, and altering the nature of the schedule in order to allow for individual work on the part of the student all entail changes in the time structure of education. At another level, the nature of cognitive or intellectual activities can be seen to be influenced by the temporal organization of the activity. For example, the amount of time that a teacher allows a student in responding to a question influences the extent of reflection upon the question.[120] At a still broader level, the temporal organization of activities may influence the nature of contemplation in a society.[121] Implicit or explicit in most educational curricula is the notion of the relation of time to the structure of attention. The concept of attention span, for example, refers to the duration of attention, implicitly assuming that certain modes of organizing attention are desirable, particularly concentrating on one thing at a time.[122]

118   Ibid., pp. 77-78.

119   Various approaches to educational innovation entail modification of timing, as do certain curriculum plans, for example, the Dalton plan and the block system of the Rudolph Steiner School; cf., Bloom, *Human Characteristics and School Learning*.

120   For one discussion of modification of the "wait-time" for answers to questions see Mary Budd Rowe, "Science, Silence, and Sanctions," *Science and Children* 6 (March 1969): 11-13.

121   Sebastian de Grazia, *Of Time, Work, and Leisure* (Garden City, N.Y.: Anchor Books, Doubleday and Co., Inc., 1962).

122   It was pointed out at the Smithsonian seminar by Margaret Mead that the concept of attention span is, in a sense, masculine in that it implies the desirability of doing one thing at a time. Yet, in the lives of most women who carry out familial responsibility, doing one thing at a time is neither possible nor desirable.

Educative institutions are not only organized in time; they also offer instruction in the appropriate management of time, both indirectly through the organization of time within the institution, and directly through a variety of procedures for rewarding those who handle time in appropriate manners and punishing those who do not, for example, late slips for tardiness, lower grades for late papers, rewards for finishing first. Both students and teachers may come to hold particular time conceptions through their participation in an educational institution. The emotion attached to such conceptions can be readily detected. It is seen, for example, on the part of instructors, in the notion of "filling time," whereby instruction is planned so that it must take up a given time unit, and there is often considerable anxiety on the part of the instructor, particularly the inexperienced instructor, that there will be time left over.[123]

The organization of time may be examined at a variety of levels, from individual, biological, and personal propensities, to social expectations and cultural conceptions. One important issue is that of the way in which time periods are segmented and marked, for example, by alarm clocks, bells, and seasonal rituals. Time divisions may be marked abstractly and mechanically, for example, by clocks and metronomes, or in terms of natural cycles, for example, by seasons and tides. Societies differ in their predominant mode of temporal demarcation, with striking differences between agricultural and industrial time—recall the changes resulting from the industrial revolution.[124] The flow or interruption of activities is another important aspect in the organization of time. The importance of interruptions and time spent waiting in line in classrooms has been noted by Jackson, as has the importance of interruptions via the telephone in office work and family routines.[125]

A few examples of the organization of time in particular institutions may suggest the importance of temporal organization and the value of systematic examination of timing in attempting to compare educative institutions and to understand the connection of one institution with another.

Temporal organization in schools is generally elaborate, entailing as it does the coordination of the activities of numerous individuals, with clearly segmented time periods, for example, bells marking the end of

123   This point was made in the Smithsonian conference by Philip W. Jackson.
124   Eliot D. Chapple, *Culture and Biological Man: Explorations in Behavioral Anthropology* (New York: Holt, Rinehart & Winston, Inc., 1970); also Edward T. Hall, *The Silent Language* (Garden City, N.Y.: Doubleday and Co., Inc., 1959); and E.P. Thompson, "Time, Work-Discipline, and Industrial Capitalism," *Past and Present* 38 (December 1967): 56-97.
125   Jackson, *Life in Classrooms*; also Hall, *The Hidden Dimension*, pp. 131-32.

lessons and specific times allowed for eating.[126] Families differ in their manner of organizing activities in time and the way in which the family's temporal organization corresponds or fails to correspond to that of the school has been considered an important factor in the child's school achievement.[127] Since time conceptions vary with cultural heritage, time has been of special importance in examining the relation of families of particular backgrounds with institutions. One example is the organization of time in the scheduling of medical appointments, where it has been shown that the time concepts of families may be radically different from those of the medical institution.[128] Another example is communities where agricultural time or cycles of nature predominate in the family's activities, and children may be taken out of school during periods of planting or harvesting (as noted in the Arensberg and Kimball study above).[129]

When one compares the temporal organization of families and schools with that of other educative institutions, one finds even more marked contrasts. In museums, too, the activities of numerous individuals must be coordinated, special events are scheduled at times deemed appropriate to insure attendance, and institutions open and close at specific hours. Yet, much of the educational activity in museums is self-timed on the part of the learner, who may go through the museum as slowly or as quickly as desired, lingering over a particular exhibit, going back again and again to reexamine a particular display, or walking quickly to another. Observations from one study of the way in which families use museums suggest that parents instruct children in appropriate time management in viewing displays by hurrying children who linger too long at one display, and moving them along in a regular manner from one area to another.[130]

Places of work may also exhibit complex modes of organizing activities in time. In industrial societies especially, work time is generally counted exactly, for example, through time sheets, time is seen as having monetary value, and ideas exist about "time-thrift" and "time-discipline."[131] Within organizations, roles vary in their temporal organization and the extent to which the individual has autonomous control over time. Time

126   Jackson, *Life in Classrooms.*
127   Leichter, "Some Perspectives on the Family as Educator."
128   Lyle Saunders, *Cultural Differences and Medical Care* (New York: Russell Sage Foundation, 1954).
129   Arensberg and Kimball, *Family and Community in Ireland.* For a vivid description see also Laura Ingalls Wilder, *Farmer Boy* (New York: Harper & Row, 1933, rev. eds. 1953, 1971).
130   Benton, "Intergenerational Interaction in Museums."
131   Thompson, "Time, Work-Discipline and Industrial Capitalism."

is often a matter of negotiation, as in union contracts concerning vacation time, compensatory time, sick leave, or maternity leave. And at work, too, the individual's handling of time is commonly a basis of evaluation, where distinctions are noted, for example, between the individual who completes work by the deadline and the one who is habitually late. In business and industry, too, innovations often entail a modification in temporal organization, for example, flexible working hours, or "flex-time" systems.[132] Institutions and positions within them also vary with respect to the extent to which the organization of time is through an "impersonal tempo." In factory work, as compared with white-collar jobs, the organization of time is related to machine operations and is thus impersonal. The individual thereby loses the possibility of control over variations in time, and, as contrasted with agricultural or crafts work, loses the "fluctuating rhythm capable of taking wide variations within the beats." Clock time, rather than time geared to cycles of nature, therefore becomes the basis of organization in industry. Here, too, one may see the way in which temporal organization in one area influences that in another, for example, the effect of work schedules on the management of family activities and responsibilities. At yet another level, as deGrazia argues, the temporal organization in the sphere of work may have a carry-over into other spheres, "since the world of industry runs on quantitative time, free time runs to the same rhythm . . . free time exists in fragments."[133]

Television offers yet another area in which it is valuable to examine temporal organization. Much of the current concern is addressed to the amount of time spent viewing television,[134] but beyond viewing time is the issue of the temporal organization of television programming. At present, most television programming—with the possible exception of public access programs—represents highly organized clock time. Programs have a regular arrangement, are scheduled in advance, and schedules are available. A particularly important question concerns the relation of the temporal organization of television programming to the structure of attention. Much television programming is organized in short discontinuous segments, particularly where advertising is interspersed with the program. Moreover, the time segments are often extremely short—generally much shorter than time segments in school

132   Kanter, *Men and Women of the Corporation*, p. 274.
133   de Grazia, *Of Time, Work, and Leisure*, pp. 300, 315.
134   Cf. Winn, *The Plug-In Drug*; for another perspective, see Hope Jensen Leichter's "The Family in Today's Educational World," in *Today's Family in Focus* (Chicago: National P.T.A. publications, 1977).

activities. This, of course, raises the question of the influence of television programming on the organization of education in other institutions and settings, for example, how watching "Sesame Street" influences the structuring of attention in kindergarten. One may ask if the short, rapid-fire, segmented, discontinuous tempo that is fostered by much television programming carries over to the organization of attention in schools and how the organization of time on television influences the organization of the family's other activities.

The organization of time in religious institutions offers one further example of the importance of temporal organization and the potential value of comparing the temporal organization of different institutions. Interestingly, today most religious institutions are organized on a weekly cycle that serves to punctuate the organization of activities in other areas, for example, Saturday or Sunday is a day for religious service, and time is made available through the cessation of activities in other institutions. Religious institutions may differ from others in allowing time for silence or meditation. Religious institutions, like schools, also serve to mark calendric cycles through ritual events, and since these calendric rituals are supplemented by other institutions such as department stores and greeting card companies, the marking of annual cycles may remain important even in nonagricultural societies, and even for families that do not attend formal religious institutions.

The organization of time and the organization of space may intersect in interesting and important ways, as in schools or prisons, where movement from one clearly demarcated place to another occurs at clearly specified times.[135] And time, like space, is subtle, with many levels of temporal organization occurring at the margins of awareness. Here, too, it is important to examine institutions in terms of the concepts of participants as well as those of the analyst.

Pedagogic and Educative Styles   A further set of dimensions in terms of which institutions and settings that educate may be compared is that of the pedagogic styles that they employ and the educative styles that they foster. In light of the literature on related subjects, the educational importance of pedagogic style and educative style is evident. Variations in teaching styles have been the subject of an extensive literature. Such distinctions as pupil-centered versus teacher-centered or authoritarian versus laissez-faire styles of teaching have been widely discussed, as have

135   Foucault, *Discipline and Punish*.

variations in the extent of support versus demand, the extent of predictability versus ambiguity, and the extent to which the steps in learning are small versus large.[136] And although the concept of educative style is comparatively new, referring to the ways in which an individual engages in, moves through, and combines educative experiences across settings, the related although different concept of learning style has been much discussed.[137] But the concepts of pedagogic style and educative style have not as yet been extensively employed in systematic comparisons across institutions and settings that educate.

The potential value of comparing styles of pedagogy across institutions and settings may be illustrated by considering where the initiative for the organization of educational activities lies, that is, the extent to which the initiative is in the hands of the teacher, others in the institution, or the learner, as well as the way in which the reactions of the learner influence the actions of the teacher. In schools the initiative for organizing educational activity rarely rests entirely with the teacher—courses are mandated by the state, lesson plans are reviewed by supervisors, schedules are set by administrators. In families, by contrast, the parent exercises potential control over the initiation of educational activities, although many parents, sometimes because of lack of resources, do not exercise the initiative that they might—indeed, some parent education programs are designed to assist parents in taking greater initiative,[138] and the parent may even abandon initiative and control to the television set. In museums, by contrast, the museum educator or curator exercises initiative in attempting to lead the viewer through a "curriculum" via a combination of text, the use of space, and the layout of the display, but the viewer is free to ignore this curriculum at will or to "study" it selectively.[139]

Closely related to the issue of where initiative lies is the question of the kinds of feedback that take place between teacher and learner. In the classroom and in the family, a transaction takes place between student and teacher so that, to some extent, the learner's response triggers

---

136   One illustrative review is contained in Madeline Hunter, "The Teaching Process," in *The Teacher's Handbook*, by Dwight W. Allen and Eli Seifman (Glenview, Ill.: Scott Foresman and Co., 1971), pp. 146-57.

137   Leichter, "The Concept of Educative Style."

138   The pamphlet series of the National P.T.A., *Today's Family in Focus*, coordinated by Steven Schlossman, is illustrative of an effort designed to assist parents in taking greater initiative.

139   A fascinating example of new techniques of museum display is "The World of Franklin and Jefferson" exhibit; for a discussion of the rationale behind this exhibit see Charles Eames, "On Reducing Discontinuity," *Bulletin, The American Academy of Arts and Sciences* 30, no. 6 (March 1977): 24-34.

a further response on the part of the teacher. In television programming, by contrast, the learner's response, while it may in the long run have a powerful effect on whether the program is continued or not, does not immediately produce a modification on the part of the teacher, that is, the announcer, commentator, reporter, or entertainer. In schools and families, for example, the speed or pace of learning may be varied somewhat to suit different learners, speeded up or slowed down in terms of their response, whereas on television, the speed is organized and given in the same manner to all. In short, the feedback process from learner to teacher is very different across institutions.

One interesting analysis compares the organization of education in schools and on television, pointing to differences in pedagogic style and the voluntary and involuntary character of attendance.[140] Gans compares television and schools, concentrating on public schools that serve urban and suburban lower-middle-class neighborhoods and network television. He argues that "in some ways the media are an even more important educational institution than the school, for they outrank it in terms of size of operation and audience, in the amount of time and the intensity of interest devoted by that audience, and in the diversity of its course content."[141] Not only are the media of tremendous importance, but they also cover curriculum content that is in some way similar to that of the schools, for "what the school calls social studies or civics, the mass media call news, documentaries, and public affairs programming."[142] Yet the style of pedagogy and the student-teacher relationship differ enormously in view of the fact that school is involuntary, whereas the audience of the media is voluntary. As a commerical enterprise, the media are geared to paying close attention to what the audience wants, for example, through ratings, surveys, and the purchase of products that are advertised. And the media engage in pedagogic styles that emphasize drama and innovative techniques—television programs with poor ratings are dropped, whereas unpopular school courses are rarely dropped. The analysis for Gans suggests policy questions about the things that each of the institutions can do best and the desirable allocation of tasks between them. This illustration indicates the value of comparing pedagogic styles across institutions.

Not only learning styles, but more broadly educative styles, may be fostered differently in different institutions and settings. A number of

140   Herbert J. Gans, "The Mass Media as an Educational Institution," *Television Quarterly* 6, no. 2 (Spring 1967): 20-37.
141   Ibid., p. 20.
142   Ibid., p. 21.

aspects of educative style may vary from one setting to another. Schools, for example, generally support single-track as compared with multichannel learning, that is, doing one thing rather than several things at a time. Television, by contrast, while it may hold attention in even more compelling ways than many school classrooms, nonetheless is not viewed in the context of rules and regulations that preclude other activities and in this sense may foster learning to do many things at the same time.

Another dimension of educative style concerns the extent to which the learner's experience is active or passive. This too is closely related to the nature of initiative on the part of the teacher. Schools and educational philosophies vary in their assumptions regarding the importance of active as compared with passive learning. Families, too, undoubtedly vary in the extent to which active learning on the part of children (and adults) is fostered. (Ironically, some parent education programs place such a heavy emphasis on the need for explicit didactic procedures on the part of parents that they may unwittingly undermine the "natural" and "exploratory" educational initiatives of the child.) Educational institutions and settings also vary in the extent to which participation of the learner emphasizes different modalities, for example, auditory, visual, tactile, physical. The assumption that television viewing is essentially passive has been a source of much of the concern about the detrimental effects of television.[143] It is, of course, possible for television viewing to be made less passive, for example, by learning aids such as workbooks, coloring books, and question-answer guides that are distributed with educational programs, or by discussion of television programs on the part of those present. This is indeed another reason why the examination of how the family mediates television is of such importance.[144] Museums offer yet another illustration of the contrasts in educative styles that are supported in different institutions. While in some respects museums support passive educative styles in that the museum-goer does not determine the nature of the display, they are at the same time open to a variety of uses—one may see school children going through displays actively taking notes and others driven by parents hardly looking at the displays at all. Some museums, moreover, have

---

143   Marie Winn's discussion of the left brain as compared with the right brain in television viewing and reading is one illustration of this concern, Winn, *The Plug-In Drug*; for a sharply differing view, see Tony Schwartz, *The Responsive Chord.*

144   A series of pictures taken by Professor Paul Byers in family homes reveals differences in posture that may presumably relate to differences in communication among family members during television viewing as compared with reading.

engaged in experiments and innovations in procedures to foster more active use of the museum.[145]

These dimensions for comparing education across institutions and settings are offered as suggestive, not as definitive. As yet, little systematic research has made comparisons across a wide range of institutions. The discussion is intended to indicate the potential value for a theory of education of this kind of comparison as well as to offer another set of concepts through which relationships among educative institutions may be examined.

Thus far, we have considered a number of concepts that may be used in looking at educational interrelationships from the perspective of institutions. The concept of institution itself, like that of community, may take on very different meanings depending on the definition selected and the methodological stance employed. Since a central educational issue today—for both program and policy—concerns the way in which the diverse institutions that educate are related to one another, it is of importance to clarify possible perspectives through which one may approach this issue of institutional relationships.

The concepts that have been examined are by no means exhaustive, nor is one necessarily superior to another, but they do suggest different questions about the nature of education in one setting as compared with that in another. Each of the concepts of relationship examined—community, systems, configuration, linkage, resonance, and mediation—approaches the problem of institutional overlap in a somewhat different way, and the comparison of institutions in terms of the content and process of their education suggests still other perspectives on the interconnections of institutions. None of these concepts has to date been employed extensively in the examination of relationships among educative institutions, although they are being used in ongoing investigation with fruitful results.[146] At this point the concepts are most helpful in directing attention to possible modes of examining institutional interconnections rather than as formalized definitions of dimensions that have been the subject of extensive empirical examination.

145   In the Discovery Room of the American Museum of Natural History, objects may be handled, touched, and rearranged. This represents one example of efforts to allow more active use of museums.

146   Some of these concepts are being employed in studies for the Center for the Study of the Family as Educator. Other studies employing some of these concepts are being carried forward by Lawrence Cremin and his colleagues, particularly Ellen Condliffe Lagemann, "A Generation of Women: Studies in Educational Biography" (Ph.D. diss., Teachers College, Columbia University, 1978).

The concepts reviewed differ in the extent to which they suggest particular structural connections, that is, roles that serve to link the school with the community, as compared with processes of connection, that is, the process by which the family criticizes and appraises the child's experience in school. The concepts also differ in the level of examination that they suggest, from looking at positions or organizations that may be visibly seen and described in tables of organization, to examining connections that must be inferred through similarity across settings, that is, resonance in imagery.

Underlying all of these concepts are two issues of special importance, first, the question of the "tightness of fit"—the closeness of connection —of one area with another, and second, the question of change. As we have seen, functionally oriented community studies often rest on an implicit, if not explicit, premise that a change in one area would imply a change in all others, that is, that the entire whole is interrelated. Yet, upon further examination, it appears that one area of the whole is often more tightly connected with certain areas than with others. The issue of the tightness of fit of one institutional area with another is further complicated by the fact that similarity and dissimilarity across settings depends on the level of analysis. That which appears dissimilar—that is, loosely connected—from one perspective may appear similar—that is, tightly connected—from another perspective.

Closely related to the issue of the tightness of the connection of one sphere to another is the issue of change. Those forms of systems analysis that have deliberately built in concepts of feedback have approached the question of change directly. Other concepts have been less explicit in their handling of change; for example, the concept of linkage, although it need not be used in a fixed, mechanical manner, has tended to suggest linking procedures at a particular moment in time, rather than the way in which such procedures develop and change over time. Concepts such as mediation, which are process concepts, on the other hand, have thus far been applied to short-term micro-processes, rather than to long-term historical change. Yet is is clear from observations of current changes in institutions such as the family that an adequate framework for examining relationships of one institution to another for educational purposes must ultimately deal with the question of change in a direct and explicit manner.

IMAGES OF THE ORGANIZATION OF
THE INDIVIDUAL'S EXPERIENCE

The question of how education in one institution or setting relates to education in another can thus be approached from an institutional perspective through employing a variety of concepts to examine relationships among institutions and through explicit comparison of the nature of education in different settings. It should be clear from the discussion thus far, however, that an institutional perspective does not fully deal with education from the perspective of the individual learner. For one thing, the diversity of institutions, situations, and settings through which different individuals move is so great that a general analysis of institutional interrelationships may have little significance for the experience of a particular individual. Moreover, as one scrutinizes more closely the various institutions and settings in which education takes place, it becomes increasingly clear that an institution, such as a school, a museum, a hospital, or a clinic, is not the same for all the individuals that participate within it. For one child, the school is the classroom teacher and a number of friends, whereas for another child, the school may be the guidance counselor, the principal, and the teacher. For one patient, the hospital may be a particular floor, nurse, or doctor, whereas for another patient it may be a waiting room.

The point becomes clear if one imagines the spaces through which an individual moves in a formal organization during the course of a day. Individuals generally encounter only a small and fairly regular portion of the total space of an institution. Even within the family, the individuals that are important to each other may vary from one person to another. For one child, a cousin of the same age may have special significance, whereas for an older sister, this cousin is of little personal importance. For an older child, a grandparent may be well known, whereas for a younger child, the same grandparent may be barely remembered. And, similarly, television may mean the news and weather for one member of the family, whereas for another, it may mean morning soap operas, and for still another, children's programs. (In fact, in much of the alarmist discussion, television is treated as if it were a unitary experience for all members of the family, while it probably varies more than has been recognized from household to household and from individual to individual.)

When one adds to the fact that individuals who participate in the same formal organization may experience very different parts of that organization, the diversity of places of work, association, neighborhood, friends, religious institutions, museums, that individuals encounter, the need for perspectives that enable one to keep the learner, whether child or adult, in central focus becomes even clearer. Moreover, the perspective of the individual learner is often lost when the focus on institutions or organizations predominates. In thinking about school-community relations, for example, the emphasis may be on the roles that link the school and the community, such as school-community coordinators, parent-teacher associations, or local school boards, while the fact that the child goes daily from family to school and back is ignored or, at best, placed in low key, as when the child becomes a "low-powered" carrier of messages.[147] Thus, while the organizational perspective is useful, it is only partial, and there is also clearly a need to increase our understanding of the organization of the individual's experience over space and through time.

A number of concepts from the behavioral sciences may be examined to suggest their possible value in working toward a greater understanding of how the individual's educational experience is structured. The concept of educative style itself is directed toward considering how the individual engages in, moves through, and combines educative experiences over a lifetime. In order to understand the variety of educative styles and the great variety of individual characteristics and propensities, it is necessary to chart the content and course of diverse educative encounters of different individuals.[148]

SOCIAL NETWORKS

A rapidly growing literature on social networks is emerging in the social sciences and is being used in a variety of areas of application that include the analysis of social supports in illness, mental health, and old age.[149]

While the literature on social networks is exceedingly elaborate, and while highly complex procedures—including intricate quantitative procedures—have been developed for measuring and tracing networks, the essential thrust of the concept for present purposes is that it focuses on the individual and those others who are significant in the individual's experience. The term *network* has been used in a metaphorical sense to suggest the "web" of social relationships in which an individual is "embedded." The concept has also been the basis for specific operational procedures for diagramming and charting social relationships, for example, drawing upon graph theory and using other forms of measure-

---

147   Litwak and Meyer, *School, Family and Neighborhood*, p. 39.

148   Leichter, "The Concept of Educative Style"; Chapple also emphasizes the importance of individual differences, cf. Chapple, "New Directions in Education in Advanced Technological Societies."

149   Hope Jensen Leichter and William E. Mitchell, *Kinship and Casework: Family Networks and Social Intervention,* 2nd ed. (New York: Teachers College Press, 1978), especially the introduction to the second edition.

ment. In all of these diverse uses of the concept, the focus on the individual is central.

A network starts from a given individual and traces the social ties of that individual, so that the network represents the perspective of a particular "ego." And the term is thus "egocentric" in that it refers to "the chains of persons with whom a given person is in actual contact, and their interconnections." Moreover, "this egocentric, personal network is of course unique for every individual." Starting from a given individual, one may trace "primary" or "first-order" network zones, that is, those individuals with whom the particular person is in actual contact. One may extend this to "second-order" zones by examining the "friends-of-friends" of those known by the individual whose network is being studied, and one can theoretically go on extending the zones to include friends-of-friends-of-friends-of-friends.[150]

Yet even as one moves out from first-order to second-order networks, the concept of personal network remains centered on the individual and, in this sense, offers a perspective on social relationships that is intermediate between the individual and the social system. As a result, the concept of network offers a mode of understanding social relationships that goes beyond the concept of a fixed system. It enables one to focus on the particular interactions of individuals and on the ways in which individuals create, re-create, and change their social relationships or, put somewhat differently, the ways in which people "fence" with values, modifying and selecting them for their own purposes.[151] The concept of network thus allows a perspective that is useful in considering the organization of a particular individual's experience, encompassing both moment-to-moment associations and encounters in formal institutions.

It is possible to trace the networks of an individual and to examine their characteristics with respect to a variety of dimensions. Some of the dimensions employed in the analysis of networks have been highly abstract and formalized, so much so that the initial content of the personal relationship is sometimes almost forgotten and the networks are "stripped of their interactional aspect." And, as Boissevain himself indicates, "this approach can lead to a rather sterile over-simplification unless it is remembered that the links are *personal relations,* which can be extremely complex."[152] In some uses of the network concept, the formal character has indeed become a matter of such central focus that

---

150 Jeremy Boissevain, *Friends of Friends: Networks, Manipulators, and Coalitions* (Oxford: Basil Blackwell, 1974), p. 24.

151 Ibid., p. 4.

152 Ibid., p. 35.

the content of the personal relationship is largely overlooked—the form is so abstracted from the context that the character of the relationship is lost. For the purpose of understanding the structure of an individual's educational experience across settings and situations, it is especially important not to lose sight of the content of the personal relations in the network.

Nonetheless, some of the formal dimensions that have emerged in the analysis of networks are useful in suggesting relationships in the organization of the individual's experience across settings. Among the dimensions that have been examined are anchorage, reachability, density, range, content, durability, intensity, and frequency[153]—or, in somewhat different although related terms, diversity of linkages, multiplexity, directional flow, frequency and duration of interaction, size, degree of connection, centrality, and transactional content.[154]

An almost limitless variety of structural dimensions can be used to describe networks. Yet some distinctions among networks are of special importance for understanding the organization of the individual's educational experience. One such distinction is that between a "tightly knit" and a "loosely knit" network. When an individual's network is tightly knit, many of those in the network know each other. By contrast, when an individual's network is loosely knit, few of those in the network know each other. Bott has hypothesized a connection between the character of a family's networks and the nature of conjugal roles.[155] Others have suggested that the structure of networks may be related to education, reflecting the extent of an individual's schooling. Boissevain argues, for example, that "the more education a person has, the greater the size of his network but the lower its density and multiplexity." In other words, persons with more schooling know a wider range of people and have broader social horizons than those with less schooling, who are likely to be more conventional because they are "vulnerable to pressure exerted upon them to conform to the traditional way of doing things." Pressure to conform is exerted in part because of the multiple links within the network. "Since the social network of a less well educated person will probably tend to be smaller, more interconnected and contain more multiplex links, we may expect that there will

---

153 J. Clyde Mitchell, *Social Networks in Urban Situations* (Manchester: Manchester University Press, 1969), pp. 20-36.

154 Boissevain, *Friends of Friends*, pp. 33-45.

155 A review of research examining this hypothesis is contained in the second edition of Elizabeth Bott, *Family and Social Network: Roles, Norms, and External Relationships in Ordinary Urban Families* (London: Tavistock Publications, 1971).

therefore be more channels through which social pressures can be placed upon him to conform to the norms of behaviour and the values held by members of his network." This in turn implies that those with less schooling are less likely to "accept new ideas or try out new techniques—to innovate—than those with more education."[156] The diversity or coherence of an individual's network is thus seen to have direct connections with education.

Since there are indications that the character of social networks is related not only to the level of the individual's schooling, but also to the nature of that schooling, the rationale for tracing the educational encounters of particular individuals from one setting to another is compelling in that it offers another perspective on the way in which education in one setting relates to education in another. A brief discussion of one of the studies at the Center for the Study of the Family as Educator may illustrate the way in which the tracing of individual networks can inform an inquiry into the structuring of the individual's educational experience. In a study of social networks and educative styles,[157] the social networks of a number of teenagers are being examined with the aim of understanding the character of these networks and the way in which individuals differ in their approaches to education. The concept of network has been employed in this research as a vehicle for tracing those individuals that are "educationally significant others" from the perspective of a particular teenager. Starting through interviews with teenagers to map those individuals that they regard as educationally significant, the research then moved to observe and interview the "significant others" in the teenagers' lives. Although it has proven difficult to maintain the distinction between "educationally significant others" and more generally "significant others"—those who have some importance to the teenager, whether that importance is defined in educational terms or not—the procedure has made possible the examination of a wide variety of encounters in which education, in the researcher's definition, takes place.[158]

It was initially intended that the research would make use of the participants' (teenagers') definitions of education, that is, the emic

---

156   Boissevain, *Friends of Friends*, pp. 86-87.

157   The study of social networks and educative styles is one of the current projects of the Center for the Study of the Family as Educator. I am grateful to Vera Hamid for skillful assistance in this research.

158   In this research the definition of education as deliberate, systematic and sustained, as discussed above, was employed, with the additional search for partially deliberate activities at the margins of awareness.

definitions, but it proved impossible to maintain this procedure and direct the inquiry to the research topic of education as it takes place in diverse settings. The problem was that emic definitions of the term *education* so often referred to schooling and did not include education in the family and neighborhood, with friends and relatives, or in settings other than schools. It was therefore necessary to search broadly for individuals and situations of significance to the teenager and then to examine these encounters in terms of the researcher's definition of education. Yet this very problem proved one of the most important reasons for tracing networks. Through network-mapping it was possible to chart the range of individuals in the lives of different teenagers. These individuals included representatives of institutions, that is, teachers, librarians, and counselors, as well as individuals encountered outside the formal organizations, that is, friends and relatives. The charting of an individual's network is only one procedure for the broader analysis of the organization of the individual's educational experience, but the charting itself revealed interesting differences in the networks of different teenagers. The networks varied in such features as ethnic composition and diversity, social class composition, and geographic spread, as well as the particular institutions that were included via this tracing, for example, the church in one network as compared with a television commercial producer in another network as compared with museums and music teachers in yet another network. These variations were striking, particularly in view of the fact that the families of origin, that is, the nuclear families of the teenagers, were similar in their social class positions.

Certain other concepts related to that of network, although somewhat different in emphasis, may also be useful in tracing or charting the organization of the individual's educational experience. The concepts of status-set and role-set have been widely used in sociology and also specifically applied to the analysis of education.[159] These concepts direct attention to the variety of "counter-positions" associated with any particular position. For example, the position of school superintendent includes the counter-positions of teacher, principal, and school board member, so that the school superintendent's role may be analyzed in terms of the way in which expectations and influences from each of these counter-positions—as well as relationships among those in the counter-positions—enter into the school superintendent's role. The concepts of status-set and role-set are thus, at one level, similar to that of

159 Gross, Mason, and McEachern, *Explorations in Role Analysis.*

network in that they include a mapping or tracing of positions, but here, too, examining the dynamics of expectations and actions within positions and counter-positions can lead to an understanding of profound questions, such as the sociological conditions that foster ambivalence.[160] If one extends the analysis that has been made of the school superintendent's role to the perspective of the child, one might, for example, consider that the status-set of the pupil attending the school would include parents, siblings, teachers, the school principal, and classmates, and this mapping could be the basis for examination of the dynamics by which pressures and counter-pressures, similar and different expectations, are brought to bear upon the child educationally from those that make up the status-set of the pupil. Thus, the mapping or tracing of networks, positions, and counter-positions through which an individual moves may help to shed light on the handling of diversity and coherence in the individual's educational experience.

The closely related concept of reference group has been widely employed in sociological analysis, directing attention to the significant others to which individuals refer in making self-appraisals and evaluations. The concept builds upon the analysis of "relative deprivation," particularly in the experience of the American soldier, where feelings of deprivation were shown to vary depending in part on the groups used as reference points in making the evaluation.[161] The concept of reference group can readily be applied to the analysis of relationships among educative institutions. The child, for example, who compares himself to a particularly accomplished older sibling may have a different sense of his educational achievement from that of a child who compares himself with a less successful classmate. It is important to note that a certain flexibility or indeterminancy inheres in the individual's selection of reference groups—reference groups may, for example, be membership or non-membership groups—and the possibilities for selection no doubt relate in part to the structure of the individual's networks as well as the properties of the groups.

160 The concepts of status-set and role-set are somewhat different in that status-set refers to positions and role-set to expectations with respect to positions. However, for present purposes, in the mapping of educational experiences the terms are sufficiently similar so that they will not be distinguished here. For a useful discussion of this literature, see Robert K. Merton, *Sociological Ambivalence* (New York: Free Press, 1976); see also Robert K. Merton, *Social Theory and Social Structure* (New York: Free Press, 1968); for a discussion that has particular bearing on relationships among educative institutions see Robert K. Merton, "The Role-Set: Problems in Sociological Theory," *The British Journal of Sociology* 8 (June 1957): 376-87.

161 For a discussion of the formation of reference group theory and its relation to the concept of relative deprivation see Merton, *Social Theory and Social Structure*, especially chap. 10, "Contributions to the Theory of Reference Group Behavior," pp. 225-386.

A rather different but related concept that may also be useful in tracing or mapping the individual's educational experience is that of field. In the work of Lewin, the analysis of the individual's life space is enlightened by formulations drawn from mathematical topology. While the mode of analysis, starting as it does from wholes rather than parts, is different in this work from that in some network thinking, there is a similarity in such notions as "connectedness of regions," where the distinction is made, for example, between "non-connected regions," "multiply connected regions," and "limited and closed regions" in terms of the space of free movement of the person. The connectedness and nonconnectedness of regions is analyzed, for example, through consideration of the forbidden and whether prohibitions extend across regions. "Regions of the forbidden which are not connected with each other" may be illustrated by prohibitions such as, "You must not cross the road alone," "You must not copy in school," "You must not be impolite to a certain person." These situationally specific prohibitions are, in Lewin's terms, "islands of the forbidden" that are nonconnected, "especially when the one prohibition issues from the parents, the second from the teacher, and the third from a good friend." Two regions are nonconnected when the transition from one of the forbidden regions to another forbidden region is possible "only by passing through the region of the allowed."[162] And while the manner of describing the dimensions of the individual's life space, the vectors or forces influencing it, and the boundaries between one region and another are quite different in Lewin's representation from the concepts employed in role theory or network analysis—although some aspects of network analysis may rest on mathematical models similar to those employed by Lewin—the underlying issues in the analysis of the structuring of the individual's educational experience are closely related.

The extent of the connection of one area with another is a matter of concern in topological psychology, as it is also in the analysis of social systems and social networks, for example, in the distinction between tightly knit and loosely knit networks. As noted above in discussing the concept of system, the degree of interconnection is handled by Lewin through distinguishing different kinds of *Gestalten*: "In order to express the degree of dependency of the parts of a dynamic whole we will speak of gestalten of greater or less unity," referring to "a group of dynamically disconnected regions, at the one extreme and at the other gestalt of the highest degree of interdependency of parts." The terms *strong Gestalten* and *weak Gestalten* may also be employed to distinguish dif-

162   Kurt Lewin, *Principles of Topological Psychology*, pp. 100-06.

ferent degrees of dynamic unity.[163] While these concepts cannot be discussed fully here in terms of their original meaning, they illustrate yet another possibility of arriving at systematic ways of defining the structure of the individual's educational experience across institutions and settings.

The concepts of network and status-set (or role-set), as well as the concepts employed in topological mapping, go beyond mere tracing or charting of the individual's experience. Yet they all suggest ways of mapping the individual's experience with respect to those individuals and situations that are educationally important, as a starting point for further analysis. These concepts also offer possible approaches to the analysis of the extent of diversity and coherence in the individual's educational experience—an issue of central educational importance.

SETTING, FRAME, CONTEXT

If one attempts to trace the organization of the individual's educational experience by following the individual over a period of time and through a variety of physical locations, one is faced with the problem of distinguishing between one setting and another. This problem assumes a somewhat different form when one starts with an individual as compared with an institution. When education is examined from the perspective of a particular institution, the boundaries between one setting and another are to some extent defined through the naming or definition of the institution. By contrast, when an individual is followed through time and space, the distinction between one setting and another is less readily apparent.

The work of Barker and Wright in the "psychological ecology" of an American town is especially useful in its discussion of issues that arise in "dividing the behavior stream."[164] In Barker and Wright's classic One Boy's Day,[165] a seven-year-old child was followed for an entire day by a team of observers and the observations of the boy's day are recorded in a book-length specimen record. The aim of the recording is "to trace in the record the whole course of the behavior which the observers saw and reported," giving "due regard for the many different things" that the boy did. Precise recording conventions are used, care is taken to distinguish the observers' interpretations from their observa-

163 Ibid., p. 174. For technical reasons, Lewin prefers not to use these particular terms.

164 Barker and Wright, *Midwest and Its Children*, especially chap. 7, "Dividing the Behavior Stream."

165 Roger G. Barker and Herbert F. Wright, *One Boy's Day: A Specimen Record of Behavior* (New York: Harper & Brothers Publishers, 1951).

tions and to retain the original flow of events, for example, by a recording convention whereby "sentences referring to different actions are never placed in the same paragraph." Thus, the aim is to record the flow of behavior with every precaution "against splitting the real units of the ongoing behavior apart so that they cannot be put together" and, at the same time, with every effort "not to join together actions which belong apart." The conventions of the record are organized so that "its organization will not prejudice any attempt to discover where different units and sequences of actions started and stopped, where interruptions occurred, where actions overlapped." Yet, even finding an appropriate sequence for the recording is complex, because many "smaller actions occurred as parts of more or less extended episodes."[166] And, as Barker and Wright analyze specimen records in order to determine "behavior episodes," it is clear that a variety of kinds of overlap may occur within the behavior stream. The behavior units may be consecutive or simultaneous, since different episodes may occur "wholly or in part, at one time," and different forms of coinciding, enclosing, and interlinking may be distinguished.[167] Despite the complications of distinguishing one behavioral episode and setting from another, Barker and Wright are able to mark off units. Techniques of filming and videotaping often temporarily avert the necessity of distinguishing units within a behavioral stream, whereas in writing verbal reports of observations of the flow of events, the issue of how to distinguish one unit from another is brought sharply into attention, and for this reason the work of Barker and Wright is particularly helpful.

The effort of their recording conventions is to avoid arbitrarily imposing units, and their theoretical frame of reference, drawn in part from Lewin, is to analyze the situation through the perceptions of the participants, with the aim of breaking through "a wall of directly observed conditions and events by means of inference" in order to "see things as the other person sees them from his viewpoint."[168] It is also clear that "situations" are defined in part in terms of the observer's concepts about the particular kinds of activities that are going on at a given moment. It is especially interesting to note that problems of transition from one definition of a situation to another are evident in the specimen records. The description of a shift from a period of play to classwork in *One Boy's Day* vividly anticipates a good deal of recent work

166   Ibid., pp. 9, 10.
167   Barker and Wright, *Midwest and Its Children*, pp. 260, 261, 262.
168   Ibid., p. 205.

on issues of how transitions from one situational definition to another are accomplished.[169]

In describing the transition from "recess" to "classwork," the following notes are included in the record, placed under the heading of "Classwork":

Scene V: Classwork
Time: 10:21-11:31

The classroom is in turmoil. A few children are in their seats but most of them are still in the process of getting settled. Some children are continuing their play activities in anything but a quiet way.

10:21: As Raymond skipped down the aisle toward his desk, he glanced around the room.

Whenever his glances met those of other children, his face lit up in friendly greeting.

At his desk he paused, as if undecided whether to sit down immediately or find something else to do.

Suddenly he turned and went to the back of the room.

He climbed onto the windowsill.

One of the little girls also climbed up on the windowsill . . . .

Just as the teacher came to the back of the room, Raymond dropped to the floor with dexterity.

Mrs. Logan repeated, with a little more emphasis, "It's time to get quiet now."

She frowned at Raymond and at the girl, who was still on the sill . . . .

While the teacher walked to the front of the room, she said, "There isn't much time to tell stories this morning. Sit up straight now! Sit up straight and put your feet under your desk where they belong! Sit up straight! If you are quiet we will have a little time to tell stories."

Raymond pulled his feet in from the aisle, straightened his hands on the desk, as though expectantly awaiting the stories.

---

169 Here the work of R.P. McDermott, particularly the analysis of a videotape of transitions in school interaction, is especially interesting. See R.P. McDermott, Kenneth Gospodinoff, and Jeffrey Aron, "The Criteria for an Ethnographically Adequate Description of Concerted Activities and Their Contexts," *Semiotica*, forthcoming. See also David Thornton Moore, "Social Order in an Alternative School," *Teachers College Record* 79 (February 1978): 437-60.

All the children had responded to the teacher's request and were ready for the stories.[170]

Just as the transitions from one segment of experience to another in school are marked by shifting definitions of the situation—definitions that require some negotiation—the transitions in life outside the school entail similar processes. In *One Boy's Day*, at the end of the day, Raymond is leaving to go home from playing with a three-and-a-half year old companion and another friend his own age, and the following description is given:

> Clifford didn't want Raymond to go in; he wanted him to stay and play. He said, "No supper, no supper."
>
> Stuart and Raymond smiled in amusement and exchanged glances over Clifford's head.
>
> Stuart said to Clifford, "Well, probably he has to eat supper. . . ." Clifford stubbornly kept saying, "No supper," in a very wistful, plaintive voice.[171]

And at bedtime, negotiations over whether or not to go to sleep reveal a similar process of transition from one setting to another.

It is clear that in the transition from one setting to another procedures are required to change the situation and define the behavior that is appropriate in the new situation. Such changes of setting may occur when the physical location is changed, but they may also occur on a moment-to-moment basis when the definition of the situation shifts.

Recent work in sociology, anthropology, and sociolinguistics has analyzed in considerable detail the way in which one unit of activity may be marked off from another as well as the transitional procedures by which shifts are made from one segment to another. As the illustration in the transitions from recess to classwork and from play to going home to supper in *One Boy's Day* reveal, breaking up the stream of behavior and shifting from one definition of a situation to another is by no means automatic. This is in part because, in a particular "current situation," many different things may be happening simultaneously. Some of them may have begun at different moments, and they may not all terminate at the same time, as in the transition from recess to classwork, where lingering moments of recess evidently intrude themselves into the period of classwork.

When one shifts from examining transitions in observed behavior to

170 Barker and Wright, *One Boy's Day*, pp. 136-38.
171 Ibid., pp. 370-71.

the analysis of the structure of the individual's attention in a given situation, it is increasingly evident that many things may be occurring at once, and the individual may be simultaneously in one space physically and in many other places in his mind. At one moment the child in school may be thinking of the argument that he had with his mother over whether to eat breakfast. At another moment he may be concentrating on the classwork when the sound of a fire engine suddenly brings to his ·mind the thought that it could be his home that is burning.[172] The analysis of the organization of the individual's experience for the purpose of understanding education must clearly take into account the structure of the individual's attention.

Even though *One Boy's Day* focuses on overtly observable behavior, it is clear that the child's attention is far from unitary. One description, for example, clearly brings to mind common forms of observable disattention. While another child is giving a report, Raymond is described in the following manner:

> In a slouching position Raymond watched Mrs. Logan with only slight interest.
>
> He sucked on his left index finger.
>
> Then he laid his head on his hands as he glanced briefly at Mattie.
>
> He studiously regarded his fingers.
>
> While Mattie finished and Susanna Hall began, Raymond, resting his elbows on his desk, chewed his fingers. He seemed to be looking out into space rather than at anything in particular. He did not appear interested in Susanna's report.
>
> He poked the fingers of one hand into the palm of the other hand in an absent-minded way.[173]

Goffman has described this kind of self-involvement as a form of disattention or what he terms "aways."[174] In the Barker record specimen, the observer clearly interprets the behavior as disattention by calling it "absent-minded." The fact that such shifts of attention are a common aspect of everyday life makes it important to understand the structure of attention as well as the observable behavior in attempting to find

172   The concept of multiple levels of attention was discussed at some length at the Smithsonian Conference, particularly in relation to television viewing.

173   Barker and Wright, *One Boy's Day*, pp. 214-15.

174   Erving Goffman, *Behavior in Public Places: Notes on the Social Organization of Gatherings* (New York: The Free Press, 1963), pp. 50-59.

meaningful ways in which the structuring of behavior can be broken up for purposes of analyzing one situation as compared with another. As Goffman indicates, the terms "current" and "situation" are themselves problematic, since "the amount of time covered by 'current' (just as the amount of space covered by 'here') obviously can vary greatly from one occasion to the next and from one participant to another."[175]

The concept of frame, introduced by Bateson[176] and developed by Goffman,[177] is useful in directing attention to the definitional procedures whereby one situation is marked off from another with respect to its "reality" status and the behaviors and interactions that are appropriate within it. An early observation by Bateson suggests the importance and subtlety of such situational definitions or frames. He noted that animals (otters in a zoo) go through very similar behavioral routines when they are fighting and when they are playing, yet the difference between fighting and when they are playing, yet the difference between fighting and playing is clearly recognizable, both by the animals themselves and by observers. This, in Goffman's terms, indicates that a "primary framework" or "schemata of interpretation" serves to define the reality status of a particular situation,[178] with respect to a particular main action or focus of attention.[179] In one situation, it is clear that "this is play," whereas in another it is clear that "this is a fight." Markers, "keys" or "cues," indicate how the "strip" of interaction is divided, and when one schema of interpretation shifts to another, and establish "when the transformation is to begin and when it is to end."[180] For example, in *One Boy's Day*, "Sit up straight and put your feet under your desk where they belong," serves to cue the transition from recess to classwork or to bracket the transformation in time. These cues also indicate "everywhere within which and nowhere outside of which the keying applies on that occasion."[181]

It is especially important that while the markers that define a situation are clearly recognized, they may nevertheless be held in the margins of awareness by the participants. In Goffman's terms, the participant "is likely to be unaware of such organized features as the framework has and unable to describe the framework with any completeness if asked,

175   Erving Goffman, *Frame Analysis: An Essay on the Organization of Experience* (Cambridge: Harvard University Press, 1974), p. 9.
176   Gregory Bateson, "A Theory of Play and Fantasy," in *Steps to an Ecology of Mind*, pp. 170-93.
177   Goffman, *Frame Analysis*.
178   Ibid., p. 21.
179   Ibid., p. 201.
180   Ibid., p. 45.
181   Ibid.

yet these handicaps are no bar to his easily and fully applying it."[182] This is reminiscent of Sapir's description of the keen alertness with which gestures are recognized in terms of "an elaborate and secret code that is written nowhere, known by none, but understood by all."[183] The process of keying or cuing the transition from one frame or one definition of a situation to another is, moreover, sufficiently subtle so that no radical change in the overt behavior may take place. "The systematic transformation that a particular keying introduces may alter only slightly the activity thus transformed, but it utterly changes what it is a participant would say was going on,"[184] and the rules that apply to the situation. Thus, the complicated and subtle procedures by which situations are defined and distinguished from one another are, on the one hand, difficult to ferret out and, on the other hand, readily apparent to those involved. Again, returning to the example of *One Boy's Day*, it is evident that while certain efforts are necessary on the part of the teacher to make the transition from recess to classwork, it is clear to the teacher, to the observer, and to the children that at a given point in time classwork is what is going on. And even where the boy is not attending to the classwork, his behavior is described as disattention by the observer, with the implicit reference to the notion that the primary focus of activity in the situation is classwork.

A variety of related concepts have also been employed to analyze the ways in which situations are defined and marked off from one another. The notion of context is particularly useful. I have argued elsewhere that methodological sophistication, particularly in the analysis of the family, can be achieved only if "contextual rigor" is sought, that is, understanding a particular behavior in terms of the definition of the situation in which it takes place.[185] Glaser and Strauss have used the concept of context in discussing the way in which "awareness contexts," that is, what interactants in a situation know about each other, influence social interaction.[186] In linguistics, the notion that "linguistic codes" vary from one context to another has recently been examined in detail,[187] with the basic idea that the meaning of a particular act or

182   Ibid., p. 21.

183   Edward Sapir, *Culture, Language, and Personality*, ed. David G. Mandelbaum (Berkeley and Los Angeles: University of California Press, 1970), p. 556.

184   Goffman, *Frame Analysis*, p. 45.

185   Leichter, "Some Perspectives on the Family as Educator.

186   Barney Glaser and Anselm Strauss, "Awareness Contexts and Social Interaction," *American Sociological Review* 29 (1964): 669-79.

187   A valuable analysis of language as it varies with different contexts, particularly in family discourse, is presented in the current research of Clifford Hill and Hervé Varenne being con-

symbol depends, at least in part, on the context in which it takes place. Here, too, the idea of cues that define a context or what Gumperz calls "contextualization cues" has been considered.[188] The educational importance of differences among contexts or situations has been examined in terms of the relation to cognitive processes.[189]

Definitions that serve to specify the reality status of a situation and to define "what is going on" within it offer an essential set of ideas for understanding how the individual's educational experience is structured in time and space. Situational shifts may be analyzed on a microscopic, moment-to-moment level, as well as in broader units—even units that extend over a period of many years in the individual's life.

These concepts do not indicate how one should divide the stream of events for particular purposes of educational analysis, but they do indicate the importance of considering a variety of perspectives in terms of which such divisions may be made. If, for example, one automatically assumes that school is one thing and home another, one may have the wrong units for analyzing differences and similarities in the nature of the education taking place.

The ideas of setting, frame, and context may be applied, of course, in the examination of behavior within educative institutions, but these ideas come to have particular importance in tracing the individual's educational encounters over time and space. The concepts of network and status-set (or role-set) enable a tracing of relationships that are important to an individual, and indeed they can be used to examine the nature of the exchanges and transactions among those in the individual's life. But a further set of concepts is needed to understand the way in which one situation in the individual's life is defined and marked off from another. For this purpose, the concepts of setting, frame, and context, although with significant differences of emphasis, offer useful possibilities. The notion of boundary in topological psychology also suggests

---

ducted through the Center for the Study of the Family as Educator; a useful discussion of context is contained in Edward T. Hall, *Beyond Culture* (Garden City, N.Y.: Anchor Books, Doubleday, 1977) particularly his chapter on "Context and Meaning."

188   John J. Gumperz, "Language, Communication and Public Negotiation," in *Anthropology and the Public Interest: Fieldwork and Theory*, ed. Peggy Reeves Sanday (New York: Academic Press, 1976), pp. 273-306.

189   Michael Cole et al., *The Cultural Context of Learning and Thinking: An Exploration in Experimental Anthropology* (New York: Basic Books, Inc., 1971); also Michael Cole and Sylvia Scribner, *Culture and Thought* (New York: John Wiley, 1974). For an analysis of natural learning situations and the transference of learning from one context to other situations see Jean Lave, "Tailor-made Experiments and Evaluating the Intellectual Consequences of Apprenticeship Training," *The Quarterly Newsletter of the Institute for Comparative Human Development* 1 (February 1977): 1-3.

ways of distinguishing areas in which one kind of activity is appropriate (the areas of the permissible) from areas in which another kind of activity is appropriate (the areas of the forbidden). And as the concepts of topological psychology have been applied by Barker and Wright in "psychological ecology," their relevance for the analysis of the structuring of the individual's educational experience through time and space has become clear. And here, as elsewhere, a central issue concerns the distinction between those conceptions that are brought into a situation and those that emerge in the situation itself.[190]

TRANSITIONS, LIMINALITY, AND MARGINALITY

Since it is clear that definitions of the situation vary significantly from one setting to another, and even from one moment to another within the same setting, it becomes essential in tracing the individual's educational experience over time and through space to understand the subtle distinctions in reality status of one situation as compared with another, whether it is serious education, play, fantasy, or make-believe. Moreover, since such differences in the frame or definition of the situation exist, the issue of how transitions from one situation to another are made has important implications for the understanding of education. Here too certain concepts from the behavioral sciences offer possible guides in examining the issues.

Transitions in the definition of a situation may take place when a shift is made in physical setting; they may also take place in the same physical setting on a moment-to-moment basis through the restructuring of the individual's attention. This makes it essential to understand the way in which memories and anticipations are woven together in the transitions from one situational definition to another. Thus, the tracing of the individual's educational encounters cannot be separated from memories and anticipations, since the present in time and space is woven together with the remembered and the anticipated. For this reason, physical objects—icons—within the home, the school, or other setting become important as they serve to trigger memories and anticipations. (In this sense too the evocative character of spaces is also of particular importance.) Since, at any moment, multiple streams of awareness exist simultaneously, it becomes necessary to analyze memories and

190   George Gonos, " 'Situation' versus 'Frame': The 'Interactionist' and the 'Structuralist' Analyses of Everyday Life," *American Sociological Review* 42 (1977): 854-67.

anticipations as well as the current focus of primary attention or, in Goffman's terms, "main involvements."[191]

In understanding education in a setting, therefore, it is important to tap not only observable events, but the "under-memories" or the "under-tastes."[192] The question of the way in which multiple strands of memory and anticipation are woven into the present has particular importance in understanding education within the family and especially the family's relation to television, where the question of the forms of imagination that are fostered or constrained by the television experience is vital. Thus, the concept of transitions, both in observable behavior and in the structure of the individual's attention, is important in analyzing the organization of the individual's educational experience and the way in which education in one setting is combined with education in another setting. The fact of moment-to-moment transitions and multiple, simultaneous strands of awareness implies that it is insufficient to examine the relationship between education in one setting, for example, home, and education in another, for example, school, in terms that presume the two physical locations are necessarily separate in the individual's attention.

The concept of liminality, as employed by Turner in the examination of periods when the individual is between statuses, for example, times of initiation during adolescence, suggests yet another level at which transitions may be analyzed. The term *liminality* is used to refer to such periods because the individual is "betwixt and between," and the transitions from one status to another often entail "rites of passage." Turner's analysis of initiation rites points to the way in which a variety of ritual and symbolic procedures may be employed to "startle neo-phytes into thinking about objects, persons, relationships, and features of their environment they have hitherto taken for granted." These rites "indicate and constitute transitions between states."[193] The transitions during liminal periods have been examined in terms of life-cycle transitions for the most part, but the concept of liminality may also be employed in the analysis of daily transitions, where one may observe certain "passage" rituals. For example, during the walk between home and school, where the memory of home lingers and the expecta-

---

191 Goffman, *Behavior in Public Places.*
192 I am indebted for the terms to Margaret Mead, who tells me that "under-taste" is a Russian image whereas "under-tone" is English. This distinction was made to her by Elena Calas.
193 Turner, *The Forest of Symbols*, pp. 93, 105.

tion of school looms, the child may engage in protective magical games, such as "If you step on a crack, you'll break your father's back."[194]

Turner's analysis of the symbolism that is used in the rites that facilitate the transition from one state to another is especially interesting and suggestive. Complex and bizarre rituals may serve to indicate that the neophyte is "neither living nor dead from one aspect, and both living and dead from another." Rituals during liminal periods may serve to symbolize the "undoing," "dissolution," and "decomposition" of previous states, and at the same time they can mark "growth" and "transformation," and the "reformulation of old elements into new patterns."[195] Although the subtle transitions from moment to moment in daily life may entail small-scale rituals that are less dramatic than the rituals employed during periods of liminality related to life-cycle transitions, they may nonetheless be vital for the analysis of the shift from one definition of the situation to another and therefore important in the analysis of the organization of the individual's educational experience through time and space.

Another related concept is that of *marginality*. The concept has an extensive history in sociology, having been applied to instances where individuals are between different cultural or status groupings, particularly those related to upward mobility or immigration, rather than between periods of life-cycle status transition. Although the focus has been distinctly different from that of the concept of liminality, marginality offers yet another image for examining the transitions in the organization of the individual's educational experience.[196] The concept is important because it directs attention to diverse values and beliefs that may exist for an individual and to the question of how the individual brings together these different cultural orientations. It also relates to the analysis of deviance, and the processes by which an individual may move outside a particular set of values and beliefs. And this in turn directs us to the basic question of how the individual selects from and combines diverse educational experiences.

An essential point about the process of transition from one setting to another and about periods of liminality and points of marginality is that a creative possibility exists in such situations. Just as Boissevain argues that those with loosely knit, more diversified social networks may be more open to innovations,[197] Turner argues that during periods

194 Again, the idea is taken from a personal communication from Margaret Mead.
195 Turner, *The Forest of Symbols*, pp. 96-97, 99.
196 Cf. Everett V. Stonequist, *The Marginal Man: A Study in Personality and Culture Conflict* (New York: Charles Scribner's Sons, 1937).
197 Boissevain, *Friends of Friends*.

of liminality, where the individual is "betwixt and between," there are particularly rich possibilities for education to take place. Turner makes an important distinction between that which is ambiguous or contradictory and that which cannot be understood in static terms. In periods of liminality, one is not dealing with "what has been defectively defined or ordered," nor with "structural contradictions," but rather with "the essentially unstructured (which is at once destructured and prestructured)."[198] In liminal transitions that are unstructured (as compared with situations that are ambiguous or contradictory in their structuring), special possibilities for education are present because the neophyte is malleable. And when rituals take advantage of this malleability, they help to create a "stage of reflection." A variety of symbolic procedures, such as disproportion, monstrousness, and mystery, may be employed to startle the neophyte into thinking about that which has previously been taken for granted. In these procedures, Turner argues, "there is a promiscuous intermingling and juxtaposing of the categories of event, experience, and knowledge, with a pedagogic intention." Through rituals that combine elements in different ways, the neophyte is forced to think. "Put a man's head on a lion's body and you think about the human head in the abstract." By altering the proportion of objects in their representation, making them huge or tiny by comparison with other features of their normal context, the same process of startling the neophyte into thinking is accomplished. Thus, liminality breaks "the cake of custom and enfranchises speculation."[199] Or, in Hall's term, liminal or marginal statuses are points when "the grip of patterned behavior" can be loosened.[200]

EDUCATIVE STYLE: THE COMBINATION OF EDUCATIONAL EXPERIENCES

A most elusive and at the same time vital issue in the analysis of the organization of the individual's educational experience is that of how the individual combines diverse experiences, both from different settings and over time. The issue is central in the concept of educative style, which directs attention to the necessity of understanding the processes of combination.[201] The issue of the combination of educational experiences from one setting to another has been dealt with classically through the concept of transference of learning. As conceived in the

198   Turner, *The Forest of Symbols*, pp. 97-98.
199   Ibid., pp. 105, 106.
200   Edward T. Hall, *The Silent Language* (New York: Doubleday, 1959), p. 212.
201   Leichter, "The Concept of Educative Style."

concept of educative style, examining the combination of experience brings together issues of the organization of external settings with those of the individual's psychological and cognitive structuring of these settings and experiences.

The issue of how the individual combines diverse educational experiences has also been examined, for example, in educational biographies, in terms that suggest the possibility of combination such as to "complement," "supplement," and "reinforce."[202] All of these terms highlight the importance of analyzing the structure of diversity in the individual's environment as well as the ways in which the individual handles diversity. Here, too, a variety of concepts in the social science literature may be explored for their possible contribution to the understanding of processes of combination.

From an institutional perspective, a central educational question has been that of the extent of continuity or discontinuity, similarity or dissimilarity, between one setting and another, for example, between the family and the school. It has been assumed that the nature and extent of similarity or dissimilarity have consequences for education, with special attention having been devoted to situations in which marked "cultural gaps" appear to exist, again, for example, between family and school.[203] Where cultural discontinuities are assumed to be present, programs have frequently been set up to increase communication and involvement and thereby to reduce the distance. An example is the new career and paraprofessional programs where it has been assumed that education can best take place where individuals of the same background are involved, and teachers (at least some teachers in inner-city schools) "speak the language of the children."[204] Difference, at least too much difference, is presumed to be educationally problematic. It has also been argued, as we have seen, that the overinvolvement of parents in the school may be problematic and that a balance should be sought in the amount of communication between school and community.[205] Overinvolvement is rarely seen as signifying too much homogeneity of values, beliefs, and experiences between the family and school; it is

202 These terms have been employed in the educational biographical studies of Lawrence A. Cremin and Ellen Condliffe Lagemann.

203 For a useful discussion of continuities and discontinuities, see Getzels, "The Communities of Education."

204 William S. Bennett, Jr., and R. Frank Falk, *New Careers and Urban Schools: A Sociological Study of Teacher and Teacher Aide Roles* (New York: Holt, Rinehart & Winston, 1970), p. vi; also, for a related discussion, see Robert K. Merton, "Insiders and Outsiders: A Chapter in the Sociology of Knowledge," *American Journal of Sociology* 78 (1972-73): 9-47.

205 Litwak and Meyer, *School, Family, and Neighborhood.*

taken rather to imply that there is too much interference of parents in the running of the school. And the suggestion is often made that the child who must move from one culture in the home to another culture in the school is in a difficult, even disadvantaged, position.

Interestingly, these assumptions are in sharp contrast to those implicit in periods of liminality, where the transition from one state to another is used to open up the possibilities of education. Clearly, an understanding of the processes of combination must clarify the different levels of similarity or dissimilarity across situations as well as the ways in which the individual selects from and synthesizes these different and similar experiences.

A number of concepts in the behavioral sciences have specifically been employed to examine situations of diversity in the structuring of the individual's experience. One such concept is that of role conflict. This concept has been explored at length in the sociological literature, with precise distinctions between various kinds of role conflict, that is, conflicts of expectation within a single position and counter-position in the role-set, as distinct from conflicts of expectation within a position stemming from different counter-positions in the role set, and as further distinct from conflicts in the different roles in an individual's life, for example, between obligations at work and obligations at home. In examining all of the various forms of role conflict, an important assumption is that conflicts arise when the individual is faced with different, and hence incompatible, demands or expectations, for example, the demand to be in more than one place at the same time or the expectation that the individual will be intimate and warm and at the same time objective and fair.[206] These constructs suggest the importance of examining the structure of the individual's educational experience across areas in which inconsistent or conflicting demands arise. Such an examination is one essential aspect in attempting to understand how experiences are combined. Analyses of role conflict have been undertaken with specific reference to education, as in the analysis of the school superintendent's role[207] and the role of teenagers in schools and the conflicting pressures on them to conform to the peer society and the expectations of teachers and parents.[208]

206   Hervé Varenne and Marjorie Kelly, "Friendship and Fairness: Ideological Tensions in an American High School," *Teachers College Record* 77 (May 1976): 601-14.

207   Gross, Mason, and McEachern, *Explorations in Role Analysis.*

208   James S. Coleman, *The Adolescent Society: The Social Life of the Teenager and Its Impact on Education* (New York: The Free Press, Collier-Macmillan, Ltd., 1961).

The analysis of role conflict suggests the great variety of ways in which different and conflicting expectations and pressures may be brought to bear on the individual. And in the analysis of role conflict, the tracing of networks, status-sets, and fields facilitates describing the extent and areas of diversity of the individual's experience. Merton's analysis of insiders and outsiders points to the fact that individuals do not have a "single status, but a status set: a complement of variously interrelated statuses which interact to affect both their behavior and perspectives." As a result, in structural terms, "we are all, of course, both Insiders and Outsiders."[209] The multiplicity of the individual's statuses—statuses based, for example, on ethnicity, sex, occupation, region, religion—is a structural source of diversity in the individual's life as well as a possible source of conflict in the definition of roles.

Closely related to the concept of role conflict is the concept of cross-pressure. The idea of cross-pressure suggests that the individual is faced with different and possibly incompatible expectations from different sources. A number of studies have focused on cross-pressures and role conflicts for adolescents, indicating the potential value of this mode of analysis in considering the individual's educational experience. Gans, for example, describes the way in which the West End Italian-American child is faced with cross-pressures stemming from the fact that the peer society emphasizes action-seeking values, whereas the school emphasizes routine-seeking values. Differences between the school and the peer society (and the ethnic community more generally) are seen to have direct effects on learning: "Emerging from homes in which learning has not been encouraged, they have been brought up in such a way that their attention span is very short. This makes studying and learning difficult. Moreover, the school—a middle-class institution—seeks to train them for a way of life that in many ways is diametrically opposed to the one which they have so far experienced." As a result, the adult routine and in particular the routine of the school "is anathema to many."[210]

In a similar manner, Coleman analyzes role conflicts and cross-pressures in the life of the adolescent, placing his analysis in the broader perspective of ideas concerning age segregation in industrial society. Coleman too assumes that pressures from the peer group often run counter to those of the adult society. Data on the structure of these cross-pressures, and particularly on the extent to which adolescents are

209   Merton, "Insiders and Outsiders," p. 22.
210   Gans, *The Urban Villagers*, p. 68.

oriented toward peers as compared with parents and teachers, were obtained by Coleman through a series of survey questions, such as whether adolescents would join a social club if their parents or their favorite teacher or their friends disapproved. In response to these and related questions, Coleman found a fairly even split between the disapproval of friends and parents, with the disapproval of teachers counting for little. Coleman argues for the importance of peers in the life of the adolescent, indicating that although "parental desires are of great importance to children in a long-range sense . . . it is their peers whose approval, admiration, and respect they attempt to win in their everyday activities, in school and out."[211] The choices that Coleman analyzes are based on hypothetical questions that assume the values of the peer culture and the values of the adult culture are divergent.

In both these analyses of adolescents, the way in which the individual combines diverse experiences is seen to relate to the structure of the external pressures. Coleman, for example, argues that the power of the peer group over teenagers derives, at least in part, from the increasing age segregation of industrial society, in which the adolescent "is 'cut off' from the rest of the society, forced inward toward his own age group, made to carry out his whole social life with others his own age" in a world apart. Adolescents therefore become part of distinct social systems "which offer a united front to the overtures made by adult society."[212] Thus, in combining peers' values with those of parents, pressures from the peer society are presumed to outweigh those from the adult world.

Both the Gans and the Coleman analyses, however, suggest that there is a certain indeterminacy in the way in which the individual puts together diverse influences and that, in fact, the selection of values and beliefs—whether to follow the views of one's parents or one's peers— varies from one individual to another. Gans, for example, indicates that even though the values of the peer-group society and the Italian-American family are in marked contrast with those of the school, there still exists "considerable variety among teenage groups. Some are embroiled in continuous conflict with the adult world, and it is they who become the most visible to the middle-class eye. More participate—at least part of the time—in school and settlement house activities, and thus are on their way to becoming routine-seekers. A rare few become middle class in the way in which the school and the settlement want all of them to

211 Coleman, *The Adolescent Society*, p. 11.
212 Ibid., pp. 3-4.

be. Thus, the teenager may *choose* [italics mine] from a variety of groupings although the choice does become numerically more limited toward the middle-class end of the scale."[213] So too, Coleman, although emphasizing the separation between the teenage world and the adult world, acknowledges that in "the state of transition that adolescents experience—leaving one family, but not yet in another, they consequently look both forward to their peers and backward to their parents."[214] And while Coleman's data may indicate the comparative importance given to peers as compared with parents—at least in response to hypothetical choices—they by no means indicate that adolescents are completely cut off from the reactions of their parents. On the contrary, Coleman himself suggests that "it is as if the adolescent culture is a Coney Island mirror, which throws out a reflecting adult society in a distorted but recognizable image." Thus, the contrasts between the peer culture and the adult culture are not total and do not exist at all levels. Moreover, as Coleman indicates, it would be a serious mistake to see adolescent culture "as a single invariant entity."[215]

These studies clearly indicate the need to understand the structure of diversity within adolescent culture itself as well as the ways in which cross-pressures and differences between parents and peers are handled differently by individual adolescents. While in answer to a hypothetical question as to whose approval or disapproval would matter most, one might respond that peers are more important than teachers or parents, such data merely raise the question of when and where actual differences are experienced by the individual and how such differences are dealt with. The idea of a Coney Island mirror that reflects back a distorted image of adult culture that is nonetheless an image of adult culture points to the importance of understanding the processes by which the individual selects and transforms experience from the outside world. An understanding of how the individual combines diverse educative experiences, therefore, must encompass both an understanding of the structure of the situation and of the way in which the individual selects from the situation.

Concepts of deviance offer another perspective on the structure of choices available to the individual in combining diverse and even conflicting influences. Merton's classic analysis of social structure and anomie suggests that where "cultural goals" and the "institutionalized means" for attaining these goals diverge, the individual has a variety of

---

213 Gans, *The Urban Villagers*, p. 69.
214 Coleman, *The Adolescent Society*, p. 5.
215 Ibid., pp. 42-43.

choices among possible modes of adaptation. These choices derive from the ways in which the individual rejects or accepts the cultural goals and the institutionalized means, with the various possible combinations resulting in different outcomes, that is, conformity, innovation, ritualism, retreatism, and rebellion.[216]

Yet another perspective on how the structure of the social world may influence the combination of the individual's educational experience may be derived from the concept of labeling. The concept of labeling directs attention to the way in which labels that are applied to an individual in one situation may be transferred to another situation.[217] A child who is labeled as less competent than a sibling may have this image carried over into his school experience, and where labels are applied through formal procedures such as testing and diagnosis, a child who is labeled as overactive or an underachiever in school may have the label transferred into the family. In other settings, for example, a museum or an after-school program, the label from the school may be unknown and therefore not be transferred, or transferred only insofar as the label has been incorporated as part of the individual's self-concept. Here, too, the way in which an individual incorporates or fails to incorporate a label is critical.

A very different perspective on the combination of educational experiences is offered by certain work in developmental psychology, particularly Kohlberg's work in cognitive development. Drawing as he does upon the theories of Piaget, Kohlberg insists that cognitive development follows certain regular patterns and that these patterns pertain regardless of the social position, ethnicity, or nationality of the child. Although Kohlberg does admit that certain variations do relate to social position, he argues that these are not essential variations in moral development. Whether one accepts the notion of fixed developmental sequence or not, Kohlberg's argument is significant for the present consideration. He characterizes "sociological notions," saying that "it is often thought that the child gets some of his basic moral values from his family, some from the peer group, and others from the wider society, and that these basic values tend to *conflict* [italics mine] with one another." Kohlberg goes on to argue that the notion of conflict and diversity in the world of the child is incorrect; "instead of participation in various groups causing conflicting developmental trends in morality, it appears that participation in various groups *converges* [italics mine]

216 Merton, "Social Theory and Social Structure," pp. 139-40.
217 Here the work of Nicholas Hobbs is especially interesting, see *The Futures of Children* (San Francisco: Jossey-Bass, 1975).

in stimulating the development of basic moral values, which are not transmitted by one particular group as opposed to another. The child lives in a *total social world* [italics mine] in which perceptions of the law, of the peer group, and of parental teachings all influence one another. While various people and groups make conflicting *immediate demands* upon the child, they do not seem to present the child with basically conflicting or different *general moral values*."[218] This position then, argues for a covergence of the experiences of the individual in moving through diverse areas of the social world, at least with respect to moral development.

However one views the particular formulation, it does point to the importance of understanding the process of selection on the part of the individual. Here, we return again to Bateson's significant insight. One may reasonably assume that the intellectual operations of which social scientists are capable also occur in everyday life. Thus, if it is possible for the social scientist to shift levels so that differences at one level become similarities at another, so too the individual in everyday life may make shifts of level. Bateson points directly to this process in saying with respect to the issue of cultural heterogeneity, *"We and the individuals whom we are studying* [italics mine] are forced to take a short-cut: to treat heterogeneity as a positive characteristic of the common environment."[219]

All of this suggests the importance of further analysis of the variety of ways in which the individual selects from and combines experience through active processes and shifts of levels in viewing the external world. Just as the concept of reflected appraisals has been important, it is equally important to understand the way in which the individual deflects the appraisals of others. As an individual moves from setting to setting, there may also be gradations in the extent to which the setting is seen as familiar. Yet artifacts, even in strange situations, may be used by the individual to create a sense of the familiar, so that here too the active symbolic processes of the individual are important.

The issue of temporal organization is also relevant to the question of how the individual combines diverse educative experiences. The extent to which early learning is definitive in setting the stage for later learning is crucial. Here some new formulations point toward greater possibilities of modification of early learning than had been presumed

---

218   Lawrence Kohlberg, "Development of Moral Character and Moral Ideology," in *Review of Child Development Research, Vol. 1*, ed. Martin L. Hoffman and Lois Walvis Hoffman (New York: Russell Sage Foundation, 1964), pp. 406-7.

219   Bateson, "Formulation of End Linkage," p. 369.

in the past.[220] A related question is whether certain kinds of learning must take place in certain sequences and at certain stages, as presumed, for example, in Erikson's theory of development.

The concept of primary, as compared with secondary, socialization offers yet another view of the relation of education at one moment in time to education at another moment in time, and the persistence of one educational experience in relation to another. Berger and Luckmann posit that "the already internalized reality has a tendency to persist," so that new contents "must somehow be superimposed upon this already present reality," with a result that "a problem of consistency between the original and the new internalizations" arises. The concept of persistence refers specifically to the structuring of the individual's experience over time. Since education in the home generally comes first, however, it also presumes that the home is the source of the primary education and that the "reality accent" of the knowledge that arises in the home is given "quasi-automatically" and applied in other situations, so that "it must be reinforced by specific pedagogic techniques, i.e., 'brought home' to the individual."[221]

This concept of the persistence and primacy of education in the home is, however, combined with a notion of the way in which significant others in the family mediate the reality of the world for the child. The child is born into a world in which "the significant others who mediate this world to him modify it in the course of mediating it. They select aspects of it in accordance with their own location in the social structure, and also by virtue of their individual, biographically rooted idiosyncrasies. The social world is, therefore, 'filtered' to the individual through this *double selectivity* [italics mine]."[222] On the one hand, this concept of primacy and persistence points to the importance of early experience in structuring reality, indicating that the process of combination is one of overlaying upon existing structures. On the other hand, the concept of filtering points to the processes by which those in the child's environment select aspects of the world. And this again suggests the need to examine the individual's selective processes.

EDUCATIVE STYLE: EDUCATIONAL AGENDAS

The concept of educative style points to the ways in which individuals engage in, move through, and combine educative experiences over a

220 Bloom, *Human Characteristics and School Learning.*
221 Berger and Luckmann, *The Social Construction of Reality,* pp. 140, 143.
222 Ibid., p. 131.

lifetime. While the concept refers to characteristics of the individual, it is not put forward as implying any fixed or single character trait. Rather, it is meant to direct attention to the quality of interactions between the individual and others in the environment. Educative style is thus conceived of as a constantly developing product of the individual's moving and multiple associations.[223]

A related concept is that of the individual's educational agenda. If, as the analysis thus far suggests, the world of the individual's educational experience is complex and diversified, at least in urban industrial societies, then the individual's selection from these diverse environmental influences and opportunities becomes vital. The notion of the individual's educational agenda is, in a sense, a counterpart to the notion of the curriculum in the family or the school. It refers not only to the long-range plans but also to day-to-day priorities for activities and the processes by which these priorities are set. Some individuals may have an agenda that structures their entire lifetime, whereas others may shift, for example, at mid-career, and structure an entirely new agenda. The agenda of an individual may be complex and clearly structured; it may also exist at the margins of awareness as an implicit set of priorities for action. In either case, the essential notion is that the individual actively engages in, redefines, and transforms the various experiences in his or her life.

The concept of the agenda directs attention, not only to the implicit or explicit priorities and processes by which the individual selects among educational opportunities and transfers or combines experiences across settings, but also to the manner in which the individual remembers and forgets. In this respect, it may be argued that to the search for ways of fostering transference of learning from one setting to another, one should add the search for ways of fostering thoughtful selection coupled with appropriate ignoring and forgetting, especially in a society in which the individual is bombarded by educational opportunities and possibilities.

In looking at the processes by which individuals select from their environment, certain concepts of personality or character structure are necessary, particularly concepts concerning the individual's response to external stimuli. Here Riesman's distinction between the "inner-directed" and the "outer-directed" individual is especially useful. A variety of other psychological concepts also point to differences among individuals in the processes by which they select from and fend off the exter-

223   Leichter, "The Concept of Educative Style." .

nal world and respond to or remain independent of external influences.[224]

SEQUENCE AND PROCESS

All of the concepts examined thus far take on their richest meaning
when conceived in relation to concepts of sequence and process. Indeed, as Whitehead argues, "lack of attention to the rhythm and character of mental growth is a main source of wooden futility in education."[225]

A developmental concept of stages of the life cycle, whether it be one
that implies fixed stages or one that is multi-stranded and more flexible,
is thus essential if one is to understand the structuring of the individual's
educational experience. Concepts about the processes and cycles of
learning itself are also important. A variety of ideas of sequence in
learning have been formulated, ranging from those that see learning and
the organization of educational activities in terms of a linear sequence,
to those that employ the concept of a spiral. In a spiral, one may return
again and again to earlier learnings, with new formulations and increasing
depth reflecting new experience.[226] As Whitehead has described so well,
education has a rhythm whereby the individual passes through "cyclic
recurrences," rather than through a uniform, steady, and undifferentiated
advance. Thus, "we pass from cycle to cycle" and "the subordinate
stages are reproduced in each cycle." Whitehead conceives of a "three-
fold cycle," whereby an alternation occurs from an emphasis on romance
or vividness and novelty, to an emphasis on precision and exactness, to
an emphasis on generalization, that represents a return to the stage of
romance but with a new synthesis. Moreover, Whitehead argues that
"education should consist in a continual repetition of such cycles,"
and that "each lesson in its minor way should form an eddy cycle issuing
in its own subordinate process. Longer periods should issue in definite
attainments, which then form the starting grounds for fresh cycles."[227]

224   David Riesman with Reuel Denney and Nathan Glazer, *The Lonely Crowd: A Study
of the Changing American Character* (New Haven, Conn.: Yale University Press, 1950). For a
clinically oriented view see Herbert Spiegel and David Spiegel, *Trance and Treatment: Clinical
Uses of Hypnosis* (New York: Basic Books, forthcoming); the large literature on "locus of control" is also relevant.

225   Alfred North Whitehead, *The Aims of Education* (New York: The Free Press, 1929;
rev. ed., 1957), p. 17.

226   See Margaret Mead, "The Conservation of Insight: Educational Understanding of
Bilingualism," *Teachers College Record* 79 (May 1978): 705-21; the "spiral curriculum" of the
Rudolph Steiner School is another example.

227   Whitehead, *The Aims of Education*, pp. 17, 18, 19.

In a similar manner, Bruner discusses the concept of a spiral curriculum and the hypothesis that "any subject can be taught effectively in some intellectually honest form to any child at any stage of development."[228] Although children learn very differently at different stages of development, following the ideas of Piaget and his colleagues, it is possible to introduce ideas that will be valuable in adult life in a form that is comprehensible to a child at earlier stages.

Such concepts of sequence and process have been developed largely in thinking about education in a particular setting, where the curriculum may be organized in a particular manner, for example, in the school, where one may introduce ideas of advanced mathematics in forms that are comprehensible to young children. The problem of sequence and process become much more complex, however, when one's purpose is to understand the relationship of education in one setting to education in another. It is clearly assumed in many compensatory education programs, for example, that a disadvantage arises when children enter school without sufficient prior education. It is therefore argued that the sequence of learning in one area must dovetail with the sequence of learning in another area. Yet the way in which an individual moves from one setting to another and combines experiences in diverse settings undoubtedly differs at different stages of the life cycle. Young children, for example, clearly engage in a range of activities outside the home very different from that of adolescents. Some interesting data from Barker and Wright's study indicate that different age groups occupy different spatial territories in the community. The activities of various subgroups in the population—infants, preschool children, young schoolchildren, older schoolchildren, adolescents, adults and the aged —are plotted in "territorial range maps," which show that although the community was remarkably open to the coming and going of children of all ages, those of different ages occupy different portions of the community. A sequence is suggested, moreover, whereby children generally add new behavior settings to their "territorial range one at a time," with their first entrance into a new setting being "brief and on an apprenticeship basis."[229] Thus, the movement through space and the institutions that are encountered vary with the stages of the individual's life cycle. Moreover, the sequence of different kinds of learning experiences varies from one setting to another. A careful sequence, moving from intuitive to analytic thinking and back, may be worked out in

228 Jerome Bruner, *The Process of Education* (Cambridge: Harvard University Press, 1960), p. 33.

229 Barker and Wright, *Midwest and Its Children*, pp. 99-101.

the school. Yet the sequence of learning via television may be distinctly different.

Rhythmic or cyclic processes are undoubtedly crucial, however one conceives of them. This implies that an understanding of relationships among institutions that educate cannot be based on a static model of the content of education in different locations. Rather, models of process are required, models that take into account the sequential structure of education within institutions as well as the way in which cycles and epicycles are meshed together as the individual moves from one institution to another. The tempo of education in the home, for example, may or may not be in synchrony with the tempo of education in the school, or the phase of learning in the home may or may not mesh with the phase of learning in the school.[230] In working toward such process models, it becomes essential to contend with the methodological problems of the study of motion.[231]

I have examined a variety of concepts that are potentially useful for an understanding of the organization of the individual's educational experience through time and space. It is not possible to reconstruct the social or institutional world merely by tracing the experience of a collection of individuals. As Goffman indicates, an analysis of the structure of experience of individuals does not necessarily address itself to or connect with the question of "the structure of social life." His own analysis of frames "is about the organization of experience—something than an individual actor can take into his mind—not the organization of society."[232] In stressing the importance of concepts that enable one to analyze the organization of the individual's educational experience, the argument here is not that it will, in itself, enable one to understand the way in which institutions are organized or the way in which institutions relate to each other, but that, given our present mode of conceptualizing, and given the ultimate goal of fostering the educational growth of the individual, it is vital to add the perspective of the learner to other levels of analysis.

CONCLUDING OBSERVATIONS

I have deliberately selected a variety of concepts and juxtaposed some that have been used elsewhere without explicit relation to each

---

230 Here the work of Eliot Chapple is especially relevant, cf. Chapple, *Culture and Biological Man.*

231 For a fascinating discussion of the "problem of motion," see Robert Nisbet, *Sociology as an Art Form* (London: Oxford University Press, 1976), pp. 94-114.

232 Goffman, *Frame Analysis,* p. 13.

other, selecting from diverse disciplines and literatures those ideas that seem to me to offer potential value in the analysis of relationships among families and communities as educators. In the process, I have undoubtedly abstracted from the original literatures in a way that sometimes gives less than full and complete coverage to earlier formulations. Moreover, I have used many of the concepts in a metaphorical sense, much as those engaged in network research have argued that the early uses of the network concept were metaphorical, that is, employed as an image without precise operational specification. While some of the concepts I have discussed have lent themselves to more specific operationalization and more empirical examination than is reported here,[233] I would argue that the metaphorical use and juxtaposition of concepts that are not ordinarily combined is entirely legitimate and appropriate in the definition of a newly emerging sphere of inquiry. My intention is not to suggest a facile synthesis; it is rather to present a panorama of concepts and levels of analysis that may be employed in inquiries pertaining to a particular question.

The picture that I have attempted to paint is necessarily complex and, in this sense, may be tantalizing—even frustrating—to those concerned with program and policy issues for which immediate answers are sought. It is clear that many vital choices today rest upon assumptions about the relationship of education in one setting, particularly the family, to education in other settings. It would be nice to be able to say that the family exerts particular kinds of educational influence that can be combined with schooling and other sources of education in particular ways. In the ferment of current interest in the family, it would be nice to be able to state that the family necessarily exerts a primary and definitive influence upon the individual's learning in other spheres and in subsequent life. It would also be nice to argue that certain kinds of institutions can best specialize in certain kinds of education, leaving other kinds of education to other institutions. But the complexity of the individual's many worlds and multiple levels of attention does not lead to formulations that are neat, simple, or definitive. On the contrary, one must argue that overly simplistic notions are in the long run far less helpful than concepts that direct attention to the subtle and complicated ways in which multiple levels of educational encounters can be examined. With our present level of knowledge, we

---

233 Some of these concepts have been subjects of extensive empirical examination in other literatures, and some, such as that of social networks and educative styles, are now being examined in research at the Center for the Study of the Family as Educator.

should not aim for a single map of the relation of different institutions in society to each other, but rather for a variety of maps that describe and specify a variety of combinations and clusterings.

It is evident, as one examines education from the perspective of the individual, that the divisions among different domains are difficult to identify. If, for example, one starts by considering the daily competencies of a particular individual and then attempts to uncover the sources through which these competencies have been acquired, one is quickly aware of the fluidity of experience and the difficulty of specifying the sources of education. It is often difficult to remember where a particular skill or an ability to carry out a particular activity was learned and whether it was indeed learned by deliberate instruction or by self-education. The examination of daily competencies also reveals the extent of redundancy or overlap between one realm of educative experience and another. Where, for example, did one learn to read a newspaper? One may point to early instruction in reading in the home, and to later instruction in reading in the school, but when one includes the question of how one selects from the many items in a newspaper those that merit one's attention, how one selects from the various newspapers those that one wishes to read, and how the reading of newspapers is combined with the viewing of news programs on television and the discussion of news with family, friends, and colleagues, the picture that emerges clearly points to extensive redundancy. Yet redundancy may in some respects be the very essence of communication.

One further point may be made about the analysis of education across institutions and settings. For an adequate understanding of educational experiences and encounters, a theory of communication is vital.[234] And here again, the notion of multiple levels arises. The complexity of communication systems has been variously described, but one essential point on which modern scholars of communication agree is that symbols have many meanings. As Turner indicates, symbols are "multi-vocal," with each symbol having "a fan of referents."[235] This implies that multiple levels of educational process and multiple meanings occur simultaneously, making it essential to understand processes by which symbols are transformed, created, and re-created by the individual.

The complexity of the analysis here may also be frustrating to those concerned with narrowly defined empirical research. My intent is not

---

234 Theodore Schwartz, ed., *Socialization as Cultural Communication: Development of a Theme in the Work of Margaret Mead* (Berkeley: University of California Press, 1975).
235 Turner, *The Forest of Symbols*, p. 107.

to argue that there is anything inherently wrong with specificity and empiricism, but it is to argue that this approach can go awry if it extracts a limited segment of human experience and analyzes it without recognition of its complex context. My argument is not against the necessary limitation of individual research inquires, but it is meant to insure that these inquires go forward with a rich sense of the broader context in which they are inevitably located. It is this point that I have emphasized in my discussions of contextual rigor.[236]

Returning to the paradox with which I began, of the family (or other institution) that disappears under scrutiny, it should now be clear that in examining the relationships among educative institutions, the paradox can only be handled by a complex set of concepts that permits multiple perspectives, a set of concepts that takes into account the organization of educative institutions as well as the ways in which individuals move through different educational settings and that focuses on the processes by which the individuals select from and transform their educational experiences over a lifetime.

236   Leichter, "Some Perspectives on the Family as Educator."

The Communities of Education

J. W. GETZELS
The University of Chicago

At first glance, it would hardly seem fruitful to raise a question about the meaning and accuracy of the time-honored dictum that the school and the community are related. The answer appears so obvious as to render the question unproblematical; everyone knows what a community is, and of course the school and the community are related.

When, however, one dares ask what specifically does *the* community to which the school is related refer to, or precisely what the term *community* itself means in this context, the answer becomes much less obvious and the question much more problematical.[1] Does the community refer to the neighborhood in which the school is located, the families whose children attend the school even if they do not live in the neighborhood, the administrative district responsible for operating the school, the political entity whose taxes support the school, or—at another level of abstraction—does it refer to a communion of minds along the lines of what the Lynds called the Middletown "spirit"—or what?

Consider the relation between the school and the community in this admittedly extreme but actual case. The Robert White School in Boston

---

1   An example of the ambiguities to which the familiar phrase "the school and the community" is liable is contained in a recent provocative article by David Nyberg, "Education as Community Expression," *Teachers College Record* 79, no. 2 (December 1977): 205-23. The article argues that most of the influence shaping the school "comes from—and should come from—*the community*" (p. 219, italics added). Until almost the very end, the reader assumes that he and the writer know what "the community" refers to. But then on the last page or two, the reader is informed that there is a "significant difficulty" in "defining 'community' " and that the writer "cannot propose a complete and satisfactory definition" (pp. 220-21); no definition of any kind is attempted. In effect, the reader had been proceeding on the implicit assumption that he and the writer agreed on, or at least knew, what was meant by community, when in fact this was not the case at all; despite its usage throughout, "the community" of which education was supposed to be an "expression" remained without specific referent.

is a private alternative school for delinquent children.[2] Its pupils are referred to it by the courts and other schools; they come from East Boston, Charlestown, Revere, Chelsea, Winthrop, the North End, and part of the West End. The school is certified by the Boston school system since it wants to maintain public school connections. School personnel come from Harvard University; financial support is provided by private philanthropy, the city of Boston, and the federal government. The directors of the school state that "the school is not yet of the community" but expect that "within the next five to seven years [it will] dissolve itself into the community taking on another form within the public school district." They are concerned that the changes wrought by the school in the children may be unfitting them for the community in which they must live. The staff asks of itself: "Have we disabled these survivors of the jungle by domestication?"

Even in this brief summary it is possible to count at least a dozen "communities," not otherwise defined, with which the school seems to be involved and which seem to be involved in the child's education. There is the geographic community from which the children come; in fact, there is more than one such community—East Boston, Charlestown, Revere, Chelsea, and so forth. There is the smaller neighborhood community in which the children's homes are located; sometimes the child's local community may be a particular block or two, or a street corner, where he "hangs out." There is the judicial community that refers the children, the academic community that provides professional personnel, the philanthropic community that supplies private funds for operating the school, and the city of Boston that certified the school and supplies the public funds. Then there is the unspecified community that, in the words of the directors, "the school is not yet of," and the community into which it is expected the school will "dissolve" itself and take on "another form within the public school district." And none of this is to say anything about the "jungle" as a setting or community (or is it?) from which the children learned more than they did in their previous schools, and which may perhaps be as related to what their present school is about as any of the other so-called communities.

Granted this is an atypical school, and we use it only as an instance. But similar complexities arise if the same analysis is applied to a more typical school. Try to delineate *the* community to which a public school in Boston, Chicago, or New York is related; or for that matter, try it even for a school in a suburb or a rural area.

2   J. Shlien and R.F. Levant, "The Robert W. White School," *Harvard Graduate School of Education Bulletin* 19 (1974): 12-18.

When I asked several teachers to take a moment to do this for their schools, one teacher mentioned a school in Chicago and listed "the ethnic community" and "the black community," explaining that "you can't understand this school without knowing them and their relation to the commercial and political communities which really call the shots." A second teacher mentioned a school in an all-white suburb and listed "the parents who live east of Rockledge Avenue and those who live west of it," adding that she did not know "whether they constitute separate communities, but each meets together against the other even though their kids go to the same community school." A third teacher said, "How about a school without a community? It is in a bombed-out central city area where no one knows anyone, and the turnover in a six-flat, which may hold two dozen families, can be 100 percent in a couple of months. The only people to whom the school is related for any length of time are the police who patrol the place."

Similar difficulties arise in more serious and presumably more informed discussions of the school and the community. The transcript of a recent conference on the subject shows a dozen references to "the community" without any indication of what the term referred to.[3] When the referent was specified, it included such diverse things as "the urban community," "the peer community," "the ghetto community," "the educational community," "the American community." Community seemed to be a geographic location or a face-to-face group in it, an entire nation or culture or one of its institutions. Despite this, when one conferee was asked what he meant when he said "the community," he replied impatiently, "Stop the nonsense. All of us know . . . "

Undefined and unrecognized diversities appear also in the methods by which relations between the school and the community are studied. Some study the school and the community by following individuals around and mapping the objective networks, which presumably are then translated into community terms; others collect subjective meanings or "cognitive maps," which are also translated into community terms. Some favor what they call the phenomenological method and seek to gain hostage on the community by naturalistic observation without prior conceptualization of what to observe; others favor the theoretical method and proceed by first conceptualizing the nature of community and then making observations guided by the conceptualization. Still others ask why not do both simultaneously, not realizing the depth of feeling among the first group that the second method leads only to

3 Conference on Families and Communities as Educators, Washington, D.C.: June 15-16, 1977.

distortion, and among the second group that the first method is quite literally impossible. And of course there are those who say that to raise these questions is mere scientism; the only method needed is common sense and good eyesight.

The point of this litany of unresolved conceptual and methodological issues is this. Depite beliefs to the contrary, there is little that is self-evident about how to identify and study *the* community or the role of the community in the child's education. If sensible examination of the relation between school and community, or the community as educator, is to obtain, the conceptual and methodological issues cannot be avoided, unpleasant as dealing with such matters may be, especially for those who like to assert solutions without troubling to specify the assumptions underlying the problems they identify, their conception of community, or the methods through which they reach the solutions they assert.

ON METHODS: HOW SHALL A "THING" BE STUDIED

A fundamental question in the study of school-community relations is the methodological strategy to be applied. The issue may be put most briefly in dichotomous terms, although this runs the danger of over-simplification to which one must be sensitive.[4]

There are those who begin from the premise that the focus of effort should be on the collection of reliable observations and data. The formulation of theory is secondary and likely to be a distraction; in any case, theorizing cannot be done without a base in data. And there are those who begin with the opposed premise that the focus of effort must be on theoretical work in the construction of heuristic conceptions. The collection of data without a base in such conceptions leads only to "blind" empiricism; meaningful observations cannot be made without recourse to some conceptual "map" (i.e., theory).

The first group points to the inevitable biases of theorizing. They agree with the position represented by MacLeod's well-known statement regarding social psychology, which holds for other of the social sciences as well:

> By the phenomenological method . . . is meant the systematic attempt to observe and describe in all its essential characteristics the world of

---

4 See J.W. Getzels, "Creativity: Prospects and Issues," in *Perspectives in Creativity*, ed. I.A. Taylor and J.W. Getzels (Chicago: Aldine Publishing Co., 1975), pp. 329-30. Also, J.W. Getzels, J.M. Lipham, and R.F. Campbell, *Educational Administration As a Social Process* (New York: Harper & Row, 1968).

phenomena as it is presented to us. It requires the deliberate suspension of all implicit and explicit assumptions . . . which might bias our observation. The phenomenological question is simply, "What is there?" without regard to Why, Whence, and Wherefore. . . . A phenomenological emphasis in psychology does not restrict a psychologist to the description of phenomena. It requires him, however, to look first at the world of things-as-they-are in its entirety before deciding which aspects of that world are to be considered important for theory.[5]

Two of MacLeod's categories of theoretical bias may illustrate the more general point. One category is the "organism-centered bias" where the essential determinants of social behavior are defined as conditions of the organism or as forces like instincts, needs, attitudes, or dispositions. The properties and functions of communities are explained by reference to a gregarious instinct or as meeting a human need for affiliation or some such presumed organismic condition. Another type of bias is the "sociological bias" where the structures and processes of society as defined by the sociologist are accepted as the true coordinates for the specification of social behavior and experience. The community is regarded as possessing the properties and functions revealed by a sociological investigation rather than as it is apprehended and reacted to by the individuals in it. In either case there is manifest bias.

The second group does not deny the possibility of bias; they maintain that conceptual and methodological bias is inevitable. The observing, perceiving, thinking organism cannot proceed without an assumptive base. One cannot look at everything, and so one must select what to look at on some grounds. If one set of assumptions is suspended, another set will sneak in anyway, unbeknown to the observer. From this point of view, instead of suspending theory, which is impossible—the language within which one sees and communicates is already "theoretical"—one should proceed within the framework of consciously held theory. In Neal Miller's words:

Pure empiricism is a delusion. A theory-like process is inevitably involved in drawing boundaries around certain parts of the flux of experience to define observable events and in the selection of events that are observed. Since multitudinous events could be observed and an enormous number of relationships could be determined among all

5   R.B. MacLeod, "The Phenomenological Approach to Social Psychology," *Psychological Review* 54 (1947): 193-94, 197.

these events, gathering all the facts with no bias from theory is utterly impossible. Scientists are forced to make a drastic selection, either unconsciously on the basis of perceptual habits and the folklore and linguistic categories of the culture, or consciously on the basis of explicitly formulated theory.[6]

The juxtaposition of the two views probably draws the issue too sharply. But the problem exists and must be faced. Shall one, for example, begin with the full knowledge of the theoretical distinction between *Gemeinschaft* and *Gesellschaft*, or more recently between the "natural community" and the "community of limited liability,"[7] or should one begin by suspending knowledge of any such ideas and look, in the words of MacLeod, "at the world of things-as-they-are in its entirety," deliberately avoiding all implicit and explicit assumptions?

It is not merely a question of personal predilection for one method over another as if all methods lead to the same research problems and the same conclusions—something like all roads leading to Rome. On the contrary, the problem and method are inextricably related, and it is sometimes difficult to determine which came first. Consider in this respect only the kinds of problems formulated by those favoring clinical methods where N = 1 is eminently sensible (Freud examines his own dreams, Piaget observes his own child, Barker studies One Boy's Day), and the kinds of problems formulated by those favoring psychometric or survey methods.

My point here is not to advocate one view over another. There is room for a variety of views, and the surest way to lose truth is to believe that one already has it; ultimately only the convergent pursuit of the manifold of approaches can lead to a full understanding of complex human events. My point rather is that one's conceptual and methodological premises—whether phenomenological or theoretical, clinical or psychometric, or whatever—have an impact on the kinds of problems that are formulated and the conclusions that are reached. When the premises are implicit and taken for granted—they are just "common sense," or, as that conferee insisted, "We *know* . . . "—the possibility of looking upon one's own formulations as tentative and demanding examination is precluded. We forget that underlying one's unquestioned

6   N.E. Miller, "Liberalization of Basic S-R Concepts: Extensions to Conflict Behavior, Motivation, and Social Learning," in *Psychology: A Study of Science*, ed. S. Koch, vol. 2 (New York: McGraw-Hill, 1959), p. 200.

7   G.D. Suttles, *The Social Construction of Communities* (Chicago: University of Chicago Press, 1972).

common sense are assumptions no less pivotal than those in the most tentative theoretical constructions. In Conant's words:

> Literally every step we take in life is determined by a series of inter-locking concepts and conceptual schemes. Every goal we formulate for our actions, every decision we make, be it trivial or momentous, involves assumptions about the universe and about human beings. To my mind, any attempt to draw a sharp line between common-sense ideas and scientific concepts is not only impossible but unwise.[8]

ON CONCEPTS: COMMUNITY, INSTITUTION, INDIVIDUAL, AND SOCIAL SYSTEM

The term *community* has numerous usages. It may refer to a restricted group of people living in a specific locality (e.g., "the Hoboken community"), an extended group with similar interests not necessarily in a specific locality (e.g., "the artistic community"), and to a group of persons or nations united by historical consciousness (e.g., "the entire Christian community").[9] The issue at the moment is not to assert a particular definition as the single "right" or even most fruitful one. It is rather to indicate the variety of possible communities and to suggest that the definition not be taken for granted as only "common sense."

Of whatever kind, communities are at once settings for educational in-stitutions and instruments of education in their own right. On the one hand, they determine the structure and curriculum of their schools. On the other, they provide the cognitive and affective experiences on which their inhabitants grow up. To be reared in Hoboken is not the same *educationally* as to be reared in Malibu Beach, even if the schools in the two places were the same. Schools are only one of the many contexts in which the child is educated. To mention only one illustrative list of such contexts, here is the one compiled some years ago by Charters and Gage:

1. teacher-pupil relationship (including parent-child)

2. classroom group

3. peer group, gangs

4. student society of the school

---

8 J.B. Conant, *Modern Science and Modern Man* (New York: Doubleday, 1953), pp. 135-36.

9 See *Webster's Third New International Dictionary* (Springfield, Mass.: G.&C. Merriam Co., 1976), p. 460.

5. social organization of the adults in the school

6. community in relation to education and the school

7. profession of education

8. society and the institution of education[10]

Though still school-bound and not exhaustive—for example, it omits mention of museums, television outlets, churches, recreational facilities—the list illustrates the variety of settings and communities of education. But a list alone, whether exhaustive or not, cannot of itself indicate the relations among its elements—in the present case, the relations among the children, the school, and the communities, and their impact on educational behavior.

One way of attempting to apprehend the interactions among individuals, institutions, and communities and their impact on behavior is to view the related elements as operating within a *social system* as the general context of behavior.[11] Specifically with respect to education, at one level of analysis a given society may be considered a social system with the school a particular institution within the system; at another level, the school may be considered a social system with the classroom an institution in it; at yet another level, the classroom may be considered a social system.

A social system embodies two classes of phenomena. There are institutions with component roles and expectations (rights and duties) that will fulfill the goals of the system, and there are individuals with component personalities and dispositions (cognitions and affects) who inhabit the system. Systematic behavior is the outcome of the interplay of these major variables: (1) institution, role, and expectation, which together compose the nomothetic or normative dimension of activity, and (2) individual, personality, and disposition, which together compose the idiographic or personal dimension of activity.

Institutional roles are complementary, each role deriving its definition and meaning from the other roles. Thus the role of teacher and the

---

10   W.W. Charters, Jr., and N.L. Gage, eds., *Readings in the Social Psychology of Education* (Boston: Allyn and Bacon, 1963), p. xvii.

11   See J.W. Getzels, "A Social Psychology of Education," in *Handbook of Social Psychology*, eds. G. Lindzey and E. Aronson, vol. 5 (Reading, Mass.: Addison-Wesley, 1969), pp. 459-537. Also, Getzels, Lipham, and Campbell, *Educational Administration as a Social Process*; J.W. Getzels and H.A. Thelen, "The Classroom as a Unique Social System," in *The Dynamics of Instructional Groups*, The 59th Yearbook of the National Society for the Study of Education, Part II, ed. N.B. Henry (Chicago: University of Chicago Press, 1960), pp. 53-82; and J.W. Getzels and E.G. Guba, "Social Behavior and Administrative Process," *School Review* 65 (1957): 423-41.

role of pupil cannot be understood or implemented except in relation to each other. In performing the role behavior expected of him or her, the teacher "teaches" the pupil; in performing the role behavior expected of him or her, the pupil "learns" from the teacher.

But it must also be borne in mind that roles are perceived and carried out by particular flesh-and-blood individuals, and no two individuals are alike even when they are performing the same role. Each individual stamps the role with the characteristic style of his own personality. Not all teachers teach, not all pupils learn—at least they do not teach and learn in the same way. Behavior is a function not only of normative expectations but also—and perhaps more importantly—of personal dispositions; behavior in a social system is always a reflection of some variable proportion of the role and personality dimensions in the complex of the entire structure of roles and interaction of personalities in the system as a whole.

The relevant elements of the framework may be represented pictorially as in Figure 1.

FIG. 1.   Elements of the normative and personal dimensions of behavior in a social system.

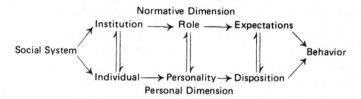

Both the institutions and the individuals in any given system—in the present case, schools and children—are integrally related to other systems and communities; the expectations of the schools and the dispositions of the children have their source in the communities in which the schools and children are embedded, and cannot be understood apart from them.

THE CONCEPTION OF COMMUNITY AND
THE VARIETY OF COMMUNITIES

The distinctive characteristics of the classic conception of community are well known. As Eggleston put it, "They are embodied in the small localised, self-contained group with shared values and ways of life which constitute a *culture* catering to *all* the needs of all the individual members."[12] But, as he goes on to say, "these tightly knit human groups

12   S. John Eggleston, *The Social Context of the School* (London: Routledge & Kegan Paul, 1967), p. 11.

of which one is unmistakably either an insider or an outsider have disappeared from large areas of modern Western society."[13] In Britian
they may be found only in the highlands and moorlands and in the Celt-
ic fringes. In the United States they may exist in the southern moun-
tain regions or in the Bible Belt areas of Utah and Idaho—if there. The
community as a single localized group serving all the individual needs
has been replaced by what some call "associations," others "networks,"
or by a variety of more or less loosely knit "communities," none con-
forming to the classic conception of community but together serving
similar functions. There has been, so to speak, a division of labor from
the classic community of which one was a part to a variety of communities to which one belongs. Or as someone put it, "neighbors" have
become "nigh-dwellers."[14]

Numerous attempts have been made to define and classify the variety
of these communities so that their impact on the institutions and individuals as well as the relations among the communities themselves might
be studied in some orderly way. A half-century ago, in perhaps the first
concerted effort in this respect, Gillette wrote, regarding the classificatory scheme he was offering, a statement that has held for other schemes
since then including the one I shall be proposing later on: "As a means
of helping analyze the community into its various kinds, I am offering
what I think of as an exploratory classificatory scheme of communities.
. . . It seeks to impress the student with the idea that there really are
different kinds of communities and that the job of locating and defining
them is a worthy undertaking."[15]

Gillette's scheme classified communities into "rural," "semi-urban,"
and "urban." The urban category was further divided into the city as a
whole and ten "intra-city" communities, including those characterized
by residential and ethnic identities, industrial and business zones, and
cultural and social interests like school, church, and recreation. Two
children living on the same city block would belong to the same residential community but also to other different communities depending
on ethnic allegiance, church membership, family, social, or recreational
interests, and so on. The two children might be exposed to the same
curriculum in the neighborhood school and might even learn the same
things there, but they would also learn very different things from the

---

13 Ibid.
14 See B.A. McClenahan, "The Changing Urban Neighborhood: A Sociological Study,"
University of Southern California Studies, Social Sciences Series no. 1, 1929.
15 J.M. Gillette, "Community Concepts," *Social Forces* 4 (1925-1926): 682.

communities to which each belonged independently. In effect, their schooling might converge, their education diverge.

At about the time Gillette was formulating his scheme, McClenahan undertook a study of an urban neighborhood as a community.[16] Although aware of Gillette's work, she developed a different classification comprised of six categories: (1) the community as a social unit, that is, a group of people in a prescribed locality who meet the more important concerns of life in common; (2) the community as an ecological or natural unit marked off by geographic barriers, lines of communication, or by limits of race or culture; (3) the community as a legal, political, or administrative unit like a municipality, school district, county, state, or nation; (4) the community as the equivalent of society; "it is the common life of beings who are guided essentially from within, relating themselves to one another, weaving for themselves the complex web of social unity"; (5) community as an ideal or mental entity; "it rests on the common and interdependent purposes of social beings . . . it is a 'union of minds' "; (6) community as a process: "Community is that intermingling which evokes creative power. What is created? Personality, purpose, will, loyalty."[17]

Twenty years and numerous studies later, Hollingshead, writing "Community Research: Development and Present Condition," still felt bound to complain that "sociologists are neither sure of what they mean by such basic terms as 'city,' 'community,' 'neighborhood,' and 'ecology,' nor are they consistent with one another in their usage."[18] He found that the concept of community was defined in at least three different ways in the extant literature: "(1) as a form of group solidarity, cohesion, and action around common and diverse interests; (2) as a geographic area with spatial limits; or (3) socio-geographical structure which combines the ideas embodied in (1) and (2)."[19]

By 1955, in the most exhaustive effort to that time at definition and classification, Hillery was able to compile no fewer than ninety-four different definitions of community.[20] He classified the conceptions into sixteen categories, which could be divided further into those specifying geographic area as a component and those emphasizing some other

16   McClenahan, "The Changing Urban Neighborhood."

17   Ibid., pp. 104-05.

18   A.B. Hollingshead, "Community Research: Development and Present Condition," *American Sociological Review* 13 (1948): 145.

19   Ibid.

20   G.A. Hillery, Jr., "Definitions of Community: Areas of Agreement," *Rural Sociology* 20 (1955): 111-23.

common characteristic. What emerged from the analysis is the notion that communities could be conceived of as groups of people in social interaction with ties or bonds having their source in geographic proximity, and/or shared goals and attitudes, and/or historic consciousness of kind. But only one element was common to all definitions: "All of the definitions deal with people. Beyond this common basis, there is no agreement."[21]

More recently—within the past two or three years—although repeating the endemic complaint that definitions of community are "loose," Hunter suggested that a "consensus" has emerged on three dimensions: "(1) community as a functional spatial unit meeting sustenance needs; (2) community as a unit of patterned social interaction; (3) community as a cultural-symbolic unit of collective identity."[22] But this formulation too came into immediate question; the claim of consensus was premature.[23] Despairing of reaching agreement in the definitional and taxonomic debate, the recent authoritative treatise *Community Studies* by Bell and Newby suggests that "rather as intelligence is what intelligence tests measure perhaps we can, for the time being at any rate, merely treat community as what community studies analyse."[24]

Despite the definitional and taxonomic difficulties, community studies do delimit their analyses to something, and investigations of community and education do relate the school to some notion of community. The trouble is that the notion is most often left implicit. One cannot proceed sensibly without adopting an explicit conception, however tentative, of what is being analyzed when one refers to the community or, more realistically, to one or another of the variety of communities.

At the risk, then, of adding yet another taxonomy that is open to question, it seems to me fruitful to think of communities, especially in relation to education, as groups of people conscious of a collective identity characterized by common cognitive and affective norms, and to order the variety of communities from those where the collective identity is most dependent on a particular locality to those where it is least dependent, although of course such ordering can only be approximate and the categories will overlap:

21   Ibid., p. 117.
22   A. Hunter, "The Loss of Community: An Empirical Test through Replication," *American Sociological Review* 40 (1975): 538.
23   See, for example, A.E. Luloff and K.P. Wilkinson, "Is Community Alive and Well in the Inner City? (Comment on Hunter, *ASR*, October 1975)," *American Sociological Review* 42 (1977): 827-28.
24   C. Bell and H. Newby, *Community Studies* (New York: Praeger, 1972), p. 32.

1. Local community (the collective identity is founded in a particular neighborhood or region). One is a member of the Hyde Park rather than the Woodlawn community in Chicago, or of the Greenwich Village rather than the Riverdale community in New York.

2. Administrative community (the collective identity is founded in a particular politically determined entity). One is not only a Hyde Parker but a Chicagoan, not only a Greenwich Villager but a New Yorker.

3. Social community (the collective identity is founded in a particular set of interpersonal relationships without regard to local or administrative boundaries). One is not only a Hyde Parker or Chicagoan but a member of a circle of people—"friends," "gang,"—with whom one regularly interacts.

4. Instrumental community (the collective identity is founded in direct or indirect engagement with others in performance of a particular function of mutual concern). One may be a member of the financial community, the union community, the philanthropic community, the school community, and so on.

5. Ethnic, caste, or class community (the collective identity is founded in affinity to a particular national, racial, or cultural group). A resident of Chicago or New York may also be a member of the Irish, Indian, Scotch, black, or upper-class community.

6. Ideological community (the collective identity is founded in a particular historic, conceptual, or sociopolitical consciousness of kind). One may be a member of the Christian, the Muhammadan, the scholarly, or the socialist community, which stretches beyond and across the local, administrative, social, instrumental, or ethnic communities.

Whichever definitional or taxonomic view is taken—even the view that a community is what community studies analyze—it is clear that the simplistic notion of the community as a single-scaled autonomous phenomenon is not tenable. People do not function in a single community but rather, as Hunter points out, in a hierarchical pattern of communities within communities, each forming a human system in itself but always related to other systems.[25] In the words of MacIver:

> It will be seen that a community may be part of a wider community, and that all community is a question of degree. . . . The one extreme is the whole world of men, one great but vague and incoherent common life. The other extreme is a small intense community within which the life of an ordinary individual is lived, a tiny nucleus of

25   A. Hunter, "Reply to Luloff and Wilkinson," *American Sociological Review* 42 (1977): 828-29.

common life with a sometimes larger, sometimes smaller, and always varying fringe.[26]

THE VARIETY OF COMMUNITIES AND EDUCATION

Preceding formulations and consequent studies of community and education typically visualized the school and the child as embedded in a community conceived as a culture with a certain ethos defined by its constituent values.[27] The quality of the school's roles and the quality of the children's personalities were related to the ethos of the community, and the specific role expectations and pupil dispositons to its values.

These formulations may now be seen as too monolithic and in need of refinement; they were based on the assumption of the self-contained autonomous community, which, if it has not disappeared altogether, is the exception rather than the rule. It is closer to reality to think of the school and the child as embedded not in a single community but in a variety of communities—of communities within communities—whose impact fluctuates throughout the life span and even in the course of meeting day-to-day needs. At one point the predominant influence on the school may come from the local community, at another from the administrative community, at another yet from the ethnic community, and so on. Similarly, at one point the greatest impact on the child may come directly or through the family from the local community, at another from the social community, at another from the instrumental community, and so on.

The cognitive and affective norms and values of the several communities may be congruent or, as is so often the case, incongruent with one another. In fact, in some ways the several communities are in competition and conflict for influence on the expectations of the school and for impact on the kinds of knowledge and dispositions the child acquires. The curricular ambiguities in the school and the motivational discords of the child reflect these conflicts. The children of the Robert White School had not acquired the knowledge and dispositions for remaining in the public schools although they had for surviving in the "jungle" in which they lived; the directors of the Robert White School were fearful that the expectations imposed by their school upon the children may disable them by "domestication" for survival in the community to which they must return.

26 Quoted in ibid.
27 See, for example, Getzels, "A Social Psychology of Education"; also, Eggleston, *The Social Context of the School.*

In any case, whatever the continuities or discontinuities among the several communities, this much is clear. On the one hand, the cognitive and affective expectations of the school derive, at least in part, from the phenomena, norms, and values of the communities to which the school is related; and, on the other, the cognitive and affective dispositions of the child are acquired, at least in part, from the phenomena, norms, and values of the communities in which the child is reared. The child learns both in and out of school; what he learns is inevitably bound not only to the communities to which the school is related but also more directly to the communities in which he holds membership independently or through his family.

The educational behavior of the child may, then, be seen as the outcome of the following dimensions in interaction: (a) The communities (local, administrative, social, etc.) as groups with collective identities defined by their patterns of cognitive and affective phenomena, norms, and values that influence the educational institutions, roles, and expectations; (b) the institutional characteristics including the pupil's role defined by its cognitive and affective expectations; (c) the individual characteristics including the child's personality defined by its cognitive and affective dispositons; (d) the communities (local, administrative, social, etc.) as groups with collective identities defined by their patterns of cognitive and affective phenomena, norms, and values that influence the developing individual personality and dispositions. By way of summary, the central concepts may be represented as in Figure 2.

Fig. 2. Dimensions of educational behavior including community, institutional, and individual elements.

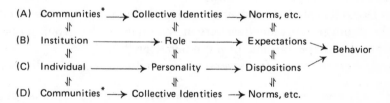

*Includes: (1) local community, (2) administrative community, (3) social community, (4) instrumental community, (5) ethnic community, (6) ideological community.

ON PROBLEMS FOR INQUIRY: EDUCATION AND THE CONTINUITIES AND DISCONTINUITIES AMONG COMMUNITIES

The conceptual change from a single community to a variety of communities as a key element in the child's education brings to light a number of issues heretofore obscured and permits the formulation of a number of neglected problems for inquiry. In this sense at least, the change is an advance, for in the words of Einstein's well-known statement, "The formulation of a problem is often more important than its solution, which may be merely a matter of mathematical or experimental skill. To raise new questions, new problems, to regard old problems from a new angle . . . marks real advance in science."[28]

In view of the revision, it is possible now: first, to order the already available observations regarding the sources of school conflict (which we shall repeat here for comprehensiveness), and second, more importantly, to identify for investigation a group of related but hitherto neglected problems, having their source in the several communities impinging on the school and the education of the child.

SOURCES OF SCHOOL CONFLICT

Three kinds of school conflict deriving from the institutional and individual dimensions (that is, *B* and *C* in Figure 2) have already been mapped and studied; they will be summarized only schematically here.[29]

1. Incongruity between role expectations and personality dispositions (between dimensions *B* and *C*). Conflicts of this type occur as a function of discrepancies between patterns of expectations attaching to the pupil (or teacher) role and the patterns of dispositions characteristic of the incumbents of the role. For example, students with high dispositions for independence and activity in a classroom with high expectations for dependence and passivity.[30]

2. Incongruity between roles and within roles (discrepancies within dimension *B*). Roles are improperly defined or are incompatible. There are three types of this kind of conflict in the school situation.

a. Disagreement within a single group defining a given role. For example, younger and older teachers in the same faculty group tended to differ in their expectations for pupil behavior.[31]

b. Disagreement among several groups defining a given role. For ex-

28 A. Einstein and L. Infeld, *The Evolution of Physics* (New York: Simon and Schuster, 1938), p. 92.

29 See Getzels, "A Social Psychology of Education," especially pp. 519-23. Also Getzels, Lipham, and Campbell, *Educational Administration as a Social Process*; Getzels and Thelen, "The Classroom as a Unique Social System"; and Getzels and Guba, "Social Behavior and Administrative Process."

30 L.G. Wispe, "Evaluating Section Teaching Methods in the Introductory Course," *Journal of Educational Research* 45 (1951): 161-86.

31 R. Prince, "A Study of the Relationship between Individual Values and Administrative Effectiveness in the School Situation" (Ph.D. diss., University of Chicago, 1957).

ample, board members and superintendents tended to differ in their expectations for the behavior of the same school administrators.[32]

c. Disagreement between two or more roles the individual is occupying at the same time. For example, the adolescent cannot ordinarily be an outstanding student and maintain respectable membership in the "gang."[33]

3. Incongruity between personalities and within personalities (discrepancies within dimension *C*). The types of conflict in category two above derive primarily from dislocations in the institutional dimension; certain conflicts derive also from the individual dimension. There are two types of this kind of conflict in the school situation.

a. Conflict arising from personality disorder as a function of incongruent dispositions (that is, in a single individual in dimension *C*). The effect of such discord is to keep the individual at odds with the institution because he cannot maintain a durable relation to a given role. An obvious example is the severely disturbed child as pupil.[34]

b. Conflict deriving from personality differences and from incongruent interpersonal perceptions (that is, among individuals in dimension *C*). Disagreement among individuals inhabiting complementary roles as to their mutual rights and obligations is not the result solely of personality disorder; there may be selective perception of expectations just as there is selective perception of objects and events in the environment. Involved here is of course the entire problem of interpersonal perception.[35]

EDUCATION AND THE VARIETY OF COMMUNITIES: PROBLEMS FOR INQUIRY

The foregoing problems deriving from the character of the school or the individual have been reasonably well mapped and studied. But the problems deriving from the impact of the variety of communities on the education of the child have scarcely been touched; the research issues have hardly been formulated in any systematic way.

There are two reasons for this neglect. First, a misleading distinction

---

32 N. Gross, W.S. Mason, and A.W. McEachern, *Explorations in Role Analysis: Studies in the School Superintendency Role* (New York: John Wiley, 1958).

33 J.S. Coleman, *The Adolescent Society* (New York: Free Press, 1961).

34 See, for example, Bruno Bettelheim, *Truants from Life* (Glencoe, Ill.: Free Press, 1955). Also, M.I. Stein, *Personality Measures in Admissions* (New York: College Entrance Examination Board, 1963), pp. 22-28.

35 R. Tagiuri and L. Petrullo, eds., *Person Perception and Interpersonal Behavior* (Stanford: Stanford University Press, 1958).

was made between education and socialization, the one somehow exclusively a function of the school and the other of the family and environment. The school was the educator, the community the socializer. This distinction is misleading; the school socializes as well as educates, and the environment educates as well as socializes.[36] Second, the environment, which influences the school and itself educates the child more directly, was conceived monotonically as a single community instead of being dealt with more realistically as a variety of communities that could be differentiated from one another analytically. Thus in Figure 2, dimensions A and D initially represented *the community* (or culture), not as in the revision the *variety of communities*.[37]

The central former issue then became the effect of the community (not communities) on the expectations of its schools and the dispositions of its children, that is, the interaction of A (as a single entity) and B, and of D (as a single entity) and C. The typical study was a comparison of pupils in one otherwise undifferentiated community (say, a lower-class community) with pupils in another also otherwise undifferentiated community (say, a middle-class community). Here, for example, is a representative formulation of the many such studies.

The child as pupil in a middle-class community:

$D \cong A$; the culture of the community in which the child is reared and the culture of the community determining the cognitive and affective expectations for the role of pupil are congruent.

$C \cong D$; the cognitive and affective dispositions the child acquires derive from and are congruent with the culture of his community.

$B \cong A$; the cognitive and affective expectations for the role of pupil derive from and are congruent with the culture of the middle-class community.

$C \cong B$; the dispositions of the child and the expectations of the school are congruent—that is, the middle-class child is prepared to do what he is required to do as a pupil.

The child as pupil in a lower-class community:

$D \not\cong A$; the culture of the lower-class community in which the child is reared and the culture of the middle-class community determining the cognitive and affective expectations for the role of pupil are *not* congruent.

$C \cong D$; the cognitive and affective dispositions the child acquires

---

36   J.W. Getzels, "Socialization and Education: A Note on Discontinuities," *Teachers College Record* 76, no. 2 (December 1974): 218-25.

37   See Getzels, "A Social Psychology of Education," p. 464.

derive from and are congruent with the culture of the lower-class community.

$B \cong A$; the cognitive and affective expectations for the role of pupil derive from and are congruent with the culture of the middle-class community.

$C \neq B$; the dispositions of the child and the expectations of the school are *not* congruent—that is, the lower-class child is not prepared to do what he is required to do as a pupil.[38]

The assumption of an undifferentiated middle-class and lower-class community makes for a neat and tidy scheme: Children in the one community acquire the dispositions needed to succeed in school and children in the other do not. In point of fact, of course, this is so only in the "ideal-type" case. In actuality, this is not true; one must be careful not to reify the ideal-type fiction into the real thing. Both groups of children are members not only of the communities identified by locality or ethnic allegiance but of other communities that also have an effect on them and on their education. Under the conceptual incubus of *the* community, the significance of these relationships—that is, among the variety of communities and their impact on education—has not received the attention it deserves.

In addition, then, to examining the continuities and discontinuities in the role and personality variables as represented by dimensions B and C in Figure 2, similar issues need to be examined in the community variables as represented by dimensions A and D, and between them and the personality and role dimensions.

1. Continuities and discontinuities among the several communities impinging upon the school (that is, within dimension A). One problem may serve as illustrative of others. In the case of the Robert White School, what were the consistencies and inconsistencies in the cognitive and affective norms and values among the following: the local community in which the school was situated, the instrumental communities (the academic and philanthropic groups) that established the school, the administrative community whose requirements for certification had to be met, the ethnic or social class communities to which the children belonged?

2. Continuities and discontinuities in the phenomena, norms, and values between the several communities and the expectations of the school (that is, the interaction between dimensions A and B). Again, a problem or two may serve as illustrative of others. In the Robert White

38 Ibid., pp. 466-67.

School, what was the relative impact of the local, administrative, social, instrumental, ethnic, and ideological communities on the character of the school? And what was the effect of the continuities and discontinuities among the communities?

3. Continuities and discontinuities among the several communities in which the child grows up (that is, within dimension D). Once more, the following problem is only illustrative. In the case of the children in the Robert White School, what was the nature of and what were the consistencies or inconsistencies in the norms and values among the local, administrative, social, instrumental, ethnic, and ideological communities in which they were reared? The same question could of course be raised for children in the same local community who did not become delinquents, or more generally for children in other communities.

4. Continuities and discontinuities among the several communities in which the child is reared and their impact on the cognitive and affective dispositions the child acquires (that is, the interaction between dimensions D and C). In the present context this is perhaps the most important issue: The communities not only determine the structure and expectations of the school (1 above) but more directly, at least in part, the knowledge and motivations of the child.

Consider in this respect the impact of the ideological community. Nearly all American children, no matter whether they have been in school or not, or how disparate the other communities to which they belong may be, learn that they are members of the American community and owe loyalty to what may be called the American creed or ideology. As Ralph Bunche observed:

> Every man in the street, white, black, red, or yellow, knows that this is the "land of the free," "the land of opportunity," the "cradle of liberty," the "home of democracy," that the American flag symbolizes the "equality of all men," and guarantees to us all "the protection of life, liberty, and property," freedom of speech, freedom of religion and racial tolerance.[39]

Even when these ideals are not fulfilled in practice, everyone has learned that he is an American, and that this creed makes him an American. In times of crisis, as in war, membership in this ideological community cements the various other communities—black and white, rich and poor, Christian and Muhammadan—into a single "American community"

---

[39] Quoted in G. Myrdal, *An American Dilemma*, vol. 1 (New York: Harper & Bros., 1944), p. 4.

taking precedence over the other communities, at least for the duration.

But there are of course the other communities that teach lessons of their own, perhaps more subtly but no less effectively. A child may be instructed through membership in one community that "children are God's blessing and should be welcomed," but in another that "you should not have more children than you can afford."[40] He may learn in his ethnic community that "education is a fine thing," but in an instrumental community that "it is practical men who get things done." Two children residing in the same local community may learn together that "the old, tried fundamentals are best; it is a mistake for busybodies to try to change things too fast or to upset the fundamentals." But in addition, through membership in one social community, one child may learn as a fundamental value that "the only thing that matters is how successful you are," and, through membership in a different social community, the other child may learn that "the kind of person you are is more important than how successful you are." Or through overlapping memberships the children may be exposed to both views, and be left without an answer to the question: "What values?" And of course each community itself may be more or less consistent or inconsistent in its norms and values.

The several communities do not expose the child only to differing values and norms. They also make available or emphasize divergent cognitive experiences and resources—television programs, museums, commercial or agricultural enterprises, recreational facilities, to say nothing of the unique experiences, resources, and forms of instruction in the home. These experiences and resources facilitate or inhibit the acquisition of particular cognitive and other skills. And it is not unlikely that what is acquired in one community may "wash out" or at least overlay what is learned in another community and in school. Although some work in this domain has been attempted, it has been fragmentary; the effect of each community was studied separately from the other communities as if the several communities were unrelated and independent of each other in their influence.[41] The central question for method-

40 These and the following instances are taken from R.S. Lynd, *Knowledge for What?* (Princeton, N.J.: Princeton University Press, 1939), pp. 60-62.

41 For one of the few studies of the effects of multiple-community memberships on educational attainment—a study clearly showing the fruitfulness of this approach—see: N. Rogoff, "Local Social Structures and Educational Selection," in *Education, Economy, and Society,* eds. A.H. Halsey, J. Floud, and C.A. Anderson (New York: Free Press, 1961), pp. 241-51. When children in a single local community or children from diverse local communities are pooled as if they lived in a single community, a linear relation is found between membership in the hierarchy of social class communities and academic attainment; that is, the familiar simple correlation

ical examination remains, that is, the impact of the several communities and of the continuities and discontinuities among them on the cognitive and affective dispositions the individual acquires.

5. Continuities and discontinuities among the several communities impinging on the cognitive and affective expectations of the school and the several communities impinging on the cognitive and affective dispositions of the child (that is, between dimensions A and D). Finally, there is the problem raised previously in simple form regarding the nature of the child's educational behavior as a function of the relation between *the community* impinging on the school and *the community* impinging on the child that must be raised in more complex and realistic form: What is the nature of the child's educational behavior as a function of the pattern of relations among the *several communities* determining the cognitive and affective expectations of the school and among the *several communities* in which the child acquires his cognitive and affective dispositions?

CONCLUSION

The term *community* is so familiar that when one speaks of the school and the community or of the community as educator, what is meant by the community is taken for granted as if there were but one possible meaning. In point of fact, the term is used in a multiplicity of ways; no fewer than ninety-four definitions have been found in the sociological literature alone. The difficulty in understanding the role of the community in educating its children through the school or more directly in its own right does not lie solely in the confusions resulting from the variety of conceptions of the community. It lies also in the failure to recognize that the geographically localized, self-contained, autonomous community has been replaced by geographically extended, loosely knit, overlapping communities. One is no longer an integral

---

between social class and educational achievement. When, however, the character of the diverse local communities is taken into account, a different and more complex relation is found not only for academic aptitude but college aspiration. In the words of the investigator, "From those at the top to those at the bottom of the social-class hierarchy, all students attending large suburban schools emerge from their educational experience relatively better equipped in academic skills, while youngsters who attend school in small villages or large industrial cities emerge from their educational environments less adequately prepared" (p. 250). The investigator goes on to comment, "The last word has hardly been said on the variety of ways young people may be affected by the community setting where they frame their career and educational goals.... [Too little] attention has been accorded the fact that education is a long-term social process, occurring microscopically in the classroom and macroscopically in a definite and describable community context" (p. 250).

part of a single all-encompassing community—of *the* community, but a member of communities—of communities within communities.

No ultimate resolution of the manifest complexities is yet possible. It is possible, however, to attempt some definitional and taxonomic clarification toward a resolution. One may think of communities as groups of people conscious of a collective identity characterized by common cognitive and affective norms and values, and may order the variety of communities from those where the collective identity is most dependent on a particular geographical locality to those where it is least dependent, although of course such ordering is approximate and the categories will overlap. Thus, one may be a member simultaneously of a local community (e.g., a particular neighborhood), an administrative community (e.g., a particular school district), an instrumental community (e.g., a particular professional group), an ethnic community (e.g., a particular national or racial group), an ideological community (e.g., a particular religious or sociopolitical group stretching beyond the local, administrative, instrumental, or ethnic communities).

The character of education offered by the school and the education acquired by the child are a function of the communities in which the school and the child are embedded. On the one hand, the communities determine, at least in part, the cognitive and affective expectations of the school; on the other, the communities determine, at least in part, the cognitive and affective dispositions of the child not only through the school but quite independently, and perhaps more importantly, through the experiences they make available in their own right and through the family.

The cognitive and affective experiences, norms, and values among the several communities in which the school and the child are embedded may be congruent or incongruent, continuous or discontinuous. In a sense, the several communities may be thought of as *cooperating* or *competing* for the expectations of the school and the dispositions of the child. To cite only the problem of values as illustrative of similar problems in cognitive and normative experiences, the child may be directed by one community to believe that "children are God's blessing and should be welcomed," and by another that "you should not have more children than you can afford," or by one community that "the only thing that matters is how successful you are," but, by another, "the kind of a person you are is more important than how successful you are."

The intent of these observations has not been to offer, much less urge, a particular conceptual or methodological solution to the complexities in understanding the relations between community and education. The intent was rather to suggest that issues that were obscured and hence closed to examination when the relations were formulated in terms of "the community and the school" may be illuminated and opened to examination when the relations are reformulated in terms of *the communities of education.*

Family-Community Linkages in American Education: Some Comments on the Recent Historiography

LAWRENCE A. CREMIN

Teachers College, Columbia University

The recent interest among students of American culture in the history of the family as educator may be said to date from the appearance of Bernard Bailyn's *Education in the Forming of American Society*. Bailyn's general argument in that volume has now become familiar. Historians of education, he maintained, had traditionally addressed inappropriate questions to the colonial period. They had asked, "When did the public school begin?" instead of, "How did colonial Americans educate their children?" The result had been a distorted picture of colonial education, one that placed undue emphasis on schooling in general and New England schooling in particular. To shift the question to how colonial Americans educated their children, Bailyn continued, would be to project the inquiry beyond the school to the real educators of colonial America—the family, the church, and the print shop—and ultimately to yield a picture not only more accurate in its own right but actually more revealing of the true significance of the nineteenth-century public school movement. As we now know, the shift portended far more than a new interpretation of colonial education; it would fundamentally alter the entire problematics of the field.[1]

1 Bernard Bailyn, *Education in the Forming of American Society* (Chapel Hill: University of North Carolina Press, 1960). On the problem of anachronism, see also Lawrence A. Cremin, *The Wonderful World of Ellwood Patterson Cubberley: An Essay in the Historiography of American Education* (New York: Teachers College Press, 1965). On the new problematics of the history of education, see Lawrence A. Cremin, *Traditions of American Education* (New York: Basic Books, 1977). The substance of the present article is drawn from a larger research project on the history of American education that has been generously supported by the Carnegie Corporation of New York.

Bailyn advanced his argument in the form of "an essay in hypothetical history," and in fact the particular hypotheses he put forward concerning the nature of the family have not stood the test of time. He maintained that in the transit of civilization from England to America during the seventeenth century, the extended family of the Old World was transformed into the nuclear family of the New World, owing principally to the selective character of the initial migration and the ready availability of cheap land in the colonies. In the absence of the extended family, and particularly of the large numbers of elderly and unmarried adult kin associated with it, traditional patterns of familial education broke down, and the ensuing crisis gave rise to schools to carry the educative functions formerly borne by the family. It was an intriguing argument, and one that made a good deal of sense in light of what was known at the time; but subsequent scholarship, some of it carried forward by Bailyn's own students, has modified it on several counts. For one thing, it is clear from the work of Peter Laslett and Lawrence Stone that the dominant familial structure of seventeenth-century England, except among the aristocracy (who did not migrate to the colonies in significant numbers), was not the extended family but the nuclear family. Furthermore, recent studies of colonial education have indicated that schooling did not emerge out of a crisis created by the transformation of the family but was itself among the elements of civilization transplanted from England, where it had already become prevalent by the time of colonization. Finally, like most historians who began to investigate the family during the later 1950s, Bailyn tended to define the family as the coresident household group and did not therefore inquire into its relationships with nearby kin. When his student Philip J. Greven, Jr., did inquire into those relationships in colonial Andover, Massachusetts, he found that the historical development proceeded not from an extended family in England to a nuclear family in New England but rather from a first generation of nuclear immigrant families to a second and third generation in which modified extended families—families in which sons settled with their wives and children in independent households nearby, remaining economically dependent upon their fathers but not coresident with them—became common.[2]

2　Bailyn, *Education in the Forming of American Society*, p. 5; Peter Laslett, *The World We Have Lost*, 2nd ed. (New York: Charles Scribner's Sons, 1971); Lawrence Stone, *The Crisis of the Aristocracy, 1558-1641* (Oxford: Clarendon Press, 1965); and Philip J. Greven, Jr., *Four Generations: Population, Land, and Family in Colonial Andover, Massachusetts* (Ithaca, N.Y.: Cornell University Press, 1970). See also the more complex analysis in Lawrence Stone, *The Family, Sex and Marriage in England, 1500-1800* (New York: Harper & Row, 1977).

Particular aspects of Bailyn's argument were flawed, then, owing to the inaccuracy of certain data on which they rested and to a limited consideration of "boundary matters" (these concern the ways in which the family is actually defined for purposes of inquiry). But the overall thrust of his argument was essentially sound. In directing historians of education to the educative functions of the family, he had provided a crucial corrective to a traditional overconcentration on the school that had obscured some of the most critical phases of educational development. And, in viewing the educative functions of the family in relation to those of other institutions, namely, the school, the church, and the print shop, he had presented a paradigm admirably designed both to test his own hypotheses and to generate better hypotheses to replace them. That this is so is clearly demonstrated by the flow of fruitful scholarship that has followed in the wake of Bailyn's essay.

Some years ago, in an article entitled "The Family as Educator: Some Comments on the Recent Historiography," I reviewed the work that had been done to 1974, concentrating on the various definitions of the family and of education that had emerged in the course of this scholarship. I also indicated there the extent to which historians of education could profit from the secondary analysis of monographs in which data or hypotheses related to education had figured centrally but which had been written with other concerns uppermost in mind. In the present essay, I should like to extend that review, concentrating on the manifold relationships between the family and other educative institutions at different times in American history. I should indicate at the outset that I am using the term "linkage" to refer to these varying relationships, well aware that it can easily be misunderstood to imply a static or mechanical or one-dimensional quality that I have no intention of conveying. I should also point out that even more than in the earlier essay I shall be dealing quite selectively with an immense literature, my effort being to highlight particular trends in the research and to illuminate certain characteristic family-community interactions in the history of American education.[3]

II

Greven's study of Andover was published in 1970, along with three

---

3 Lawrence A. Cremin, "The Family as Educator: Some Comments on the Recent Historiography" in *The Family as Educator*, ed. Hope Jensen Leichter (New York: Teachers College Press, 1975). I should make explicit that I am using the phrase "secondary analysis" here in the way social scientists use it in referring to the reanalysis of data originally gathered for other purposes.

other, books that attempted to shed additional light on the relationship between family and community in colonial New England: John Demos's *A Little Commonwealth: Family Life in Plymouth Colony*, Kenneth A. Lockridge's *A New England Town: The First Hundred Years*, and Michael Zuckerman's *Peaceable Kingdoms: New England Towns in the Eighteenth Century*. (My book *American Education: The Colonial Experience, 1607-1783* also appeared that year, building on the data presented in the other volumes as well as on my own research in communities outside New England.) I reviewed the several works with respect to household and kinship in "The Family as Educator," paying special heed to the revision they forced in some of Bailyn's hypotheses. It is important, however, to go beyond the material on the family to that on the New England community at large, from the time of settlement to the coming of the Revolution. The Lockridge volume is especially valuable in this respect. Scrutinizing the town of Dedham between 1636 and 1736, Lockridge identifies two distinct stages in the evolution of the community, an initial stage (1636-1686) in which the founders managed fairly successfully to build a utopian community and a later stage (1686-1736) in which a quite different community emerged as a result of diversity and dispersion. During the first half century, Lockridge maintains, Dedham's founders created a "Christian Utopian Closed Corporate Community": "Utopian because theirs was a highly conscious attempt to build the most perfect possible community, as perfectly united, perfectly at peace, and perfectly ordered as man could arrange. Closed because its membership was selected while outsiders were treated with suspicion or rejected altogether. And corporate because the commune demanded the loyalty of its members, offering in exchange privileges which could be obtained only through membership, not the least of which were peace and good order." During the later period, the movement of the second and third generations out from the center of the township yielded a very different community, one fragmented into a number of independent and frequently antagonistic towns, where individualism, contentiousness, litigiousness, and disharmony sharply challenged the impulse toward consensual communalism.[4]

---

4 John Demos, *A Little Commonwealth: Family Life in Plymouth Colony* (New York: Oxford University Press, 1970); Kenneth A. Lockridge, *A New England Town: The First Hundred Years: Dedham, Massachusetts, 1636-1736* (New York: W. W. Norton & Company, 1970); Michael Zuckerman, *Peaceable Kingdoms: New England Towns in the Eighteenth Century* (New York: Alfred A. Knopf, 1970); Lawrence A. Cremin, *American Education: The Colonial Experience, 1607-1783* (New York: Harper & Row, 1970). See also Sumner Chilton Powell, *Puritan Village: The Formation of a New England Town* (Middletown, Conn.: Wesleyan Uni-

The Demos study portrays the family that was at the heart of this evolving community. Its locale is colonial Plymouth, and, just as Lockridge is carefully hesitant about easy generalization from Dedham to America, so is Demos hesitant about generalization from Plymouth to America. But the argument for generalization is nevertheless implicit in both volumes. "Let me . . . be quite candid about my belief that family life in Plymouth was not at all unique," Demos maintains. "There were, I think, broad lines of similarity to the typical case in the other American colonies, particularly those embraced by the term 'puritanism.' The family is, after all, an extremely fundamental and durable institution: it often provides a kind of common denominator, or baseline, for a whole culture whose various parts may differ substantially in other respects." What becomes overwhelmingly clear from this study is the utter centrality of the family to every aspect of colonial life. It served, either regularly or occasionally, as a business, a school, a vocational institute, a church, a house of correction, a hospital, an orphanage, and a poorhouse. The congregation was a cluster of families, voluntarily joined—at least in the initial years—for purposes of worship; the town was a cluster of families, voluntarily joined—again, at least in the initial years—for purposes of civil government. The community was for all intents and purposes a group of families, with the church and town serving as institutions for articulating and implementing extrafamilial policies.[5]

What, then, can one derive about family-community linkages in colonial education from these five volumes? A good deal, I think, both directly and inferentially. Lockridge and Demos, for example, both make much of the close pattern of settlement during the early period. The effort to build a godly community was served spatially by what the anthropologist Conrad Arensberg has called a "dense collective experience," in which families collaborated to achieve certain clearly articulated goals, notably that of pious behavior. One linkage between family and community was from family to family, with all adults, especially heads of households and in particular town and church officials, having responsibility for scrutinizing public behavior. Indeed, one of the earliest educational ordinances enacted by the Massachusetts General Court was the law of 1642 empowering the selectmen of each

---

versity Press, 1973); and Darrett B. Rutman, *Winthrop's Boston: A Portrait of a Puritan Town, 1630-1649* (Chapel Hill: University of North Carolina Press, 1965). The quotation from Lockridge may be found on pages 16-17.

5 Demos, *A Little Commonwealth*, pp. viii-ix.

town to "take account from time to time of all parents and masters, and of their children, concerning their calling and employment of their children, especially of their ability to read and understand the principles of religion and the capital laws of this country," and authorizing them, with the consent of any court or magistrate, to "put forth apprentices the children of such as they shall [find] not to be able and fit to employ and bring them up." Incidentally, to highlight my earlier point about the multiple roles of the family, to put forth children as apprentices was to assign them to other families in the township in the interest of their education.[6]

Beyond the linkage of family to family, there was the abiding linkage of family to church. The church was the originator or mediator of much in the realms of knowledge, values, attitudes, skills, and sensibilities that was publicly deemed necessary to be learned and lived. Ministers taught congregations directly, through formal sermons ordinarily preached on Sundays and Thursdays as well as through catechizing, household visitation, and public ceremonial. Ministers also taught congregations indirectly, via heads of families, who mediated their preaching and enjoined household members to carry it into effect in their daily lives. Conversely, congregations, and particularly those members who were heads of households, remained in continuing dialogue with their ministers on matters of doctrine, the assumption under Congregational polity being that ministers were *primi inter pares* and therefore obliged to be attentive to the religious interpretations of their congregants. In addition, the church taught through the institution of church discipline, whereby transgressors of the moral code (which embraced many aspects of diurnal living) were subjected to censure, public confession, correction, and restoration. As Zuckerman observes, church discipline constituted a powerful process of consensual regulation and instruction. "When a New Englander was driven to stand before his assembled neighbors and confess his transgression, more than mere punishment was involved. All societies punish the behavior they define as criminal or immoral, because violation of their ordinances is a challenge to the legitimacy of the normative order and so cannot pass unrebuked; but in the punishments meted out by the churches of Massachusetts the offender himself acknowledged his recognition of the morality he had violated. He as well as his pastor and his peers attested to the justice of his humiliation. He was the object of the community's punishment, but

6   Conrad M. Arensberg, "American Communities," *American Anthropologist* 57 (1955): 1150; and Cremin, *American Education: The Colonial Experience*, pp. 124-25.

simultaneously he was a member of the community which was punishing, so that even in the act of retribution the solidarity of the society was not upset. Only the offender who failed to confess stood outside that social order; only he truly sinned, because he asserted his own inclinations and impulsions, his own will, against the standards of the community." In addition, it should be noted, the church served continuously as a forum for the exchange of ideas, as a marketplace for the transaction of business, and as a rostrum for the communication of news.[7]

There were schools, too, though they were neither as significant nor as pervasive as the churches in their educational influence. Moreover, as has already been suggested, the data in the Demos, Greven, and Zuckerman studies, as well as in my own volume on colonial education, demonstrate that schools were not only a significant element in the original configuration of education transplanted from England, they also developed frequently as extensions of the family, rather than as surrogates for it, as Bailyn assumed. In other words, where schools did appear there were generally strong and abiding family-school linkages deriving from an overlapping of sponsorship, support, control, and management.

The close linkages between families, between families and schools, and between families and the congregations and polities into which they were organized go far in explaining the educative basis and power of the colonial New England community. It was not merely a matter of spatial arrangment, of close physical contiguity, that threw small numbers of individuals into face-to-face interaction; it was also a matter of timing. As Arensberg has observed, "Frequent daily intercourse of neighbors and townsfolk, continuous contact of the young people among themselves at each age of growing up, as well as enforced frequent sabbatarian communion, meant a dense collective experience, a chance for internalization of these rigidities of repetitive role and habit, of readiness to seek consensus coupled with a stubbornness of egalitarian judgment about which much has been written." When "repetitive role and habit" conform to an explicitly formulated *paideia*, in this instance, Puritanism, communal life itself becomes educative, with social institutions complementary and mutually supportive of a particular version of character. Such, indeed, has been the educative basis of most utopias. When the New England community dispersed and fragmented, however,

---

7 Zuckerman, *Peaceable Kingdoms*, p. 62. On church discipline see also Kai T. Erikson, *Wayward Puritans: A Study in the Sociology of Deviance* (New York: John Wiley & Sons, 1966).

as individual households and groups of households moved out over the countryside, the power of contiguity and repetitiveness in sustaining a particular *paideia* was diminished, and that ethic gave way to alternative and frequently conflicting versions of the earlier Puritan ideal. Even then, the family, the church, and the school remained powerfully linked educators, engaged thereafter in the transmission of diverse rather than common views of piety and the good life; hence, the individualism, the contentiousness, and the disharmony Lockridge found in the second and third generations of Dedham settlement.[8]

A final comment seems appropriate about the communities portrayed in the Greven, Demos, Lockridge, and Zuckerman volumes. They were, in effect, small, autonomous societies existing very much in isolation. Yet the fact is that the communities of colonial New England—and of all colonial America—were part and parcel of a larger Anglo-American, indeed, Western, society and that their families, churches, and schools were linked by various forms of communication and exchange to geographically distant elements of that larger society. As I have remarked elsewhere, colonial American communities were in constant contact with the cultural centers of Great Britain and Continental Europe: Families studied a didactic literature prepared and printed in London and Edinburgh; churches and schools employed pedagogical styles that derived variously from France, Switzerland, and the Dutch Republic; and amateur scientists exchanged data with their counterparts in a dozen European cities. The point is not to deny the significance of the local and indigenous; it is merely to argue that, even in the earliest period of colonial development, educational institutions in general and the family in particular were already mediating diverse external influences and communities were not simply isolated geographical localities.[9]

III

If the recent work on the colonial American community has focused on the social history of the New England town, recent scholarship on the nineteenth- and twentieth-century American community has concentrated on the social history of the city. Many of the studies—though by no means all of them—have been quantitative in approach, analytic in emphasis, and comparative in orientation, and have emphasized such matters as the nature of family structure, the extent of social mobility, the "texture" of neighborhood life, and the relationships among urban

8 Arensberg, "American Communities," p. 1150.
9 Lawrence A. Cremin, *Public Education* (New York: Basic Books, 1976), pp. 33-34.

institutions. A few have attempted to examine particular cities in their entirety—one thinks of Sam Bass Warner's work on Philadelphia, Stephan Thernstrom's on Newburyport and Boston, Roger W. Lotchin's on San Francisco, and Michael H. Frisch's on Springfield, Massachusetts—but even these have concentrated either on particular periods of transition or on such special problems as social mobility. Moreover, beyond the usual assertions about the multiplication of institutions, the growing complexity of diurnal life, and the movement from *Gemeinschaft* to *Geselleschaft*, their generalizations have been partial at best and frequently contradictory. Thus, Thernstrom's statements about the lack of mobility in Newburyport are countered by his discovery of a good deal more mobility in Boston, while Lotchin's findings regarding the almost "anarchic" individualism of San Francisco ("There was a constant reconciliation of things, a continuous renegotiation of the social contract") conflict with Frisch's regarding the tense but enduring sense of cultural cohesion in Springfield. The majority of the studies have concentrated on particular problems or aspects of life in a given city or a particular segment of a city's population, and it is these that have proved most valuable in extending our knowledge of family-community linkages in education.[10]

One of the most illuminating veins of material in this respect is that dealing with immigrant communities and the problems they faced in the process of becoming Americanized. Josef J. Barton's *Peasants and Strangers: Italians, Rumanians, and Slovaks in an American City, 1890-1950* explores two fascinating sets of educational relationships—those between families and voluntary associations and those between families, schools, and work—and their bearing on social mobility. In founding mutual benefit societies, popular circulating libraries, and various kinds

10 Sam Bass Warner, Jr., *The Private City: Philadelphia in Three Periods of its Growth* (Philadelphia: University of Pennsylvania Press, 1968); Stephan Thernstrom, *Poverty and Progress: Social Mobility in a Nineteenth Century City* (Cambridge: Harvard University Press, 1964); idem, *The Other Bostonians: Poverty and Progress in the American Metropolis, 1880-1970* (Cambridge: Harvard University Press, 1973); Roger W. Lotchin, *San Francisco, 1846-1856: From Hamlet to City* (New York: Oxford University Press, 1974); and Michael H. Frisch, *Town into City: Springfield, Massachusetts, and the Meaning of Community, 1840-1880* (Cambridge: Harvard University Press, 1972). The quotation from Lotchin is on pp. 342-43. With respect to the problem of space, mentioned earlier in connection with the colonial community studies, Alan R. Pred's *Urban Growth and the Circulation of Information: The United States System of Cities, 1790-1840* (Cambridge: Harvard University Press, 1973) is especially interesting, particularly for its consideration of the flow of information, via newspapers and the postal service, between and among cities. Also, despite the fact that it deals with a Canadian city, Michael B. Katz's *The People of Hamilton, Canada, West: Family and Class in a Mid-Nineteenth-Century City* (Cambridge: Harvard University Press, 1975) is relevant here.

of fraternal organizations, the Italians, the Rumanians, and the Slovaks of Cleveland were re-creating in the New World institutions of popular education they had known in the Old. Linked as these voluntary associations were to the immigrant family and the immigrant church, they served at once to sustain the language and culture of the ethnic subcommunity and as ethnic mediating agencies (as distinguished from nonethnic mediating agencies such as the public school) between the immigrant family and the dominant American culture. In his analysis of intergenerational mobility and the particular role of schooling in fostering it, Barton is especially cogent with respect to the multiplicity of linkages involved. "The son's transition from the status of his parents to that of his adult occupational role," he points out, "was mediated by schooling; hence education was a second important source of mobility. The acquisition of an occupational role involved two stages: the transition from the status of the family to a certain level of educational achievement, and the step from a given educational category to an occupational status. The assertion, then, that education is an important means of mobility implies at least three things: first, that there is a strong connection between education and subsequent occupational status (that is, education determines occupation to a large extent); second, that there is a high rate of educational mobility, so that children coming from different social strata have about the same chance of reaching various educational levels; and third, that there are no appreciable delayed effects of the father's status on the son's career, in the sense that the father's status exerts little impact on the son's choice of occupation beyond its influence on education. The isolation of these three processes allows one to examine in some detail the actual pattern of education and mobility in immigrant families." If one translates "status of the family" into educational terms, Barton's study becomes an analysis of the interaction among three principal educative settings—household, school, and work.[11]

Kathleen Neils Conzen's *Immigrant Milwaukee, 1836-1860: Accommodation and Community in a Frontier City* is similarly instructive, particularly for the care with which it examines the mediating role of the ethnic community in the process of Americanization. Like Barton, Conzen gives a good deal of attention to *Vereinswesen*, the plethora of music groups and drama societies, mutual benefit associations and debating clubs, gymnastic organizations and church societies, fraternal assemblies and tavern circles, political pressure groups and benevolent

11 Josef J. Barton, *Peasants and Strangers: Italians, Rumanians, and Slovaks in an American City, 1890-1950* (Cambridge: Harvard University Press, 1975), p. 135.

associations, organized by the immigrant community to perpetuate and enhance its cultural life in the New World; and she explicates the inextricable ties between these voluntary associations and the families, churches, and parochial schools that the Germans saw as crucial to the transmission of their native culture. Furthermore, in an imaginative critique of the standard notion of the role of the ghetto in immigrant assimilation, Conzen points out that the Germans of Milwaukee clustered together not because they were driven to it by the dominant American society but rather because conditions in Milwaukee at the time of their arrival permitted the sort of spatial congregation and economic, political, and cultural participation that postponed their assimilation. Put otherwise, Milwaukee became more and more German as the Germans became more and more American, with German families, churches, parochial schools, voluntary associations, and newspapers serving as critical elements in the process.[12]

Arthur A. Goren's *New York Jews and the Quest for Community: The Kehillah Experiment, 1908-1922* sheds still more light on these phenomena. The situation of the Jews in New York was distinguished by the fact that a liberal, prosperous, and relatively Americanized middle-class German Jewish community already existed in the city when large numbers of impoverished orthodox East European Jews began to arrive during the 1880s and 1890s. The Kehillah—"kehillah" is the Hebrew word for "community"—represented an effort by the earlier group to mount a widespread program of community development, involving schools, synagogues, lodges, and mutual benevolent societies, in order to prevent the disintegration of the new Jewish community on the Lower East Side and the consequent spread of crime, delinquency, and other forms of social pathology. The anticipated linkage in this instance was between the East European Jewish families and the community institutions sponsored and subsidized by the German Jews. The effort was defeated, however, not by the failure of the Kehillah to take root but by the rise of competing schools, synagogues, and fraternal organizations with linguistic, doctrinal, and ethnic ties to the East European Jews themselves. In effect, the linkages with the community network the sponsors were attempting to bring into being gave way in the face of more powerful linkages with institutions that the East European Jews found more compatible.[13]

12 Kathleen Neils Conzen, *Immigrant Milwaukee, 1836-1860: Accommodation and Community in a Frontier City* (Cambridge: Harvard University Press, 1976).

13 Arthur A. Goren, *New York Jews and the Quest for Community: The Kehillah Experiment, 1908-1922* (New York: Columbia University Press, 1970).

Several clusters of studies in the field of urban history have dealt quite specifically with the relationship between the family and one or more of the other educative agencies. Carl F. Kaestle, Maris A. Vinovskis, and Selwyn K. Troen, for example, have used census materials and other statistical data to explore the simple—though difficult to answer—question of when children left the family to attend school and when they left school to engage in full-time work at different times in American history. Kaestle and Vinovskis argue, contrary to traditional views, that the age of school entry actually rose in pre-Civil War Massachusetts, in response to arguments from educators and physicians that attending school too early was morally and physically harmful to youngsters (obviously a correlative of the argument in favor of domesticity, namely, that the family was the ideal context for early moral and physical development). Thus, the proportion of children under four in the public schools of Massachusetts declined from approximately 15 percent in 1850 to less than 1 percent in the late 1880s. Likewise, the proportion of youngsters over thirteen leaving school for work increased significantly between 1860 and 1880, though the rates differed considerably for males and females. In a similar analysis of St. Louis youngsters during the post-Civil War period (c. 1880), Troen presents the following data:

Education and Employment from Ages Five to Twenty, by Percentages, c. 1880.

Age	Attending school	Employed	Unknown	Total number
5	19.5	0.0	80.5	625
6	56.2	0.0	43.8	657
7	80.6	0.2	19.2	573
8	89.0	0.4	10.6	546
9	90.1	0.6	9.3	494
10	90.9	2.1	7.0	573
11	89.3	3.6	7.1	524
12	82.0	9.4	8.6	545
13	70.7	17.5	11.8	532
14	48.9	33.0	18.1	585
15	35.1	43.1	21.8	536
16	19.3,	60.0	20.7	576
17	11.6	64.2	24.2	541
18	5.4	68.7	25.9	710
19	3.7	71.1	25.2	678
20	1.7	76.1	22.2	769

The two studies address themselves to one aspect of the family-school-work linkage, namely, the ages of transition from one context to the next, far more precisely than had earlier been possible. Incidentally, it should be noted that youngsters obviously remained in the family while they attended school and that many also remained in the family during the first years in which they engaged in full-time work.[14]

David Tyack's *The One Best System: A History of American Urban Education* focuses on a quite different element in the family-school linkage, namely, the element of control. Tyack argues that, in the rural hamlets of pre-Civil War America, there was relative consonance between the educational aims and approaches of the local district schools and the educational aims and approaches of the local families that provided their clienteles. The burgeoning cities of post-Civil War America, however, saw a growing dissonance between the educational aims and approaches of the local school systems, dominated as they often were by white, Protestant, American males on school boards and in school superintendencies, and the aims and approaches of the immigrant or black families that constituted significant segments of the school clienteles. Compulsory attendance laws preserved the linkage, Tyack maintains, but the relationships became increasingly strained and unsatisfactory in the view of clienteles that were outside the "mainstream."[15]

Another cluster of studies has illuminated the relationships between urban families and the urban church. Building on earlier work of Charles I. Foster and Clifford S. Griffin, which clearly delineates the configuration of church, public school, Sunday school, Bible and tract society, and religious publishing house that the Protestant evangelical movement of the 1830s and 1840s used so successfully in its mission work, Carroll Smith-Rosenberg sketches the development of the mission movement in New York City in *Religion and the Rise of the American City: The New York City Mission Movement, 1812-1870*. What becomes even

14 Carl F. Kaestle and Maris A. Vinovskis, "Education and Social Change in Nineteenth-Century Massachusetts: Quantitative Studies" (Washington, D.C.: National Institute of Education, Project Number 3-0825, December 31, 1976); and Selwyn K. Troen, *The Public and the Schools: Shaping the St. Louis System, 1836-1920* (Columbia, Mo.: University of Missouri Press, 1975), p. 122. See also the analysis by Lee Soltow and Edward Stevens, based on data gathered for the 1860 federal census, in "Economic Aspects of School Participation in Mid-Nineteenth Century United States," *Journal of Interdisciplinary History* 8 (1977-1978): 221-43. For a more ethnographic approach to family-school relationships during the nineteenth century, based largely on diaries and autobiographies, see Geraldine Jonçich Clifford, "Home and School in 19th Century America: Some Personal-History Reports from the United States," *History of Education Quarterly* 18 (1978): 3-34.

15 David B. Tyack, *The One Best System: A History of American Urban Education* (Cambridge: Harvard University Press, 1974); idem, "The Tribe and the Common School: Community Control in Rural Education," *American Quarterly* 24 (1972): 3-19. The linkages with child-care facilities in the twentieth century raise similar questions. See, for example, Margaret O'Brien Steinfels, *Who's Minding the Children: The History and Politics of Day Care in America* (New York: Simon and Schuster, 1973).

clearer from Smith-Rosenberg's analysis is the vast disjunction between the people managing the mission programs in the city's slums and the clienteles to whom those programs were directed. Again, two quite different family-church linkages are illuminated: one between the families of the middle-class men and women who entered the mission movement in large numbers and the mission churches, societies, and homes that the movement sponsored, and the other between those churches, societies, and homes and the impoverished families to whom they ministered. The latter relationships were variously successful, ranging from the few instances in which "moral regeneration was accomplished" (for which read "education, as viewed by the sponsors, was effective") and the much larger number of instances in which it was not. Needless to say, the studies of immigrant subcommunities described earlier offer another perspective on the configuration of educative institutions established by the immigrants themselves, so that the Irish residents of the Five Points neighborhood in New York City, where the New York Ladies Home Missionary Society of the Methodist Episcopal Church established its House of Industry, were not different in their rejection of the effort from the East European Jews of a later era in their rejection of the Kehillah.[16]

Still another cluster of studies has dealt with the relationship between the family and various institutions of rehabilitation, such as the reform school, the penitentiary, and the mental hospital. The pathbreaking monograph in this realm is David Rothman's *The Discovery of the Asylum: Social Order and Disorder in the New Republic*. Making creative use of the concept of "social control," which exercised a considerable hold on the imagination of social historians during the 1960s and early 1970s, Rothman argues that the various rehabilitative institutions that took form in the United States during the pre-Civil War era arose as a special response to the social mobility and turbulence of the time, and that, while their sponsors employed a rhetoric of reformation and regeneration, their policies were those of custodianship and control. The leitmotif of the Tyack and Smith-Rosenberg studies, of middle-class reformers creating community institutions for lower-class clients, sounds through the Rothman volume as well. But, beyond this, Rothman il-

16 Charles I. Foster, *An Errand of Mercy: The Evangelical United Front, 1790-1837* (Chapel Hill: University of North Carolina Press, 1960); Clifford S. Griffin, *Their Brothers' Keepers: Moral Stewardship in the United States, 1800-1865* (New Brunswick, N.J.: Rutgers University Press, 1960); and Carroll Smith Rosenberg, *Religion and the Rise of the American City: The New York City Mission Movement, 1812-1870* (Ithaca, N.Y.: Cornell University Press, 1971).

luminates two additional aspects of the family-community linkage. First, he makes abundantly clear the extent to which the family metaphor suffuses the nineteenth-century discussion of rehabilitative institutions in the United States. And, second, he demonstrates the relative powerlessness of rehabilitative programs, despite all the rhetoric, in the face of the relentless competing education of families, peers, and the institutions of organized crime. Similarly, Steven L. Schlossman explores the gap between rhetoric and reality with respect to the nineteenth-century reform school in *Love and the American Delinquent: The Theory and Practice of "Progressive" Juvenile Justice, 1825-1920*, giving particular attention to the proceedings of the children's court in Milwaukee and the linkages between the probation system and the families of the children who came within its orbit.[17]

A final cluster of studies has dealt with the relationship between the family and various institutions of full-time employment. This has been a leading area of scholarly concern in recent years, with the result that the inquiry has proceeded along many lines. The Handlins' *Facing Life: Youth and the Family in American History* uses autobiographical material to trace changes over the entire span of American history in the ways young people have chosen, prepared for, and entered upon the occupations to which they would devote their lives. Other studies have focused on particular groups, places, or age strata. Thus, Horace Mann Bond's *Black American Scholars: A Study of Their Beginnings* concentrates on the specific role over several generations of particular families and particular communities (with particular churches) in nurturing individuals who would go on to the doctorate. Similarly, Nancy F. Cott's *The Bonds of Womanhood: "Woman's Sphere" in New England, 1780-1835* portrays the special role of friendship networks among women, not only in heightening a consciousness of women's roles, but also in facilitating the movement of particular individuals into authorship, politics, and, later, employment outside the home; while Daniel J. Walkowitz's "Working-Class Women in the Gilded Age: Factory, Community and Family Life among Cohoes, New York, Cotton Workers" and Tamara K. Hareven's "Family Time and Industrial Time: Family and Work in a Planned Corporation Town, 1900-1924" stress the role of family and kin relationships at different stages of the life cycle in

---

17 David J. Rothman, *The Discovery of the Asylum: Social Order and Disorder in the New Republic* (Boston: Little, Brown and Company, 1971); and Steven L. Schlossman, *Love and the American Delinquent: The Theory and Practice of "Progressive" Juvenile Justice, 1825-1920* (Chicago: University of Chicago Press, 1977).

determining who would go to work, when, with whom, and for what periods of time.[18]

Richard Sennett's *Families against the City: Middle Class Homes of Industrial Chicago, 1872-1890* takes a quite different approach in exploring the interplay between the particular work family members engaged in and the patterns of relationship within the household. "There was a hidden unity in the work experience of family members and family groups in Union Park," Sennett maintains. "The strains in family balance and continuity caused by work, the goad of family responsibilities on the worker, and the effect of intensive conditions of family life on work achievement, all were bound together, I believe, by the position of the family as the only coherent primary group in the individual's relation to the immense, growing city of Chicago. The hypothesis I shall advance is that the family was used as the immediately available tool by which men such as those in Union Park tried to shield themselves from the disorder and diversity of the city; it is this shielding process which explains the configurations of family and work in 1880." It is also that shielding process that led, in Sennett's analysis, to the intensification of middle-class family life during the later nineteenth century, when the nuclear unit began to serve as a buffer against the turbulence of the city. Joseph Kett's work on adolescence goes in still another direction, stressing the ill-defined situation of teenagers from the early nineteenth century to the present, living as they have between their growing desire for independence and the stubborn fact of their semi-dependence, with the family providing the chief context in which much of the tension has been felt, articulated, resolved, and left unresolved.[19]

18   Oscar Handlin and Mary F. Handlin, *Facing Life: Youth and the Family in American History* (Boston: Little, Brown and Company, 1971); Horace Mann Bond, *Black American Scholars: A Study of Their Beginnings* (Detroit: Balamp Publishing, 1972); Nancy F. Cott, *The Bonds of Womanhood: "Woman's Sphere" in New England, 1780-1835* (New Haven, Conn.: Yale University Press, 1977); Daniel J. Walkowitz, "Working-Class Women in the Gilded Age: Factory, Community and Family Life among Cohoes, New York, Cotton Workers," *Journal of Social History* 5 (1970-1971): 464-90; and Tamara K. Hareven, "Family Time and Industrial Time: Family and Work in a Planned Corporation Town, 1900-1924" in *Family and Kin in Urban Communities, 1700-1930,* ed. Tamara K. Hareven (New York: Franklin Watts, 1977). See also Virginia Yans McLaughlin, "Patterns of Work and Family Organization: Buffalo's Italians," *Journal of Interdisciplinary History* 2 (1971-1972): 299-314; and idem, *Family and Community: Italian Immigrants in Buffalo, 1880-1930* (Ithaca, N.Y.: Cornell University Press, 1977).

19   Richard Sennett, *Families against the City: Middle Class Homes of Industrial Chicago, 1872-1890* (Cambridge: Harvard University Press, 1970), pp. 141-42; Joseph F. Kett, *Rites of Passage: Adolescence in America, 1790 to the Present* (New York: Basic Books, 1977); and idem, "Growing Up in Rural New England 1800-1840," in *Anonymous Americans: Explorations in Nineteenth-Century Social History,* ed. Tamara K. Hareven (Englewood Cliffs, N.J.: Prentice-Hall, 1971), p. 116.

IV

Another vein of recent scholarship that has yielded important insights concerning family-community linkages in education is the one dealing with the slave community of the pre-Civil War South. The work in this area has been part of a broader revision of black history in the United States, in which time-honored generalizations about the survival (or disappearance) of transplanted African traditions, the prevalence of the matrifocal family, and the absence of a significant black community have been giving way in the face of new data and fresh inferences from those data. Among the many works that might be cited are John W. Blassingame's *The Slave Community: Plantation Life in the Antebellum South*, Eugene J. Genovese's *Roll, Jordan, Roll: The World the Slaves Made*, Herbert G. Gutman's *The Black Family in Slavery and Freedom, 1750-1925*, and, most important for an understanding of education, Thomas Lane Webber's "The Education of the Slave Quarter Community: White Teaching and Black Learning on the Ante-Bellum Plantation."[20]

We now know that nuclear families embedded in a network of kin were the rule rather than the exception among blacks on the antebellum plantation, that these nuclear families maintained highly significant linkages with the quarter community both on the plantation and beyond, and that within the quarter community the clandestine black church, with its rich traditional admixture of liturgy and folklore, was among the most influential institutions, perhaps the most influential of all. The work of Webber in particular has persuasively demonstrated that an educational configuration of black household, black church, and various black peer groups succeeded in nurturing among blacks abiding notions of black equality, opposition to slavery, and the promise of ultimate justice, at precisely the time white teachers (often aided and abetted by subordinate black associates) were insistently teaching contradictory ideas of white supremacy, black inferiority, and the justice of slavery. The dynamics of education within the black subcommunity were not unlike those within the immigrant subcommunities of many cities, in that children and adults were subjected to competing systems

---

20   John W. Blassingame, *The Slave Community: Plantation Life in the Antebellum South* (New York: Oxford University Press, 1972); Eugene J. Genovese, *Roll, Jordan, Roll: The World the Slaves Made* (New York: Pantheon Books, 1974); Herbert G. Gutman, *The Black Family in Slavery and Freedom, 1750-1925* (New York: Pantheon Books, 1976); and Thomas Lane Webber, "The Education of the Slave Quarter Community: White Teaching and Black Learning on the Ante-Bellum Plantation" (Ph.D. diss., Teachers College, Columbia Univeristy, 1975). For a comparative perspective on these works, see the several relevant papers in Vera Rubin and Arthur Tuden, eds., *Comparative Perspectives on Slavery in New World Plantation Societies* (New York: The New York Academy of Sciences, 1977).

of education, though it should be understood that the stubborn realities of color and slavery did make for certain inescapable differences.

These comments on the education of the slave-quarter community call to mind a final genre of scholarship that should be mentioned in connection with the study of family-community linkages in American education, namely, the "do-it-yourself" genealogy that has followed the publication of Alex Haley's *Roots* and its subsequent dramatization on network television. Actually, the growing interest in family history antedated Haley's book, deriving from a more general concern with the family that had been developing since the early 1960s, a concern that was heightened considerably by the celebrations associated with the American Bicentennial (the Smithsonian Institution's Conference on Kin and Communities was but one manifestation of the heightened interest). Thus, a plethora of manuals has appeared during the past two or three years encouraging people to inquire into their own familial origins and providing checklists of questions to be asked and evidence to be sought. To take one of the better examples, Jim Watts and Allen F. Davis's *Generations: Your Family in Modern American History* includes a number of autobiographical, biographical, genealogical, and contextual readings intended to serve as models for individual historical inquiry, beginning, incidentally, with an essay by Haley describing his own effort to recover his familial history; and it also offers advice on how to gather the data necessary for the enterprise. What is especially admirable about the Watts and Davis volume, however, is the complexity of the historical questions it raises and, as one aspect of that complexity, the attention it gives to what have here been called family-community linkages. Not all the manuals are so sophisticated as the Watts and Davis volume, of course; but, to the extent that popular historiographical inquiry is guided by complex analyses like this one, it promises to uncover a good many fresh and important data, at the same time eliciting a growing public understanding of the nature of the broader enterprise that has here been defined as education and the role of family-community linkages in the educational process.[21]

---

21   Alex Haley, *Roots* (New York: Doubleday & Company, 1976); and Jim Watts and Allen F. Davis, *Generations: Your Family and Modern American History* (New York: Alfred A. Knopf, 1974). See also, among others, Dan Rottenberg, *Finding Our Fathers: A Guide to Jewish Genealogy* (New York: Random House, 1977); Jeanne Eddy Westin, *Finding Your Roots: How Every American Can Trace His Ancestors—At Home and Abroad* (Los Angeles: J.R. Tarcher, 1977); and Harriet Stryker-Rodda, *How to Climb Your Family Tree: Genealogy for Beginners* (Philadelphia: Lippincott, 1977).

V

I have conceived of education in this essay as the deliberate, systematic, and sustained effort to transmit, evoke, or acquire knowledge, attitudes, values, skills, or sensibilities, and any learning that results from the effort, direct or indirect, intended or unintended. This definition obviously projects inquiry beyond the schools and colleges to a host of individuals and institutions that educate—parents, peers, siblings, and friends, as well as families, churches, synagogues, libraries, museums, settlement houses, and factories. And it clearly focuses attention on the relationships among the several educative institutions and on the effects of one institution's efforts on those of another. What is needed most for a sound historical understanding of these relationships—or linkages, as I have called them here—is a variety of investigations that study them in their own right, with explicit educational questions uppermost in mind; and, indeed, it is precisely that sort of investigation that Kaestle, Vinovskis, Troen, Tyack, Bond, and Webber carried out in the monographs described above. Meanwhile, until such studies become plentiful, the kind of secondary analysis of extant monographs that has constituted the burden of my commentary here can surely produce at least two sorts of fruitful insights: first, into the shifting relationships among educative institutions at different times in American history and, second, into the character and operation of the relationships themselves.[22]

Even on the basis of the preliminary analysis I have undertaken here, several conclusions may be ventured in both realms. The linkages between family and community, and in particular between family and church, obviously gave education in colonial New England much of its characteristic flavor and power, especially during the seventeenth century. In that period in which Lockridge sees the successful creation and maintenance of a utopian commune in Dedham, the several components of the configuration of education there were sufficiently complementary and mutually reinforcing that a powerful cumulative influence was achieved. In the later period he describes, however, dispersion and diversity led to a situation in which multiple configurations of education exerted conflicting and often contradictory influences. To be sure, the nineteenth and twentieth centuries have seen the creation of communities not unlike seventeenth-century Dedham in their educational characteristics—John A. Hostetler describes such communities in *Hutterite Society*, as does Laurence Veysey in *The Communal Experience: Anarchist and Mystical Counter-Cultures in America*—though it should be noted that modern agencies of transportation and communication have made it difficult for such communities to preserve their identity through mere geographical isolation. But most American communities, with the larger cities in the vanguard, have experienced a steady proliferation of educative institutions and a steady multiplication of educational configurations in the face of continued ethnic, religious, and racial diversification and of incessant geographic and social mobility—indeed, nothing has so impressed the first generation of historical demographers investigating American urban history as the hitherto unrecognized turnover of population in any given year. Increasingly, most local communities have embraced multiple configurations of education, and most configurations of education have comprised institutions mediating nonlocal influences. Formal schooling has become more and more important, as has the education proffered by external places of work on the one hand and external media of communication on the other—first, newspapers and magazines and, later, cinema, radio, and television. And families and churches have made their adjustments to these changes, partly by accommodating to the newly significant institutions, partly by mediating their influence, and partly by turning them to their own purposes.[23]

Within this historical context, there is much to be said about the nature of the linkages themselves. I have used the phrase "configuration of education" to refer to the patterning of relationships among educative institutions that tends to develop at a particular time and in a particular place. These relationships, as is clear from the discussion above, can be political, pedagogical, or personal; they can involve the teachers or the students or both; they can be strong or weak, symmetrical or asymmetrical, consonant or dissonant, enduring or transitory. And, at least during the nineteenth and twentieth centuries, they have usually involved more than two institutions, so that to explicate family-church or family-school linkages is ordinarily to consider but one segment of a larger educational configuration. This being the case, virtually all the linkages discussed here must ultimately be viewed in the context of larger configurations of education (a task that is easiest in the instance of slave or immigrant subcommunities); and virtually all need to be analyzed from additional perspectives. Kaestle, Vinovskis,

22   For an elaboration of the theory stated here, see Cremin, *Public Education*, chap. 2.

23   John A. Hostetler, *Hutterite Society* (Baltimore: The Johns Hopkins University Press, 1974); and Laurence Veysey, *The Communal Experience: Anarchist & Mystical Counter-Cultures in America* (New York: Harper & Row 1973).

and Troen increase our understanding of the movement of clienteles into school and out of school, thereby explicating the "personal" side of household-school and school-work linkages; but they provide little insight into the political or pedagogical relationships between home and school or between school and work, having chosen not to raise questions in those realms. Tyack, on the other hand, suggests a good deal about the political and pedagogical relationships between home and school and complements the material in the Kaestle, Vinovskis, and Troen studies, albeit the data for the several investigations are drawn from different locales. Similarly, Walkowitz's research on the recruitment of women to the factories of Cohoes, New York, reveals the pervasive influence of family and kin relationships in the determination of which women went and at what time, while Sennett's work on middle-class families in Chicago emphasizes the pervasive influence of the employment market on the quality of familial life. In the former studies, a discussion of family-church linkages would doubtless have been helpful; in the latter, a discussion of family-school linkages would surely have added a good deal. Ultimately, proper analysis of family-community linkages in the education of a particular time and place must explore the family's relationships with all the other significant components of the prevailing educational configuration.

Perhaps the most difficult question to ask with respect to all these linkages, or *sets* of relationships, involves the ways in which they produce similarity or dissimilarity, continuity or discontinuity of behavior, as individuals move from one educative experience to another. The problem emerges most clearly in the case of the slave and immigrant communities, where alternative configurations of education vied for the loyalty of clients, with the configurations of the black or ethnoreligious subcommunity on the one side and the configurations of the dominant white American community on the other. One can concentrate all one wishes on the relationships between and among the institutions themselves, but, until the actual influence on clients moving from one institution to another is investigated, the story will at best be

24 For the concept of the bifurcated education, see Cremin, *Traditions of American Education*, p. 66; and idem, "Americanization: A Perspective," *UCLA Educator* 19 (December 1976): 5-10. For the theoretical problem of tracing an individual's relationships with "educationally significant others," see Hope Jensen Leichter, "Some Perspectives on the Family as Educator," in Leichter, ed., *The Family as Educator*, pp. 1-43; and idem, "The Concept of Educative Style," *Teachers College Record* 75 (1973-1974): 239-50. For the concept of the educational biography, see Cremin, *Traditions of American Education*, pp. 145-53; and Ellen Condliffe Lagemann, "A Generation of Women: Studies in Educational Biography" (Ph.D diss., Teachers College, Columbia University, 1978).

half-told. It is here that the techniques of educational biography and prosopography can be useful, though we have only begun to learn how to ask questions so as to obtain insights that are significantly educational.[24]

The Conservation of Insight —
Educational Understanding of
Bilingualism

MARGARET MEAD

The American Museum of Natural History, New York

Today, when peoples of different academic generations gather to discuss a problem, it is almost routine to say, "Let's not reinvent the wheel," and then follow this with what often appears to others as a restatement of something they already know. The discussion then proceeds with boredom, irritation, and sometimes despair on the part of those who feel they have heard this all before, because it seems that all attempts to apply the insight derived from science and experience are repetitious and therefore, by definition, inefficacious.

I think this is a false metaphor. The wheel involves a very simple set of principles that can be applied to an ox cart or an eight-cylinder car and, once invented, is very difficult if not impossible to ignore. There are sufficient prototypes in nature, from tumbleweeds to logs used as rollers, for launching a canoe, so it is very difficult to imagine how it could not have been invented over and over again in different parts of the world. Yet the whole of the Americas, before Columbus, was without it.

The kinds of insights to which people refer when they are discussing conceptions and practices that involve human beings and the current state of the societies in which they live are of a very different order. They involve the continuing active participation of human beings, human beings subject to aging, to political vicissitudes, to changes in climate of opinion and knowledge.

In a country like our own, 200 years after our organization as a nation state, in an age in which the sciences, human as well as physical, have grown at an unprecedented rate, the expectation of change is built in and the hope that change will represent progress is balanced by the fear that we will lose the advances we have made. The American fear of loss of status, if that status has to be shared by others, which has pervaded our class structure and dictated our attitudes toward residence, has also permeated our educational decisions for over a century. It has been expressed in the distinction between the private academy for the children of the privileged and the public school for the unprivileged, the series of attempts to extend the period of free education (first into the high schools and then to higher education), the dual school system of the South, and the separation of pupils and resources by residential segregation in the North. Who is to be educated, with whom, and for what, has been a central theme in the working out of American democracy and has provided an ever-changing framework within which new and old educational theories have been reargued.

Those who have initiated change within one set of circumstances have aged within it, returning periodically to the fray to lament that the reforms they advocated were never really carried out. Younger educators, facing a new version of old problems, fresh from the fray, hear these laments as dirges from the past. While these complaints may sharpen their zeal, they also inject some notes of disenchantment into educational policies, a disenchantment that is either accentuated or diminished by the turn of events within the country and in the context of accelerated planetary communication. It therefore seems to me that it would be worthwhile to develop a model or a set of models within which the point could be made that although some part of a program or policy has been developed in the past, nevertheless there is a difference the next time around; the advocacy of free education for all children, informed attention to individual differences, accent on the disadvantaged or on the gifted, homogeneous classes that facilitate a sense of worth, or heterogeneous classes that stimulate different capacities of gifted children—the list can be as long and detailed, or as short and broad, as one likes.

One model is a simple historical one: the careful specification of the contexts (in the late nineteenth century, before World War I, after World War I, etc.) in which the degree of urbanization; the nature of transportation, immigration and in-migration; the use of economic resources; the degree of communication with and modeling on news about changes in German, Russian, and Chinese schooling, are worked out carefully in relation to the condition of education. With our new computer tools, it would be possible to devise an instrument through which any number of variables could be graphically introduced so that all of these contextual factors could be grasped, as in the kind of graphic presentation used by the Club of Rome and refined in later versions of successive Club of Rome reports.[1] Each time statistics are introduced—for example, how many children attended how many grades of school or what percentage of literacy existed—this could be seen in the context of the size of the student population, or the degree of urbanization of the country, or types of immigration from countries of high or low literacy. Each point of advocacy—class size and class composition, location and type of structure of school buildings, per capita resources spent on each pupil in different areas—could be seen in context before statements about the success or failure of new programs could be dismissed with, "We tried that in 1932"; "In the end we always fall back"; "No matter what sort of experimental college we try to invent, they all end up as four year B.A. colleges"; or statements about decentralization or aggregation of pupils in consolidated schools like the Gary, Indiana, model in the decade before World War I or the advocacy of educational parks in the 1960s.

In this way we might get rid of the boredom that generations of students have felt over the recitation of educational history, which in context can be fascinating, but separated from the wider context often does seem repetitive.

One also might draw on the Gesell-Ilg spiral model of human development and combine it with an evolutionary aspiration. In the Gesell-Ilg model,[2] the developing child is seen as returning periodically to the same set of developmental problems, each time at a chronologically older level, so that this recurrence presents a second, third, fourth, chance to work out the same problems. The spiral model can also be applied to cultural evolution so that each solution of, for example, the problems of communication—speech, glyphs, script, telegraphy—represents a more complex solution to the same problem of communication with greater speed over greater distance.

In human affairs, we also have to take account of the periodic swings that can be attributed to generational conflict. In any society in which change is expected, there is also a rebellion of one generation against the preceding generation, whether this is the biological parent, the

---

1   Mihajlo Mesarovich and Eduard Pestel, *Mankind at the Turning Point* (New York: Dutton, 1974); and Donella H. Meadows et al., *Limits to Growth: Report of the Club of Rome's Project on the Predicament of Mankind* (New York: Universe Books, 1972).

2   Margaret Mead, "On the Implications for Anthropology of the Gesell-Ilg Approach to Maturation," *American Anthropologist* 49, no. 1 (January-March 1947): 69-77.

teacher, or the style setter in some creative field. These pendulum swings may result only in nonsignificant changes which appear as fashion, or they may represent a spiraling effect. In a field like education, where the contribution and point of view of each age grade is bound to be infused with a certain amount of rejection of their own education as well as the usual rebellion against the senior generation, there may be expected to be even more of a pendulum swing than that which occurs in a field like the arts. Every time a pendulum swings, like the return to the three Rs and the McGuffy readers, it is condemned as a simple repetition. Then we lose a chance to point out what may in fact be a spiral effect rather than a simple pendulum swing with the next generation returning to the same position. The possibilities of finding and accentuating some new level that can transform the simple pendulum swing into a spiral can be enhanced or reduced by the willingness of the participants in any debate to inspect the difference in circumstances surrounding the discussion.

Furthermore, increasing knowledge of human behavior adds another dimension. True, we can find the same kind of pendulum swing, which can be attributed to intergenerational conflict, within science itself, so that scientific insights may be neglected for a decade or several decades. But there is a steady accumulation of unassailable knowledge that must be taken into account by educators if they wish to make advances deeper than changes in fashion.

To the changes in situation, changes in the world at large, precipitating events, generational conflict, and changes in fashion, we must add the steady increase in scientific knowledge. Within such a complexity, we can advance one step further in judging which insights from previous educational innovations we do indeed wish to conserve. Can insight be conserved or must each generation remake the same discoveries in order to have the sense of authentic participation? Anthropologists face this problem over and over again, as young students go out into the field and rediscover "culture," or some aspect of culture, about which they have read and heard but which, because they have not experienced it, they do not actually *know*. The desire to name the fresh discovery may be overwhelming and so jargon is born, jargon which insulates groups of practitioners from each other and from the wider groups of concerned citizenry on whom all applications of scientific insights depend.

As an illustration of the way in which we can systematically invoke this system of complexities, I have chosen to sketch out the relationship between anthropological theory and problems of bilingual education as they have occurred during my scientific lifetime. This began with my first piece of research on the relationship between language spoken at home and the performance of Italian children on intelligence tests.[3] During my senior year in college, I was completing a major in psychology and planning to take an M.A. in psychology, but already preparing to shift to anthropology. My mother, who had made a study[4] of the adjustment of Italian immigrants in Hammonton, New Jersey, was making a restudy and had consulted Professor Boas in connection with her physical measurements of Italian children. He suggested to me that I take advantage of my mother's records of the community and make a study of the relationship between the amount of Italian spoken in their homes and the Italian school children's intelligence test scores.

The situation within which this question was raised was the preoccupation with intelligence tests that resulted from the application of psychological tests during World War I. In the post-World War I climate, with its accompaniment of zenophobia and reaction, these tests scores had been used to claim the innate inferiority not only of Afro-Americans but of people of Mediterranean stock who had been crowding to our shores in great numbers. Immigration laws were being designed to limit the numbers of such immigrants. Attempts were made to suggest that children who spoke a foreign language might have difficulty in school, but these were countered by an insistence that this might be true in kindergarten but would soon disappear. The whole question of language was neglected within the racial discussions of the day, which were focused on the superiority of Nordics,[5] northern Europeans who had a better record of adjustment in American schools than did southern Europeans.

American cultural anthropology has a basic premise that social and cultural differences between groups of human beings, as distinct from differences among individuals, are due to experience and not to genetics.[6]

---

3 Margaret Mead, "Group Intelligence Tests and Linguistic Disability among Italian Children," *School and Society* 25, no. 642 (April 1927): 465-68; idem, "The Methodology of Racial Testing: Its Significance for Sociology," *American Journal of Sociology* 5 (March 1926): 657-67.

4 Emily Fogg Mead, *Italian on the Land: A Study in Immigration*, U.S. Bureau of Labor Bulletin 14, (May 1907), pp. 473-533.

5 Madison Grant, *The Passing of the Great Race: Or the Racial Basis of European History* (New York: Scribner, 1918; 4th rev. ed., New York: Scribner, 1936).

6 During the 1920s there was a fairly lively interest in "culture-free tests," which followed the development of performance tests for the nonliterate used in World War I. Beatrice Blackwood (*A Study of Mental Testing in Relation to Anthropology* [Baltimore: Williams Wilkins Co., 1927]) summarized a number of these attempts and, throughout the ensuing years, there have been periodic attempts to develop such tests culminating in such investigations as those

The results of my research could have been predicted: There was a direct relationship between the amount of Italian spoken at home, itself related to the date of immigration of the parents, and the scores on intelligence tests, which were themselves related to expected performance in American schools.

Here the issue was simply the consequences of speaking a different "mother tongue" and my study did not raise the question of bilingualism itself. But in the course of searching the literature, I found a study made in Wales, which contained some very interesting points. Children who spoke Welsh at home, played in Welsh, and were taught at school in English performed worst; children who spoke English at home, at play, and at school performed best; and the children who spoke Welsh at home, but played and were taught in English were intermediate. The author claimed that the disadvantages of this bilingualism extended into the university years.[7]

During my subsequent years of field work, and in the process of learning Oceanic languages myself, I became interested in the way a two-year-old American child handled his bilingual competence in Samoan and English. This competence, which disappeared with his return to the United States, crippled his capabilities in writing English right up to his attainment of a graduate degree. Later, working among the Omaha Indians, I found undertones in the writing of Indian adolescents, who were educated only in English, that suggested a negative relationship between the two languages. In both cases, one of a mother tongue and one of a second language spoken in the community and not at home, the relationships between the two languages were negative. Through

of Charles Osgood ("Objective Indicators of Subjective Culture," in *Issues in Cross Cultural Research, Annals of the New York Academy of Sciences*, vol. 286, ed. Leonore Loeb Adler [New York Academy of Sciences, 1977]). Although the emphasis has shifted from attempts to develop tests that can adequately test children of very different cultures or detect special competencies developed in primitive cultures (Michael Cole and Sylvia Scribner, "Developmental Theories Applied to Cross-Cultural Research," in *Issues in Cross Cultural Research*; Michael Cole, "An Ethnographic Psychology of Cognition," in *Cross Cultural Perspective on Learning*, eds. R.W. Brislin, S. Bochner, and W.J. Lonner [New York: Halsted/Wiley, 1975]; and Michael Cole, J. Gay, J. Glick, and D. Sharp, *The Cultural Context of Learning and Thinking* [New York: Basic Books, 1971]), they have indirectly contributed to a background for the question of the relationship between bilingualism or multilingualism and manifestations of intelligence either in school or formal test situations.

7 D.J. Saer, "The Effect of Bilingualism on Intelligence," *British Journal of Psychology* 14 (1923): 35-38; and see B.S. Bloom, *Compensatory Education for Cultural Deprivation* (New York: Holt, Rinehart & Winston, 1965), which has been criticized for the methods used—a procedure frequently used to discredit unacceptable ideas. I cite it here in terms of its suggestiveness, a suggestiveness it took a long time to realize.

the years between 1925 and World War II, I collected a variety of cases of this sort, still under the stimulation of the original Welsh study and the possibilities that it suggested of continuing mental handicap.

While little attention was paid to the effect of foreign languages spoken by European immigrants' children, the treatment of language in American schools was affected by the decision after World War I to demand a high school education for every child. There had been a slow infusion of children from less literate backgrounds into the American school system in the early years of the century to which American schools responded by impoverishing the curriculum. Greek, which had been a requirement the generation before, almost completely disappeared, followed by a reduction in the requirement of Latin. With the entrance of more pupils of immigrant and working-class backgrounds, Spanish began to replace French and German, as both easier and more suitable for "commercial courses." The arguments in back of this reduction of the importance of learning at least one second language were a compound of contempt for the capabilities of the newcomers and a belief that the old idea that "Latin trained the mind" was false and there was no transfer of learning from studying one subject to studying another. (A recognition that one poorly learned subject interfered with learning another, while one well-learned subject facilitated learning another, had to wait for a much more sophisticated understanding of learning.)

During the thirties and forties, though there was little interest in bilingualism as such, an attempt was made to allow for students of foreign origin in a variety of intercultural activities. The customs, the songs and food, the dance and dress, of various cultural groups were recognized within the schools and within the community. But the expression of this movement toward cultural pluralism was hampered at the language level because so many of the immigrants had been nonliterate and spoke only a dialect. Attempts to introduce them to the standard language of their countries of origin often proved embarrassing and, after some valiant educational battles for Italian, it would be found that the Italian students elected to study French where no special competence would be expected of them. Also, within the movements of culturally impoverished white populations during the depression, there was a beginning recognition that they too spoke a dialect and that communication between pupil and teacher was hampered when the referents of the same word were very different. Echoes of the study of the canal-boat children in England (the alleged deficiencies of which have again been hauled into a politicized struggle in the 1970s)[8] entered the American scene during World War II when we struggled with the kinds of education appropriate for children who came from bare surroundings with little discipline; these children needed the discipline of the old-style kindergarten more than the currently fashionable freedom of the new-style nursery school, which was devised for middle-class children who came from homes where they were too constrained to neatness and order.

During World War II, I was involved in developing the anthropological study of food habits and we made a series of studies of the food habits of various ethnic groups in the United States.[9] For the first time a new dimension beyond that of familiarity with and use of the mother tongue was introduced into the problem of bilingual education. We found a close association between love of food, home, and speech among Italian children and began to see the poorer early performance of Italian children in school as due to the contrast between the home atmosphere and the relative coldness of the American school room. This contrast did not hold for children of German immigrants, who were brought up in homes where eating correctly was used as discipline, so that the demands of the home dining table and of the school were more congruent. Research work on the food habits of black and white children in the South also provided new insights into stylistic contrasts between home and school as some of our black research workers introduced, as a criterion of nutrition, whether people "used manners" and "said grace."

These observations on home style could be further interpreted in the light of the extensive studies of class differences in the South made during the thirties.[10] Discussions of education, of the capacity of children to benefit from an education in terms of caste and class, presaged the emphasis on cultural deprivation and dialectical differences in speech that were to surface two decades later.

Also at the same period, when the military draft on the one hand and

8   Cyril Burt, *The Backward Child* (London: University of London Press, 1937); and Arthur Jensen, "Heritability of IQ," *Science* 194, no. 4260 (October 1976): 6.

9   Margaret Mead, "The Problem of Changing Food Habits," in Report of the Committee on Food Habits, 1941-1943, *National Research Council Bulletin* 108 (Washington, D.C.: National Academy of Sciences, 1943).

10   Allison Davis, Burleigh B. Gardner, and Mary R. Gardner; directed by W. Lloyd Warner, *Deep South: A Social Anthropological Study of Caste and Class* (Chicago: University of Chicago Press, 1941); Allison Davis and John Dollard, *Caste and Class in a Southern Town* (New Haven, Conn.: Yale University Press, 1937); Allison Davis and John Dollard, *Children of Bondage: The Personality Development of Negro Youth in the Urban South* (Washington, D.C.: American Council on Education, 1940): and W. Lloyd Warner, Robert J. Havighurst, and Martin B. Leob, *Who Shall be Educated? The Challenge of Unequal Opportunities* (New York: Harper and Brothers, 1944).

racial conflict on the other focused attention on ethnic and racial differences in literacy and competency, there was a renewal of discussion about the relationship of schooling and competence. The little book *The Races of Mankind* by Ruth Benedict and Gene Weltfish,[11] which included a disturbing statement about the superiority of black children schooled in unsegregated schools in the Northeast over some white children schooled in inferior schools in the South, was distributed by the Navy and banned by the Army. But here the emphasis was upon the way schools could iron out differences in home backgrounds—differences that appeared in records of achievement or intelligence tests—rather than upon the effect of dialects spoken at home. Under the heading "differences in experience" we were of course already beginning to deal with problems that could later be related to effects of bilingualism. I remember pointing out to teachers of the children of Appalachian migrants in California that the word "cup" called up very different images to a teacher who paired "cup and saucer" in her mind and to a child who had never seen a saucer.

Linguists had not yet been involved in the question of the consequences of bilingualism or monolingualism. However, during World War II, when it became necessary to educate large groups of Americans to deal with foreign languages, linguists were brought in to devise new methods of language learning under the program of the American Council of Learned Societies. Entirely new methods of teaching languages with saturated daylong practice were introduced. These methods focused attention not only on the inadequacy of our language teaching, but also on some of the psychological consequences of a kind of monolingualism that results in thinking of the *words* in other languages as translations of the English *names* for objects.

After World War II, the demand for translation and the invention of simultaneous translation aided by electronic transmission devices introduced new questions. To what kind of experience could the expertise of those Russian émigrés who developed simultaneous translation be attributed? Concurrently, we were making a study of various Eastern European Jewish groups, recognizing the importance of their multilingualism. There were also clinical reports of a kind of paranoia in which hearing voices was sometimes displayed by children of immigrant multilingual parents who reserved one language to quarrel in.

As Israel received its mass of Asian Jews, new insights developed on

11 Ruth Benedict and Gene Weltfish, *The Races of Mankind* (New York: Viking Press, 1947).

the degree to which the children of Asian immigrants found difficulties in schools built on a European model when they were compared with children of European backgrounds. In the United States, in the international atmosphere of the immediate post-World War II period, there were a variety of experiments in teaching foreign languages—especially Russian and Chinese—or attempts by embattled classicists to introduce the new methods into the teaching of Latin and Greek. Meanwhile, the Modern Language Association resisted the new methods so that, in the mid-1950s, one could find Latin taught as a living language, French as a dead language (that is, learned entirely from texts), and a course in the nature of language itself in the same school.[12]

While during the late 1940s and early 1950s the active attempts at racial integration had been somewhat moderated because of full employment, by the mid-1950s it became clear that there would be serious employment difficulties for black youth as the need for unskilled labor decreased and automation produced structural unemployment. Renewed agitation for racial equality—the civil rights movement—began. In the light of earlier studies of cultural deprivation and the continuing criticisms of test results, which anthropologists had produced intermittently, there was renewed interest in school situations where black children who spoke a dialect were taught by middle-class white teachers who spoke standard English, or where Puerto Rican and Mexican children presented all the difficulties of both cultural difference and language difference when they entered school. After flurries of resistance, in which civil rights leaders resented the idea of speaking a dialect, serious research into Black English and bilingual and bicultural education for non-English-speaking children began. Linguistics, as a separate scientific discipline, was introduced into the field of education, peaking in the late sixties. The emphasis throughout has been on kinds of communication that are impeded—between teacher and children, or children and fellow pupils, or teachers and parents—when a cultural barrier has to be crossed rather than upon the effect upon the child learner of being bilingual or multilingual. The use of film and film analyzers and the development of the subdisciplines of kinesics, proxemics, and paralinguistics provided a scientific background for analyzing a variety of classroom problems.[13] In short, we have extensive documentation today about the way in which differences in culture and language, or dialect

12 Margaret Mead, "An Anthropologist's Search for a Good Linguistic Education for Her Child," *Parents League Review* 12 (1978).
13 Courtney B. Cazden, Vera P. John, and Dell Hymes, eds., *Functions of Language in the Classroom* (New York: Teachers College Press, 1972).

and standard language, or caste and class differences within one culture affect the child's performance in a school designed for children of the majority culture, a school in which success can be positively predicated on the successful passing of standard tests that have been validated within the same system.

Outside the immediate educational system, anthropologists and anthropological linguists have also been building up a corpus of experience. In 1958, Paul Garvan organized a symposium in which the consequences of differences in the status of two languages were extensively explored.[14] In an earlier paper, Gregory Bateson had suggested that it was not enough for two speakers of a lingua franca, from different statuses, to be able to discuss any subject in that lingua franca because for the most part they would never be led to conduct such conversations.[15]

On the practical level, with the extraordinary dispersion of foreign nationals all over the world, in the complex networks of international organizations, multinational corporations, and armies of occupation, the question of the effect of bilingual education on child residents abroad has been raised by hundreds of parents, anxious about their children's intellectual development. Does bilingualism impair not only performance in school, but actual mental functioning? There was a great deal of evidence to show the enormous advantages enjoyed by those who had command of more than one language who had broken the rigid links that tied the names of objects in one language unbreakably to the objects themselves. The long history of intellectual achievement by Jews and Armenians who, by minority status, have always been forced to speak more than one language could be cited. And yet, experience with children in bilingual situations was puzzling, as aptly summed up by Chester Christian: "In an important sense, the education of those who speak two langauges can never be equal to the education of monolinguals; it must be inferior or superior. Whether it will be one or the other depends heavily on whether literacy is provided in one or both languages."[16]

These present-day findings are based primarily on the study of bilingual situations to which the relevance of literacy has long been

14 Margaret Mead, "Discussion of the Symposium Papers," in "Urbanization and Standard Language: A Symposium Presented at the 1958 Meetings of the American Anthropological Association," *Anthropological Linguistics* 1, no. 3 (March 1959): 32-33.

15 Gregory Bateson, "Pidgin English and Cross Cultural Communication," *Transactions of the New York Academy of Sciences* 6, no. 4, series 2 (1944): 137-41.

16 Chester C. Christian, "Social and Psychological Implications of Bilingual Literacy," in *The Bilingual Child*, ed. Antonio Simoes, Jr. (New York: Academic Press, 1976), p. 38.

known, for example, in comparing the failure of American and most English-speaking peoples to produce high levels of literacy in English when children were taught from the beginning only in English, as compared with the success of the Dutch in the former East Indies who introduced children to literacy in their original languages and produced students who found it easy to become literate in several European languages. These relative successes have been known for three decades but have only recently been recognized by American educators under the pressure of the criticism of our failure to educate minority children. The insight of three decades ago had to be focused by events, fostered within a climate of opinion, and provided with resources and research done with the contemporary style of educational research in happy alliance with linguists and anthropologists.

So we have new, well-defined knowledge of the relationships between the language spoken at home and the educational achievement of the child, which now draws on the many researches that previously fell on deaf ears and might quite easily—but incorrectly—be defined as reinventing the wheel. Meanwhile, a nagging question remains: Is there still, in fact, a difficulty in bilingualism that impairs or compromises mental functioning? (I am using the older term *mental* because of the peculiarly jargonish connotation of the word *cognitive* at present.) The Welsh study of five decades ago suggested a difference in *emotional* weight in three areas—home, play, and school. This is different from the status questions and the comprehension questions that have concerned so many recent research workers. It is not a matter of a child in a vocabulary-poor home not knowing the name for red, although differences in color can be perceived; or feeling lonely and frightened because he doesn't know how to ask for the toilet in English. This is also different from the problem of how paralinguistic phenomena affect communication, teaching, and learning.

It has nagged at my mind through all the years that I have thought about questions of bi- and multilingualism. The early instance of the American child who ceased to remember any Samoan, but whose command of English was impaired and in whose writing Samoan constructions persisted, was followed by many other instances of apparent suppressions of languages learned in early childhood, suppressions that in some cases could be recovered under stress of great emotion. Edward Sapir fifty years ago questioned the integrity of speaking more than one language and Robert Louis Stevenson wrote a charming essay on the dishonesty of speaking a foreign language. Yet in the late 1940s, I had a brilliant young collaborator who could deal, with complete intellectual efficiency, with any subject, using exclusively her Russian, German, French, or English competence, acquired in successive periods of schooling. There seemed to be as much evidence on one side of the argument as on the other, with circumstances of relative status and use being the determinants of whether a bilingual was indeed inferior or superior to a monolingual.

It is only very recently that I have begun to develop a new theoretical approach, informed by accumulating evidence, which has led me to go back and pick up a number of leads that date back many decades. We have assumed that bilingualism and multilingualism are virtually the same thing, when compared with monolingualism, and from the standpoint of whether or not one is imprisoned in one intellectual system, this is of course true. There is also abundant evidence that the first step —the first new language, the first new cuisine—is the hardest and that after that first break away from prison the next language, the next cuisine, the next culture, is easier to learn. But the accumulation of small observations suddenly made me ask: Haven't we made a mistake not to differentiate more between bilingualism and multilingualism, attributing the *virtue* or advantages of multilingualism to bilingualism and neglecting the differences in which bilingualism may produce severe mental handicaps, while multilingualism does not? Isn't it possible that bilingualism is another kind of trap as severe in its own way as monolingualism?

Once this question is asked, a whole new vista opens up. All the evidence that has been so carefully assembled on the asymmetries and confusions that accompany learning two languages fall into place. Every dualism contains possible destructive potentialities of polarization. The ambivalences inherent in human development are always available both in the parent-child situation, based upon the inevitable dependency of the child, and in human attempts at turning such complementary situations into egalitarian, symmetrical relationships.[17]

The efforts of educators in the last twenty years to establish bilingualism have been motivated by political and humanitarian ideas of egalitarianism and attempts to compensate for and reduce the superior advantages of children who speak a majority language over those who speak a minority language. As such, they touch the very center of the relationship between school and community, both in immediate relationships between each school and the local community and in the ques-

---

17 Margaret Mead, "End Linkage: A Tool for Cross-Cultural Analysis," in *About Bateson: Essays on Gregory Bateson*, ed. John Brockman (New York: Dutton, 1977) pp. 169-231.

tion of how schools—elementary, secondary, and higher—prepare for membership in the larger communities of nation, continent, hemisphere, and planet. The teaching of other languages opens the student's mind to other systems of thought and feeling, other cultures and other periods of history, and breaks the rigidity inherent in one language. But if only one other language is taught, and if that language is one already loaded with affect through economic, social, and religious disparities, inequalities, and historical and cultural contact, there may be more disadvantages than advantages.

Supporting evidence is found in the accounts of the serious and responsible efforts of middle-class English-speaking Canadian parents who send their children to French-speaking schools, producing different —less satisfactory—results from those achieved when French-speaking children go to English-speaking schools, even in a province where French is the majority language rather than English. Here, social class and economic situation are held constant; the situation is not intensified by parents who speak two languages, and both give access to literate traditions that are strictly comparable and distinguished.[18]

The contrasting evidence concerning the high achievement of multilingual groups like Eastern European Jews and Armenians, and the extraordinary integrative capacities of a multilingual country like Switzerland, no longer seems to contradict evidence of the possible handicapping effect of bilingualism. The extraordinary capacity of Russians reared under the old regime of several governesses and tutors, each of whom spoke no Russian, which made the invention of simultaneous translation possible, becomes equally relevant. Bilingualism, and especially bilingualism developed in some compensatory effort to absorb immigrants, increase social mobility, equalize inequalities as a step toward openness and membership in the world, can be a trap. It becomes, as so many analyses of past and recent experiments in relationships between majority and minority languages have shown, a worse trap if there is no literacy in the mother tongue.

But once it is recognized that it is the potential antagonism in all dualism and all polarizations that is harmful, the next step is easy to take and has some of the delightful simplicity that all good educational innovations have. Simply introduce a third language. The third language need be only enough to give children a sense that there are many systems of speech and writing so that they are not boxed in forever by two

18 Merrill Swain and Henry C. Barik, "Bilingual Education for the English Canadian: Recent Developments," in Simoes, *The Bilingual Child*, pp. 91-100.

languages with different emotional weighting. A UNICEF Christmas card with "Merry Christmas" in many scripts, a song with the same tune and words in three languages, a game in which the words from a third language are kept intact, opens the way. At later educational levels, this is the function that was performed by Siamese in the traditional preparation of young Englishmen for the foreign service or by television lessons in Russian or Swahili for the internationally minded neighbors of the Army language school in Monterey, California.

I have brought this discussion from my earliest wonderment about the effect of a language spoken by an immigrant, minority group of children to my present state of understanding that involved over five decades of relevant research and continuing quest for more knowledge to make a rough sketch of the way in which a growing body of scientific knowledge in dynamic psychology and cultural anthropology[19] can illuminate, decade by decade, a continuing problem. Each generation of research workers that has attacked the question has brought more insight. Many have been as lacking in historical and comparative perspective as the opponents of Mediterranean immigration were of the history that made an absurdity of their prejudices. Similarly, Jensen's ignorance of concepts of race and hybridization make his attribution of a lesser ability to handle abstractions in children classified as black than in children classified as white equally alarming. In both cases the preservation or inclusion of a minimal degree of existing knowledge would have been a corrective.

A lifetime of pursuit of a problem, a lifetime in which a research worker returns again and again to the same problem, can follow the spiral model rather easily. Our problem becomes how, other than by apprenticeship to one teacher, we can bring to students of education a form of preparation for their task that can conserve the insights of the past and at the same time infuse them with a sense of discovery and personal creativity.

BIBLIOGRAPHY

Bateson, Gregory. *Naven*. Cambridge, England: The University Press, 1936.
Bateson, Gregory. "Pidgin English and Cross Cultural Communication." In *Transactions of the New York Academy of Sciences*, series 2, vol. 6, no. 4. New York: New York Academy of Sciences, 1944.
Benedict, Ruth, and Weltfish, Gene. *The Races of Mankind*. New York: Viking Press, 1947.

19   Claude Levi-Strauss, *Mythologiques*, 4 vols. (Paris: Plon, 1964-1971).

156

Blackwood, Beatrice. *A Study of Mental Testing in Relation to Anthropology*. Baltimore: Williams Wilkins, 1927.

Bloom, B.S. *Compensatory Education for Cultural Deprivation*. New York: Holt, Rinehart & Winston, 1965.

Brockman, John, ed. *About Bateson: Essays on Gregory Bateson*. New York: Dutton, 1977.

Burt, Cyril. *The Backward Child*. London: University of London Press, 1937.

Cazden, Courtney B.; John, Vera P.; and Hymes, Dell, eds. *Functions of Language in the Classroom*. New York: Teachers College Press, 1972.

Christian, Chester C. "Social and Psychological Implications of Bilingual Literacy." In *The Bilingual Child*, edited by Antonio Simoes, Jr., pp. 17-39. New York: Academic Press, 1976.

Cole, Michael. "An Ethnographic Psychology of Cognition." In *Cross Cultural Perspectives on Learning*, edited by R.W. Brislin, S. Bochner, and W.J. Lonner. New York: Halsted/Wiley, 1975.

Cole, Michael; Gay, J.; Glick, J.; and Sharp, D. *The Cultural Context of Learning and Thinking*. New York: Basic Books, 1971.

Cole, Michael, and Scribner, Sylvia. "Developmental Theories Applied to Cross-Cultural Research." In *Issues in Cross Cultural Research, Annals of the New York Academy of Sciences*, vol. 286, edited by Leonore Loeb Adler, pp. 366-73. New York: New York Academy of Sciences, 1977.

Davis, Allison, and Dollard, John. *Caste and Class in a Southern Town*. New Haven: Yale University Press, 1937.

Davis, Allison, and Dollard, John. *Children of Bondage, the Personality Development of Negro Youth in the Urban South*. Washington, D.C.: American Council on Education, 1940.

Davis, Allison; Gardner, Burleigh B.; and Gardner, Mary R., directed by W. Lloyd Warner. *Deep South: A Social Anthropological Study of Caste and Class*. Chicago: University of Chicago Press, 1941.

Gordan, Joan, ed. *Margaret Mead: The Complete Bibliography 1925-1975*. The Hague: Mouton, 1975 (s.v. linguistics, language, and education).

Grant, Madison. *The Passing of the Great Race; Or the Racial Basis of European History*. New York: Scribner, 1918; 4th rev. ed. New York: Scribner, 1936.

Henry, Nelson B., ed. *Community Education: Principles and Practices from World-Wide Experience*. 58th Yearbook of the National Society for the Study of Education, Part I. Chicago: University of Chicago Press, 1959.

Jensen, Arthur. "Heritability of IQ." *Science*, October 1976, p. 6.

Levi-Strauss, Claude. *Mythologiques*. 4 vols. Paris: Plon, 1964-1971.

Mead, Emily Fogg. *Italian on the Land: A Study of Immigration*. U.S. Bureau Labor Bulletin, May 14, 1907, pp. 473-533.

Mead, Margaret. *An Anthropologist at Work: Writings of Ruth Benedict*. Boston: Houghton Mifflin, 1959.

——. "An Anthropologist's Search for a Good Linguistic Education for Her Child." *Parents League Review*, 12 (1978) (in press).

——. *Continuities in Cultural Evolution*. ("The Dwight Harrington Terry Foundation Lectures on Religion in the Light of Science and Philosophy.") New Haven: Yale University Press, 1966.

——. "Discussion of the Symposium Papers," in Urbanization and Standard Language: A Symposium Presented at the 1958 Meetings of the American Anthropological Association," *Anthropological Linguistics*, vol. 1, no. 3, March 1959, pp. 32-33.

——. "End Linkage: A Tool for Cross-Cultural Analysis." In *About Bateson: Essays on Gregory Bateson*, edited by John Brockman. New York: Dutton, 1977, pp. 169-231.

——. "Group Intelligence Tests and Linguistic Disability among Italian Children." *School and Society*, vol. 25, no. 642, April 1927, pp. 465-68.

——. "Margaret Mead." In *A History of Psychology in Autobiography*, vol. VI, edited by Gardner Lindzey. New York: Prentice-Hall, 1974, pp. 293-326.

——— "The Methodology of Racial Testing: Its Significance for Sociology." *American Journal of Sociology*, no. 5, March 1926, pp. 657-667.

———. "On the Implications for Anthropology of the Gesell-Ilg Approach to Maturation." *American Anthropologist*, vol. 49, no. 1, January-March, 1947, pp. 69-77.

———. "The Problem of Changing Food Habits," In Report of the Committee on Food Habits, 1941-1943, "The Problem of Changing Food Habits," *National Research Council Bulletin*, 108, 1943, pp. 20-31.

———. "Professional Problems of Education in Dependent Countries" *Journal of Negro Education*, vol. 40, no. 3, Summer, 1946, pp. 346-57.

Meadows, Donella H., et al. *Limits to Growth: Report of the Club of Rome's Project on the Predicament of Mankind*. New York: Universe Books, 1972.

Mesarovich, Mihajlo, and Pestel, Eduard. *Mankind at the Turning Point*. New York: Dutton, 1974.

Osgood, Charles. "Objective Indicators of Subjective Culture." In *Issues in Cross Cultural Research, Annals of the New York Academy of Sciences*, vol. 286, edited by Leonore Loeb Adler. New York: Academy of Sciences, 1977.

Saer, D.J. "The Effect of Bilingualism on Intelligence." *British Journal of Psychology*, 14 (1923): 35-38.

Simoes, Antonio, Jr., ed. *The Bilingual Child*. New York: Academic Press, 1976.

Spindler, George, ed. *The Making of Psychological Anthropology*. Berkeley: University of California Press (in press).

Swain, Merrill, and Barik, Henri C. "Bilingual Education for the English Canadian: Recent Developments." In *The Bilingual Child*, edited by Antonio Simoes. New York: Academic Press, 1976.

Warner, W. Lloyd; Havighurst, Robert J.; and Loeb, Martin B. *Who Shall Be Educated? The Challenge of Unequal Opportunities*. New York: Harper and Brothers, 1944.

Wax, Murray L.; Diamond, Stanley; and Gearing, Fred O., eds. "Early Childhood Experience and Later Education in Complex Cultures." In *Anthropological Perspectives on Education*, pp. 67-90. New York: Basic Books, 1971.

New Directions in Education in Advanced Technological Societies

ELIOT D. CHAPPLE
Rockland Research Institute, Orangeburg, New York

Education is, after all, the process by which individuals at any age and in any situation acquire new or modified patterns of interaction and the cultural skills associated with them. Its product, therefore, consists of the interaction forms or roles or subroles necessary for participation in every kind of institution. Thus education today is omniranging; it cannot be limited to the schools and the families with whose shaping influences we have been long concerned. What we need to investigate more clearly, at this point in time, is the fundamental changes in the linkages among institutions and the bearing these changes have on education as we have traditionally known it.

Cremin, in his article in this issue, from the vantage point of the historian, has pointed to the ways in which surrogate institutions began to appear in the nineteenth century—the asylum, the reform school (and prison), and the poor house—as substitute "families" for limited populations of individuals. In the early development of these institutions, so well described by David Rothman in *The Discovery of the Asylum*, a rigorously defined structuring of institutional life was established on the theory that individuals placed within them required not merely the replacement of a family environment (hypothecated to be available within brick walls), but also familial roles (set up by staff) to which the inmates had never been exposed.[1] As part of the theory, real family members, if such were available, were regarded as sources of possible infection, and all visits were systematically restricted.

What has been happening in the last few decades goes precisely in the opposite direction. It is far more encompassing, involving every

---

1   David J. Rothman, *The Discovery of the Asylum* (Boston: Little, Brown, 1971).

segment, every organizational unit, of society. I refer to the increasing trend away from segregating those whose patterns of behavior are considered alien to society (even if not always antisocial or asocial) behind walled-in complexes. The trend has been particularly noticeable with respect to asylums for the mentally ill or retarded, while almshouses have been almost completely eliminated by welfare payments. Correctional institutions are still the subject of bitter controversy, with strong voices for and against their elimination, but the delinquent and the criminal, the mentally ill and the retarded, pose unsolved problems in achieving the reality of "reeducation." All this is further complicated by the need for a complementary reeducating process for the unaccepting members of the community to which it is assumed patients and inmates should return. Even the residential units of private agencies, where the myth of family surrogation was carried on by reiterated use of terms for family relationships, are disappearing.

To a considerable degree, this trend toward "deinstitutionalization" (whether or not it is supported by hard evidence as to its cost-effectiveness) derives from the spread of educational processes throughout society that have long gone unrecognized. Ironically, it is also coincident with much public dissatisfaction concerning the efficacy of the schools, the primary turf of the educators. But even more fundamental are the shifting linkages among the constituent institutions of our society. The term *institution* is used here to categorize the organizational systems we see in families, schools, churches, government, business and industry, associations and societies of all sorts, which are a consequence of the accelerations of changing technologies. These differentially influence the individual person, affecting those interactions with all other individual persons that make up his or her idiosyncratic network.

We have long obscured our understanding of what goes on with the particular human beings in any social context by the continuing tendency, common to researchers and officials alike, to take the easy way out and group remarkably different persons and the roles they perform under single labels—teachers, pupils, trainees, males, females, the aged—the list is endless. Then we manipulate the labels, using statistically illegitimate procedures from which to generalize about teachers or managers or politicians or blacks or Puerto Ricans. The illegitimacy of the statistics derives from the unhappy but necessary requirement that "random" samples must be taken from homogeneous groups; yet this is obviously not the case. The ambiguities are made worse by blind faith in the universal applicability of the Normal Law (and the statistics of large numbers derived therefrom), without recognition that rigorous assumptions have to be satisfied before any law (equation) for any frequency distribution can be used.[2]

It appears difficult for many to realize how much each person differs from every other, anatomically, biochemically, physiologically, neurologically, and interactionally; but the evidence is incontrovertible.[3] Every human being represents a unique identity, the resultant at any given time of a long and complex process of individualization. J. W. Getzels, in the 1977 symposium, emphasized the most rigorous, scientific definition of the phenomenon: So far as he was concerned, $N = 1$. What we actually observe at any moment in time is one discrete person, though we quickly interpose an abstraction and make the hypothesis, when two *ones* are present, that they interact.[4] And so we may, provided that we define the criteria leading to the abstraction and recognize that if two persons are in view, the criteria we have selected define our result. This does not mean that uniformities may not be determined by comparing what we can observe (and measure) in each *one* we examine. But I stress this here because both Ginsburg and Fuller, on the basis of physiological (behavioral) genetics, and I have insisted that rat_1 is not rat_2, and $mouse_1$ is not $mouse_2$, even if they derive from the same strain or laboratory stock.[5] One can scarcely argue, then, that $human_1$ equals $human_2$.

The reality we have to accept is that individual personalities differ remarkably from one another in the patterns of interaction that characterize them, in their levels of activity and initiative, in the degree to which they are aggressive or dominant, in how well they adjust to differing others, and, above all, in their vulnerability to stress occurring in adjusting or failing to adjust to others with widely diverging patterns.[6] Recognizing these as the observable evidences of individualization, we can begin to look at how culture, embodied in developing technologies and the specialization they require, proliferates the division of labor, and structures and constrains the interactions of people.

Follow any person throughout a day, and then day to day, and, with-

---

2   Alvan Feinstein, *Clinical Biostatistics* (St. Louis, Mo.: Mosby, 1977).

3   Eliot D. Chapple, *Culture and Biological Man* (New York: Holt, Rinehart & Winston, 1970).

4   Eliot D. Chapple, "Measuring Human Relations: An Introduction to the Study of the Interaction of Individuals," *Genetic Psychology Monographs* 22 (1940): 3-147.

5   Benson E. Ginsburg in *Methodology in Mammalian Genetics*, ed. W. J. Burdette (San Francisco: Holden Day, 1963); and John L. Fuller, "Physiological and Population Aspects of Behavior Genetics," *American Zoologist* 4, no. 2 (May 1964).

6   Chapple, *Culture and Biological Man.*

out considering that further extensions of the observation process depend on the development of sophisticated sampling, assume that this one and many other ones with whom he or she comes into contact are included in the omniranging eye of the investigator. What is immediately evident from our collection of data is that we can abstract a succession of geometric relations, the spatial distancing in three dimensions between our individuals, varying in time during the day, the week, the month, and by location in particular spaces, restricted in our society by the obvious barriers imposed by architectural technology exhibited in physical structures of all sorts, and in the architectural spacing and constraints of land-use in roads, parks, and so forth, superimposed on and modifying natural environmental boundaries.[7]

But beyond that, with this handy endowment of the inquirer with magical vision—unblocked by environmental obstructions, natural or man-made—we also detect repetition in who interacts with whom. We can thus begin to describe each relationship in the network in terms of frequency of contact, of who initiates it, of how long it lasts, and much more, being at the same time able to measure the degree of adjustment and the occurrence of stress and the reactions thereto. Depending on the degree of adjustment, that is, whether synchronous intervals take place or whether asynchrony is so pronounced that severe reactions occur, we begin to see shifts within networks as people endeavor to avoid those who distrub them and seek out those to whom they adjust well.

Cultural constraints, however, tend to be overriding. Not only may spatial barriers be such as to compel individuals to interact with those who disturb them, or to prevent them from spending time with those with whom they achieve adjustment, but repetitive interactions also depend on cultural sequences, the ordering of actions, whether in the kitchen, on the job, in the church, on the team, or wherever. Thus both in specialization—the performance of a limited sequence of actions out of a much longer total sequence—and in the division of labor—each sequence being performed by a specialized person (in that organizational situation)—the completion of the sequence begins or follows the completion of others. And it is here that the interaction forms, or role segments or subroles, elaborate more complex patterns than we include in the bare bones of an individual's network. We can identify highly differentiated interactional sequences, built on wide permutations in the constituent actions that have to be performed.[8] In our society,

7   Ibid., chap. 10.
8   Ibid., chap. 11.

these actions may involve acting on materials, often with the aid of other material objects (tools, machines, etc.), on pieces of paper with all the elaborate symbolic elements to be managed, or on people (teaching, selling, interviewing).[9]

Moreover, these sequences and their spatial diversification are linked together, connecting institutions to one another, through the movement of materials, paper, or people. In economic and governmental institutions, we call these the work-flows. As we know, they are highly complicated and elaborated. In other organizations, such as churches, legislative gatherings, and school rooms, they take on the form of ritual techniques, of parliamentary ordering, and, in the educational processes, are half-ritual, half-procedural. They provide the cultural matrix of much of teaching, learning, and execution of learning that constitute the role patterns of teacher and student. As these sequences extend to *include more than one person in any position,* hierarchical organization develops, not merely in its traditional meaning of supervision and control (drawn vertically on an organization chart) but also following the direction of these work-flows. Their interplay results in internal segregation of organizational units, each having internal cohesion that opposes it to other units. In modern technology, countervailing sequences become established, designed to stabilize the work-flow sequencing. These consist of controls of quality assurance, procedural standards, cost accounting—able to speed up, slow down, or stop the free-running patterns of the work-flow sequence. Segmentation, isolation, instability, are accentuated as the technology and the spatial distances become more complex.[10]

My intention here is not to describe how complex organizational systems, or more inclusive systems of systems, develop, but to make evident how change, reorganization, readjustment, and the splitting away of previously coherent systems bring about their effects (and why they do not). To indulge in not quite outrageous oversimplification, there are two ways in which changes in organizations come about (within organization I include the interactional systems built from the cultural dimensions, through which complex technological and symbolic processes can be reduced, ranging from the nuclear family to A. T. & T. and General Motors, for reasons I have discussed at length in many publications over the years). The first way to bring about change is to shift people within an organization or out of it completely. All these

9   Eliot D. Chapple and Leonard R. Sayles, *The Measure of Management* (New York: Macmillan, 1961).
10   Chapple, *Culture and Biological Man.*

individual personalities have achieved some state of balance or im-balance by having to interact with one another. All sorts of interventions make this possible. Changes in members of a group are natural, through birth, death, illness, and so forth. Many are cultural, altering the organizational linkages previously existing—getting married and setting up a new home; moving from one grade or one school to another; being promoted or fired or transferred; joining a new institution, whether it be a corporation, a church, a profession; winning or losing an election.

The second and easier way to bring about change is to change the spatial arrangements, to change the sequencing by technological or other logics, for example, by altering the routes and frequencies through which technological symbols are produced, as in accounting. As a consequence, if the new arrangement holds, the organizational structure is inevitably changed since these are the constituent elements that determine the sequencing on which the process is built, no matter what the official superstructure looks like on the chart. Everyone knows the incessant warfare that goes on in organizations about office location, proximity to the boss, avoidance of transfer to the boondocks. Less commented on, but even more powerful in their impacts on relationships, are changes in work-flows altering who interacts with whom, and, more inclusive, introduction of a new manufacturing technique, a computer, or a merger with another corporation or religious group.[11]

With this as background, let us now examine what has been happening in our modern world—the radical shifting going on in the networks of individuals and the linkages of institutions (organizations), internally and externally. We must remember that this has to include the smallest units we participate in as well as the largest. Taking educational systems as our starting place, and deferring consideration of the family until later, what we call "the school system" has clearly undergone major changes. For most young people in the early part of this century, except a specially selected group who attended high school because they hoped to go to college (colleges then were limited in number and enrollment), grammar school was the end of the educational experience. Many dropped out long before they reached the eighth grade, depending on the particular state's legal requirements; but the primacy of the grammar school was evidenced in the importance of the graduation ceremonies, the power of the principal, and, for many years, the

11   For illustrative material see Chapple and Sayles, *The Measure of Management.*

prevalence of class reunions. After World War I, however, the restrictions on the employment of young people became more rigid, and farming and fishing, the primary industries where familial need had some impact, became less and less important as employers, a development hastened by the technological revolution in farming that rendered most juveniles superfluous.

The laws preventing the young from going to work gradually increased the age at which schooling could be ended and emphasis on formal achievement standards reduced the chances of starting early, particularly for those desirous of being something more than laborers. These restrictions were reinforced by the great migrations and thus the availability of cheap adult labor, the feast-and-famine nature of business where people could be laid off wholesale, and, by mid-century, by the necessity of obtaining substantial technological know-how for a "good" job. As high schools began to take in a much higher proportion of those not college bound, they had to develop trade and business courses to satisfy the requirements of business and government. This influence carried over to the college level, where the influence of civil service and professional requirements, going hand in hand, began to reduce the traditional concern with scholarship almost to a minimum. Just as the trade unions were able to rigidify the building codes to restrict the possibility of loss of work by their members by bringing powerful pressure on political units, so the civil service establishment, acting for professionals, pseudo-professionals, and specialists, continually worked on state and local legislatures (and the federal government, of course) to increase the hurdles of examinations, experience, and job specifications to protect their own.

Thus high schools redirected much of the purpose of education, either with vocational and college tracks running side by side or, in many cities—particularly where industrial needs could be effectively delimited—through the establishment of vocational high schools (even though these often exhibited a rather unstable existence). Grammar schools lost their predominant place, though the ambiguities in age-level achievement were advanced by the popularity of the junior high schools, essentially institutions designed to provide greater elaboration of social and ritualized activities for those forced to remain in school for a longer period. They imposed a high school simulacrum presumed to aid students in coping with the structuring that existed in the high school itself and that college would ultimately impose. Underlying this drive for expansion was a primarily vocational (getting a job) emphasis. Whatever the official rationale for the belief that now everyone should go to college, the old normal school became a college, and various trade schools have followed suit. Most colleges, of course, aspired to become universities.

By World War II, sophisticated technology had become more and more essential both in business and in the armed forces. Extensive training programs were developed to meet the needs that even the high schools had largely left untouched. Since then, training for every kind of position has become an all-inclusive preoccupation of business and government. This has been reinforced by the educational benefits provided to veterans under various servicemen's benefit laws, resulting in a mammoth surge in the size and number of colleges, universities, and two-year colleges, and the formation of extensive statewide systems of education. Not only did sputnik set off a frantic preoccupation with competition in the exact sciences, engineering, and medicine; a similar trend took over the business schools with the folk belief, so implemented as to be self-fulfilling prophecy, that an M.B.A. or a certificate from one of the innumerable crash courses for managers, designed for "comers," picked and supported by their companies, is almost essential for any kind of advancement.

This preoccupation with education for the leaders of corporate or governmental units has spread like wildfire throughout the world. There are probably few if any countries, Third World or other, that are not sending students to the United States for "advanced" learning, or, through the aid of multinational corporations, setting up little replicas of the Harvard Business School or MIT.[12] Though the college-age population is declining, due to shifts in the birth rate, educational expertise in the sciences, engineering, law, medicine, and business is spreading internally within large organizations, who emphasize and subsidize these repositories of specialized knowledge on which their growth depends.[13] Similar shifts are affecting the professions. Even physicians are increasingly having to participate in postspecialization training. For many specialties, and in more and more states, requirements for such refresher courses are being mandated.

Beyond that, the technology of communication has been revolutionized, both by high-speed air transportation, reducing the time

---

12   In the summer of 1978, USC will offer a twelve-month course on high-level management practices for Asian excutives. UCLA will offer a similar course plus a series of shorter courses in Asian cities. These are two among many.

13   Many large corporations have for years run their own conference facilities, but usage has now expanded to commercial as well as university-owned centers for executive training programs.

needed to bridge spatial separation, and by satellites doing the same for audiovisual contexts. Yet we must recognize that all these are dependent on the basic technological revolution made possible by computerization. Its elaboration in many directions is changing the linkage and network systems by which large organizations used to operate. Not merely do highly developed controls facilitate the efficiency and speed of operations, but highly automated equipment is designed to maximize computer controls and eliminate hand labor.[14] In addition, possession of know-how—the capacity to make those simple discriminations necessary for decisions, once the distinguishing property of middle management and, if truth be told, of higher management also—is being replaced by computers.[15]

To deal with complex systems by the old hand methods, whether it involves running continuous-flow chemical plants, managing huge inventory accumulations, trying to stay on top of the multiplicity of financial transactions characterizing banking, government, and large corporations, is literally impossible without computerization. Specialization and the division of labor have become almost infinitely segmented, and the march goes on.

Large law firms are computerizing court decisions for easy recall, estate planning is now being managed by sophisticated computer systems, and even the medical profession, still clinging to its "clinical" verbiage, is desperately trying to bridge the gap between subjective and intuitive statements, which vary with each doctor, by exploring the potentials of computerized systems (supported by the physicians' fear of malpractice suits, intervention by public advocate groups, and the need to justify their services—and those of the hospitals they utilize— for third-party payments like Medicaid and Medicare).

Underlying all this proliferation of organizational complexities is a fundamental principle of anthropological biology I first described in 1940 (literally, but unpublished, in 1933), and expanded on in *Principles of Anthropology*, written with Carleton Coon and published in 1942.[16] In the context of this paper, it states that when

14 Redesigning and retooling in automobile plants is proceeding at such a rapid pace that it is estimated that there will be at least a 10 percent reduction in semiskilled employees by the 1980s. At one Chrysler plant, 20 electronic welding machines will perform 540 spot welds in assembly or 75 percent of what was formerly done by hand. Force reduction is expected to spare only computer personnel, machine operators (highly skilled) and engineers, the developers of new car and plant (and machine) designs.

15 Chapple and Sayles, *The Measure of Management*.

16 Chapple, "Measuring Human Relations"; and Eliot D. Chapple and Carleton S. Coon, *Principles of Anthropology*, rev. ed. (New York: R. Krieger, 1978).

changes in temporal patterns of interaction are set in motion, the stresses produced in each of the human beings involved (assuming the source of the stress is not immediately removed) have to be compensated for by changes in other relationships, and often the establishment of new ones, in the attempt to achieve a new state of stability. Knowing the quantitative properties of the individual's particular network, one can calculate what interactional changes will be required to achieve a compensatory adjustment.

In terms of this principle, technological and/or individuality changes can often be compensated for within the organizational system, ordinarily with very considerable periods of disturbance before the new adjustment is reached. The internal organizational mechanisms are comparable to those now to be discussed. However, in more complex situations, where several institutions are linked together, a new organizational structure has to appear through which stabilization can take place. In these conditions where linkages overlap, the institutions (organizations) are said to have "tangent" relations to one another because at least one person is being acted upon in common by individuals from, say, the two separate institutions tangent to one another.[17]

The standard example I use as introduction to the process is the instability in the relationships of families and schools. The same individual is *son* to *parents,* but also *pupil* to *teachers.* In theory, the daily time budgeting of interactional activities by each should avoid overlap, but school is superordinate to family within laws and regulations (whether in education or not) and conflict between school and family is endemic, even if often latent.[18]

A further principle then states that where individuals in two (or more) institutions are tangent to one another through their interaction with third persons, in this case, the son as pupil, an organizational system will be created more or less automatically. The likelihood of its appearance is a function of individual characteristics—susceptibility to disturbance, initiative, energy, activity, and other properties of the person's interaction rates. In this instance, parent-teacher associations appear as compensatory mechanisms to increase the degree of adjustment of home and school. (We need not discuss here how parents can often bring pressure on teachers through the associational means and how the compensatory system serves to try to counterbalance the hierarchical authority of the teacher.)[19]

17 Ibid.
18 Ibid.
19 Ibid.

If one scans the organization linkages with these two principles in mind, the number and extent of such organizational systems, often themselves extremely complex structurally, parallel closely the institutional segmentation that the advanced technologies have created. But one must remember not to be trapped by the semantic labels for these compensatory systems—associations, societies, clubs, committees, conferences, and a remarkable number of other terms that may, to some extent, disguise the compensatory processes that the tangent relations (linkages) have activated. Moreover, a fundamental rule derived from the above principles holds that, wherever one identifies such a structure (committees being a particular variant in government and corporate activities), its existence indicates that there is a basic organizational weakness in need of examination and correction.[20]

The more this compensatory proliferation increases, the more serious the centrifugal forces that rend the total organizational system. Often one sees attempts by a highly stable system—for example, the Mormon Church or the Roman Catholic Church, or major corporations—to try to incorporate all these spheres of instability and the people involved within their hierarchical control. Or, as a special case, extremely important in many scientific and cultural organizations and in government, one person may be selected to "represent" the people involved where, unconsciously, they know that tangent relationships and potential disturbances (sometimes benefits) exist. The delegate, representative, or whatever he or she may be called serves as an early warning signal, usually prefatory to the attempt to merchandise some kind of joint committee for the two organizations at the point where potentially serious changes are anticipated. It is also through this compensatory network that common techniques, practices, and procedures are widely introduced when both, or many, sides recognize that impending technological changes need to be controlled so as not to be entirely destructive.

Meanwhile, the school system per se, including the colleges, is losing out in the educational competition. The specialized schools—business, medical, law, and engineering schools—are flourishing where they have focused their teaching efforts on mastery of the advanced technologies. Moreover, in-house training programs, conducted either by employees of the corporation or government or by consulting firms or faculty members of professional schools, are spreading.[21] It is

20   Chapple and Sayles, *The Measure of Management.*

21   Large corporations increasingly are unwilling to participate in training programs such as the Labor Department's program for Vietnam veterans, in spite of cost reimbursals. They

important to realize that this process is going on outside the schools of education. They are almost completely excluded from this vast proliferation of specialized training courses. The term *training* ought not to be taken narrowly. Much of it is highly sophisticated and eagerly sought after for whatever reasons, but educationists have had little to do with this reorganization of the teaching-training emphases.

This widespread shift in the institutional balances in the structure of society is not merely a fashion of the times. It is a result of the impacts on organizations of continuing technological change, which force the further elaboration of the complexities of organizational systems and the proliferation of linkages between their constituent corporate subsystems (with a host of others as well as with equally complex units of governments at every level). As regulatory intervention increases so rapidly, coincident with technological growth, working relationships are established with a wide variety of professionals—not one advertising agency, one accounting firm, one law firm, one engineering firm, but a multiplicity, depending on the multiplication of the products.

As the organizational systems become more enveloping, by mergers, by growth, and by gaps and ambiguities in the control systems, large institutions become segmented into more and more discrete unit systems no longer tied together by the natural work-flow sequencing of a product line. Thus the system of linkages elaborated for conglomerates, national and multinational, are primarily financial, relying on accounting as a means of control. But this, by its very nature, is highly unstable, so the component parts, those divisions or branches of what were once independent companies, are no longer viable on their own. As a consequence, a plant may have been in a given community for a hundred years, with the lives of its employees, their families, and community institutions built around it. Tomorrow, the order comes to close down the plant; costs are too high and demand for the product is falling. Now parts will be made in Taiwan or Singapore and assembled somewhere a thousand miles away.[22]

Thus, corporate and governmental consolidation, forced and facili-

---

have made it clear that they have their own sophisticated programs and prefer to do the training themselves. Even Navy recruitment is following a similar course with the illiteracy shown even by high school graduates. They have begun their own remedial reading programs to try to remedy these deficiencies.

22   Zenith, the last U.S. integrated TV producer, is closing down all but two plants and having the parts made in Southeast Asia. This multinational dispersal of manufacturing components is now called, ironically, production sharing.

tated by technological change, is resulting in the spread of different forms of education through the society. Schools as educators are declining in acceptance, not simply because fewer births took place in the appropriate years past, but because, with few exceptions, the school is no longer the principal educator; it provides only the ingredients, the substructures, on which education in the corporate and technological world can build.[23] A college degree is today a requirement for any job above that of a laborer; yet, except in the specialties, and often only with an advanced degree, it has no market value except as an entry certificate.

Moreover, what once was a primary influence in stabilizing the strengths of the schools and the community was the family system, with its "roots," including at least several generations and a good proportion of kin, in a fixed location, the home town. This is disappearing, particularly for those in the corporate and governmental world (and also for the migrants seeking to enter the system, leaving their own countries behind). Breakdown in the families of the managerial group began with the dogma that a prospective executive needs "wide" experience. Hence he should be moved from one part of the country to another to be exposed to a variety of different problems and responsibilities. As corporations grew in size, plant fixity in its initial location became dispensable, unlike the migrations of plants in textiles and shoes in the thirties to new but permanent locations primarily to escape the unions and obtain cheap labor. As multinational corporations spread throughout the world, however, this process has accelerated. Though they have become larger and larger, they are more vulnerable to the impacts of the financial markets. Today, the old three-generation family is gradually disappearing from the same neighborhood, the same city. Kin and long-established friends, held together by activities and interactions they indulged in that were once a constant part of living, are now scattered to the winds. Where they live, what schools, churches, clubs, and societies they find, afford commitments that can only be temporary and uncertain.

The three (or more) generation family has lost its hierarchical power over its members. Wherever you move, new relationships have to be

---

23 Both the Navy program to counteract illiteracy and, at high levels, the insistence on specialized education, usually at the graduate level except for engineers, plus focused training programs within the corporation or by corporate-subsidized commercial or nonprofit training organizations, the latter either the offshoot of universities or made up of faculty on what is supposedly extramural time, appear to be among the fastest growing enterprises in the country, the Armed Forces being forced into it by their difficulties in filling their recruitment needs.

established, and adjustment is by no means easy to accomplish. Whatever systems of acceptance a community may provide (many are commercial), the new person, the new family, are strangers, with all the emotional stresses created when they move. Through transfer or termination, they try to locate within bridgeable distances of those they know and can depend on. Little wonder that the strongest bond is between the siblings and their spouses, their children, and the close friends that each has formed.[24] As this process goes on, repeating itself over long periods of time with little sign of mending, the family system becomes an affine network, built on the connecting bonds of siblings and their spouses. Families are no longer able to contribute effectively to the stability of the institutions of the communities to which they move. Strangers, with acquaintances who are usually also strangers, make up a floating population, with little chance of establishing significant relationships with the "locals" (the shopkeepers, real estate agents, etc.), the small permanent population of a suburban town or urban complex.

The end result has, therefore, been the disarticulation of families from the schools and, to a large degree, from the political forces operating in the community. Most transients can have little real impact on community institutions, given the likelihood that at any time they may have to move away, however much they may hope that this might prove their permanent home. True, schools and their quality are of concern while parents have children living with them. Yet the lack of roots (and influence) means that the control of the school system will be maintained by the locals, broken only temporarily by the intervention of a remarkably charismatic outsider.

As strangers, though they might wish for better schools, this largely irrevocable impermanence means that the primary focus of their living and the asset that promises continuity is their property. Its current cash value, which perhaps they can increase, is the guarantor of being able to live successfully in a new community. Whatever threatens the amount of cash realizable if they have to sell endangers their own future. Perhaps the next community may have better schools or those here may improve, but this is secondary. Bond issues to benefit the schools mean increased taxes, reducing their equity. Moreover, they believe themselves to be vulnerable to other "strangers," those "undesirables" who could reduce their property's value. Equally important

---

24 Eliot D. Chapple, "Families and Communities in Today's Realities: The Reawakening of the Living Past" (Paper presented at the Smithsonian Institution, Washington, D.C., 1976).

is the degree to which the essential services protecting their own safety and that of their home and neighborhood are to be counted upon.

In the hierarchy of values in this period of rapidly accelerating technological change, schools are no longer the focus of community pride as was true in earlier times. Just as the family has undergone (or is undergoing) fundamental change, so the schools in company are losing their primacy. Education as it is carried on in the schools of the community has become equivalent to other services, to the police, fire department, sanitation. Perhaps it is even falling lower in the scale of essentiality as dangers to life and property are spreading, no longer limited to the inner cities, but throughout the country. This is not to say that education itself is endangered, as we have seen. The crucial question is whether the schools and families as educators are relegated to the periphery as the corporate and governmental systems take over their primary educational functions.

Education and the Transfer of Inequality from Generation to Generation

PETER R. MOOCK

Teachers College, Columbia University

Human capital economics provides a theoretical framework for analyzing the decisions of individuals to incur costs for education. The model predicts that an individual will choose to add to his or her stock of human capital—i.e., to invest—so long as the discounted value of the returns that accrue over time exceeds or at least equals the value of the present consumption foregone.[1] While there are many ways to raise productive capacity—such as migrating (from an area with a smaller to one with a larger stock of complementary capital, physical or human)[2] or marrying (which, despite the tax laws, can yield similar benefits via specialization and economies of scale)[3] —education is probably the clearest example

The author gratefully acknowledges the critical reading of this article in draft by William Garner, Hope Jensen Leichter, Victor Levine, Joyce Moock, Harold Noah, and Jeffrey Siedenberg.

1 Because of the "time value of money," reflected in market interest rates, future returns (or future costs) must be "discounted to the present" to make them comparable to present flows. The roots of human capital theory can be traced to the very early writings of political economists. Adam Smith wrote in 1776 of investment in human capital (*An Inquiry into the Nature and Causes of the Wealth of Nations*, vol. 1 [London: Macmillan and Company, 1869], pp. 106-07) in terms that are fully recognizable in light of current theory. But only in the last 20 years has human capital emerged as a primary concern of professional economists. A landmark occasion in the development of this concern is the 1960 presidential address to the American Economics Association of Theodore W. Schultz ("Investment in Human Capital," *American Economic Review* 51 [March 1961]: 1-17). For a recent appraisal of the heuristic value of human capital theory, the reader is referred to Mark Blaug, "Human Capital Theory: A Slightly Jaundiced Survey," *Journal of Economic Literature* 14 (September 1976): 827-55.

2 Larry A. Sjaastad, "The Costs and Returns of Human Migration," *Journal of Political Economy* 70 (October 1962): 80-93.

3 Gary S. Becker, "A Theory of Marriage, Part I," *Journal of Political Economy* 81 (July/

of human capital investment, and one of the most significant in terms of total resources expended.[4] Indeed, the enhancement of an individual's capacity to "do things" (not just market-related activities, but *all* things in life) is a reasonably accurate if not sufficiently specific expression of what economists and others mean when they speak of "education."[5]

Looking just at formal schooling and investment in learning on the job, Mincer has shown that differences in the accumulation of human capital may account for as much as 55 percent of the variation in the weekly wage rate of white, nonfarm, nonstudent American males up to age sixty-five.[6] The effect of education on "household production" is more difficult to observe, but the evidence we have suggests that education enhances efficiency in nonmarket activities just as it seems to do in paid employment.[7]

Michael has shown that the effect of additional education on family consumption patterns is similar to the effect of additional money income;[8] in other words, a family with more education than another

---

August 1973): 813-46. Reprinted in Theodore W. Schultz, ed., *Economics of the Family: Marriage, Children, and Human Capital*, A Conference Report of the National Bureau of Economic Research (Chicago: University of Chicago Press, 1975); and Gary S. Becker, *The Economic Approach to Human Behavior* (Chicago: University of Chicago Press, 1976).

    4   For estimates of the full costs of *formal* education (schools, universities, and government training programs) alone, see Elchanan Cohn, *The Economics of Education* (Cambridge, Mass.: Ballinger Publishing Co:, 1975), pp. 108-12.

    5   We may compare the definition of a historian: ". . . education [is] the deliberate, systematic, and sustained effort to transmit, evoke, or acquire knowledge, attitudes, values, skills, or sensibilities, as well as any outcomes of that effort." Lawrence A. Cremin, *Public Education* (New York: Basic Books, 1976), p. 27.

    6   Jacob Mincer, *Schooling, Experience, and Earnings* (New York: Columbia University Press, 1974), chap. 5.

    7   There are at least three interpretations of the positive relationship between education and earnings. First, as already noted, education may render workers more productive. Second, education may simply identify those who are, for whatever reasons, already more productive. This is the "screening hypothesis." For a discussion, see Paul Taubman and Terence Wales, *Higher Education and Earnings: College As an Investment and a Screening Device*, A Report Prepared for the Carnegie Commission on Higher Education and the National Bureau of Economic Research (New York: McGraw-Hill, 1974); presented in summary form in Thomas F. Juster, ed., *Education, Income, and Human Behavior*, A Report Prepared for the Carnegie Commission on Higher Education and the National Bureau of Economic Research (New York: McGraw-Hill, 1975). Third, education, like union membership, may sort workers into separate, noncompeting labor groups, for reasons that have nothing to do with productiveness. For a discussion of the third hypothesis, see V. Lane Rawlins and Lloyd Ulman, "The Utilization of College-Trained Manpower in the United States," in *Higher Education and the Labor Market*, A Volume of Essays Sponsored by the Carnegie Commission on Higher Education, ed. Margaret S. Gordon (New York: McGraw-Hill, 1974). Whereas either of the latter hypotheses could provide an explanation of the education-earnings relationships in the *external labor market*, neigher seems to make much sense in reference to the *internal (intra-household) labor market*. By far the most reasonable explanation of an observed relationship between education and *household production* is that education makes individuals more productive.

    8   Robert T. Michael, *The Effect of Education on Efficiency in Production* (New York:

family generally behaves as though its money income were higher, even when money income is actually the same. Leibowitz finds that the educational attainment of the mother of a preschool child is related positively to the IQ of the child when tested later in school, and to the final educational attainment of the child, and she finds these relationships in multiple regression runs in which she controls for other determinants of intellectual development, including the *time* of the mother spent in caring for the preschool child.[9] In sum, education seems so important a determinant of individual well-being in American society that an understanding of the reasons for differences in the *propensity to invest* in education is crucial to the development of a sound and equitable social policy.

II

Within the human capital framework, the individual's propensity to invest in the formation of human capital is greater, the smaller the interest cost of financing the investment and the greater the rate of return on each dollar invested.[10] As a decision-making model, the human capital framework applies less well, presumably, to children than it does to adults. The very young have not yet assumed responsibility for the way in which resources—time and money—are allocated. They are, typically, decision takers, rather than decison makers. For them there are few, if any, alternatives to an externally prescribed course of action.

The transition from helpless infant to responsible adult is a gradual one. There is no single developmental landmark that divides childhood from adulthood, although many communities celebrate the transition at some point in ritual fashion, as with the Christian confirmation or Jewish bar mitzvah. An important *rite de passage* shared in early life by virtually every modern-day American is entry into school. Although many decisons will continue to be made for the child—by parents and, now, *in loco parentis* by teachers and other school personnel—school entrance marks the first important break with parental authority. To some extent, the individual's progress through the educational system and success thereafter lie, from this point forward, in his or her own hands.

National Bureau of Economic Research, 1972); presented in summary form in Juster, *Education, Income, and Human Behavior*.

9   Arleen Leibowitz, "Home Investments in Children," *Journal of Political Economy* 82 (March/April, 1974, Part II): S111-31; reprinted in Schultz, *Economics of the Family*.

10   Gary S. Becker, "Human Capital and the Personal Distribution of Income: An Analytical Approach" (Ann Arbor: Institute of Public Administration, University of Michigan, 1967); reprinted in Gary S. Becker, *Human Capital*, 2nd ed. (New York: Columbia University Press, 1975).

But, by the time a child enters school and assumes partial responsibility for the future, considerable investment has already taken place. In particular, the child's parents have incurred costs in the child's behalf that will affect his or her propensity to invest in education over time. Ignoring innate differences in ability, which the author believes can never be identified with any great rigor, or measured with tolerable precision, we can assert that the greater the preschool investment of the parents in the child's behalf, the greater the individual's incentive to invest in forming additional human capital, because the rate of return on each dollar of investment will be higher, and because the financing cost usually will be lower.

The rate of return on educational investment is high for individuals from advantaged backgrounds because; as students, they are efficient relative to other individuals; they have learned how to learn. Also, at least in the past in this country, they have received a disproportionate share of available subsidies in education (scholarships, fellowships, admission to publicly funded universities), so that the price of a given course of study has been lower on average for individuals from advantaged backgrounds than for others. Finally, because of family connections, they are likely to be more successful at marketing whatever amount of human capital they acquire.

The cost of financing education (i.e., the interest cost on the capital investment) is usually lower for such individuals, which is the second reason for their greater propensity to invest. There are often family funds to cover both tuition and living expenses during the schooling period, whereas less advantaged individuals, to invest to the same extent, would need to borrow funds in the commerical capital market. Moreover, when it *is* necessary to borrow from sources outside the family, the rate of interest may be lower for those from advantaged backgrounds because of family collateral and reputation and because of these individuals' demonstrated scholastic ability.

What we are suggesting is that children are already highly disparate in capacity by the time they enter school at age six; and that differences in capacity at the point of school entrance, an important step in the progression toward individual emancipation, explain differences in the propensity to invest in the formation of further human capital and, ultimately, differences in income.

III

How would we go about measuring capacity at the point of school entrance? Since units of capacity cannot be observed directly, and since tests of ability are often considered suspect, our measure may need to be a monetary one. With adults, we could look at differences in their market wage, which can be assumed to measure differences in capacity.[11] Except under special circumstances, however, children are prohibited by law from working for wages even if they, or their parents, would choose otherwise. Thus we cannot look to market value as a measure of a child's capacity but must, instead, consider the cost of producing it.

The costly inputs in the production of early human capital are the flow of purchased goods and services and the flow of parental time allocated to the child.[12] Considerable research on the determinants of ability in young children has focused on the availability in the home of *material* resources, which are relatively easy to measure. Some recent studies, however, indicate that the quantity and quality of parental time inputs may be as important, if not more so, than the input of purchased goods and services.[13]

In the "classical" American family, in which sex roles are sharply defined—the father specializing in market work, the mother in housework—the "direct" (money) costs of child care are the responsibility of the male breadwinner, whereas the "indirect" (time) costs fall largely on the woman. This family stereotype, in which there are two parents

11   The capacity, at least, to do market work. One's wage, however, is only a rough measure even of this since (1) an individual's full compensation includes significant nonmonetary components (for a discussion of the importance of the nonmonetary components of full compensation, see Robert E.B. Lucas, "Hedonic Wage Equations and Psychic Wages in the Returns to Schooling," *American Economic Review* 67 [September 1977] : 549-58; also, Smith, *An Inquiry into the Nature and Causes of the Wealth of Nations*, pp. 105-06; Samuel Bowles, "Schooling and Inequality from Generation to Generation," *Journal of Political Economy* 80 [May/June 1972, Part II] : S237-39, and (2) during most of an individual's working life, a portion of full compensation is simultaneously reinvested in training on-the-job, an implicit transaction between employee and employer that registers explicitly in the accounts of neither (see Becker, *Human Capital*, chap. 2).

12   Since the child's own time has no market value, we will ignore this factor in discussing the formation of early human capital. The omission is based on the unavailability of data and cannot be justified theoretically. On the one hand, it may be true that variation in the *quantity* of own time across children is small, due to the absence of any market alternative. On the other hand, however, the *quality* of own time becomes increasingly disparate across children between birth and school entrance, as already stated, and a fully specified production function for early human capital would include the stock of human capital in period $t-1$ as an input in the production of capital in period t. In other words, one input in the production of capital in any period is the output of this same process in the period before. See Yoram Ben-Porath, "The Production of Human Capital and the Life Cycle of Earnings," *Journal of Political Economy* 75 (August 1967): 352-65.

13   For a review of some studies by economists of the impact of parental time inputs, see Peter Moock, "Economic Aspects of the Family As Educator," *Teachers College Record* 76, no. 2 (December 1974): 92-104; reprinted in Hope Jensen Leichter, ed., *The Family as Educator* (New York: Teachers College Press, 1975).

present, the male engaged in market employment and the female fully occupied at home, can be misleading in light of current facts and figures. Given the rising incidence of marital instability in America, it is predicted that four out of ten children born in this decade will spend at least part of their childhood years in single-parent families.[14] Moreover, as a reflection of the growing participation of all women in market work, the mother of a preschool child today is about as likely to be in the labor force as to be out of the labor force. In 1973, 48 percent of women with children under six spent at least some time in market work during the year; 16 percent worked fifty or more weeks. Taking the child as the unit, instead of the family, 45 percent of children under six were children of working mothers; 14 percent were children of mothers working fifty or more weeks.[15]

In other words, current data indicate considerable diversity in family organization and employment patterns. The working mother may be an aberration in some people's minds, but she is not so in reality. Despite this, however, the fact remains that significant numbers of women do stay home to care for young children, delaying, interrupting, or terminating valuable market careers. To each of these women (or to the family unit of which she is a member), the benefits of the increased time that staying home allows her to spend with the child must be worth, *at least*, the loss of market income; otherwise, she would choose to engage in market employment and find cheaper substitutes (e.g., day-care facilities) for her own time in child care. Any attempt, however, to cost the input of a mother's time in caring for her preschool child is fraught with methodological pitfalls.

First, the fact that a particular woman with a preschool child is not employed is not proof that she *would be* employed without the preschool child. Even if she had been employed up until the child's birth, the decision to bear the child and the decision to drop out of the labor force may have been made simultaneously. There is no certainty that the birth of the child *caused* her to quit her job. Unless it is true that the presence of the child is the sole cause of her market inactivity, then it is incorrect to count the full amount of the earnings that she forgoes as a cost of the child. But if not the *full* amount, then what *fraction* should be assigned to raising a child?

Second, since "earnings forgone" cannot, by the nature of the beast,

14 Kenneth Keniston and the Carnegie Council on Children, *All Our Children: The American Family under Pressure* (New York: Harcourt Brace Jovanovich, 1977), p. 4.

15 U.S. Department of Commerce, Social and Economic Statistics Administration, *Current Population Reports: Consumer Income* (Series P-60), no. 98 (January 1975), pp. 110-15.

be observed directly, some approximation of this cost element must be found. Provided that the woman has been employed sometime in the past, we might measure the current value of her time in market work by her last wage. Depending on how long it has been since she quit, however, labor demand conditions are likely to have shifted, and her market skills to have depreciated. Alternatively, we might estimate her wage by observing the average wage of other women who are currently employed and who possess all the relevant characteristics of this woman. Of course, the specification of "relevant characteristics" is a matter of some conjecture.

Third, even if we knew exactly what the woman, were she now employed, would be earning in monetary terms, we would not know her *full compensation*. An employee's full compensation for work performed consists of his or her own *money wage*, including all contributions withheld from the worker's paycheck, plus benefits (payments "in kind," such as free or subsidized meals, and "intangibles," such as job prestige or the desirability of geographic location), plus any *on-the-job training* that is financed out of the individual's earnings flow and the future returns to which belong to the individual. For any particular individual in any particular period, money wage may account for only a small fraction of full compensation.[16]

Fourth, there are almost certain to be significant economies of scale in child care. Once a family has taken on the responsibility of a first child, the cost of caring for a second child (who is reasonably close in age to the first) is presumably much reduced. What fraction, however, of the family's total outlay of resources on child care is the *marginal* outlay? On what basis should we allocate the full cost of the woman's time input between the two (or, where there are more than two, among the several) children?

Despite these conceptual and informational problems, studies that would quantify the costs of child rearing are not without precedent. In a study for the U.S. Commission on Population Growth and the American Future, Reed and McIntosh estimated the average indirect costs in 1969 of a *first child* in the United States.[17] By concentrating on first children, the authors avoid the question of how to allocate costs in the situation of a family with two or more children.

16   Refer footnote 11 above.
17   Ritchie H. Reed and Susan McIntosh, "Costs of Children," in *Economic Aspects of Population Change*, ed. E.R. Morss and R.H. Reed, vol. II of *Research Reports*, Commission on Population Growth and the American Future (Washington, D.C.: U.S. Government Printing Office, 1972).

The first step in estimating market *earnings* forgone is to estimate market *time* forgone. Noting that married women of childbearing age without children under fourteen years of age performed on average 1,000 hours of market work in 1969, Reed and McIntosh make the assumption that this same number of hours would have been worked by the typical woman who has a child under fourteen had she not been encumbered by the presence of the child. To get an estimate of work time given up typically by the mother of a child of a particular age, Reed and McIntosh subtract from 1,000 hours the amount of time worked, as predicted by a regression equation that controls for factors such as race, age, educational attainment, and employment status of the husband.

By this procedure, they estimate work time lost by the mother due to the presence of the child to be 894 hours in the child's first year. Work time lost declines gradually during the child's preschool years, reaching 711 hours in the sixth year. In the seventh year, when the child has entered school, the figure plummets to 380 hours. In other words, the mother of a child in school spends considerably more time in market work on average (620 hours) than the mother of a preschool child (106 hours in the first year, climbing gradually to 289 hours in the sixth year) but spends less time than a married woman without children (1,000 hours).

The next step in estimating earnings forgone is to put a price on each hour lost. For this, Reed and McIntosh use the average wage of women in 1969, and then, to get separate estimates of earnings forgone according to educational attainment, use the average wage of women in each of four educational categories.[18] Espenshade updates their results by applying 1977 wage figures. According to his results, the average indirect cost of a first child from birth to age six in the United States is $20,073 currently. For mothers with an elementary school education, it is $15,347; with a high school education, $18,997; with a college education, $24,752; and with more than a college education, $31,396.[19]

The research of Espenshade allows us to compare the indirect (time) costs of child care with the direct (money) costs. Again following a methodology proposed by Reed and McIntosh, Espenshade estimates the current direct costs of a first child in the United States. His figures are for the maturation period from birth through four years of college.

18   Ibid.
19   Thomas J. Espenshade, "The Value and Cost of Children," *Population Bulletin* 32 (April 1977): 1-47.

According to his calculations, averaged across regions, the monetary out-lay on food, shelter, clothing, medical care, educational services, and the like is $44,156 following a low-cost plan, and $64,215 following a moderate-cost plan.[20] By prorating these averages, we can estimate the direct costs of a first child from birth to age six to be $13,197 and $20,062, following the low-cost and moderate-cost plans respectively.

The research cited here implies that the market earnings given up by a woman due to the presence of a first child typically equal or exceed the sum of direct purchases made in behalf of the child. The total costs of raising a first child to age six would appear to be somewhere in the neighborhood of $40,000 on average in the United States today. There is additional research suggesting that the marginal cost of each subsequent child is about half that of the first, or $20,000 on average.[21] In short, the "price" of children today is quite astoundingly high.

IV

Although the *average* family may expend the equivalent of $40,000 over six years on a first child, and $20,000 on each subsequent child, a significant minority of American families lack the resources permitting such lavish care. Even in the case of a two-parent family in which both parents are employable full time (35 hours per week) at the minimum wage ($2.30 per hour), the total of their potential pretax earnings is just $8,050 per year, $48,300 over six years. At least four-fifths of this potential earnings flow would be required for child care, to maintain (in dollar terms) one or more preschool children at the level of the national average. Given the many alternative claims on income, this family would be unable to provide child-nurturing inputs to this extent.

A child in this family would have to forgo some of the desiderata enjoyed by the typical American child. The sacrifices would include certain toys, books, and items of clothing deemed "unnecessary" or "too expensive." Living space would be at a premium in this family; there would be small likelihood of a separate room, all to the child's self, as a place for quiet and reflection. Both parents might feel compelled to continue working, even if the only alternative supervision for the child were that of an untrained or disinterested baby sitter. The nutritiousness of diet is often a neglected factor in low-SES (socioeconomic status) homes, due to a combination of ignorance and financial incapacity.

20   Ibid.
21   Boone A. Turchi, *The Demand for Children: The Economics of Fertility in the United States* (Cambridge, Mass.: Ballinger Publishing Co., 1975), chaps. 3 and 4.

Of course, the hypothetical family just described is not destitute. In many American homes, conditions are worse—the market value of parental time is lower than in this home, and the paring of child-nurturing inputs necessarily more extensive. Particularly hard hit are single-parent families and families in which the principal breadwinner cannot find employment.

It is true that the dollar value of resources expended is not a perfect measure of *effective* inputs in the production of early human capital. Some families make particularly good use of resources expended. They are "efficient" producers of child care. Other families make poor use; they are "inefficient" producers of child care. One family may lavish expensive purchases on a child, without much attention given to their instructional or nutritional value or to the danger of "spoiling" the child, while another family sees that every dollar spent counts significantly toward the child's development.

Certainly, all hours of time are not equal. Two women, commanding identical market wages, may quit jobs to care for their respective children, but the one may be an attentive and loving mother, while the other, perhaps unconsciously, resents the interruption of her market career and, by staying home, actually retards the child's development. A third woman may continue to work during her child's preschool years yet, by devoting most of her evenings and weekends to child-rearing activities, spend as much time with the child as she would have spent had she quit her job. Moreover, because she continues her career, her attitude toward the child may be more healthy than it would have been, and therefore her time with the child more productive. A fourth woman may engage in labor-force activity but come home so exhausted or preoccupied each day that she ignores, or, worse, abuses her child.

The wage rate, which reflects quite well productivity in market work, may be a poor measure of productivity in child care. A woman or man may lack the education and training necessary to secure a high-paying job but may, nevertheless, make an extraordinarily good parent. Although the odds are against it, many individuals do move from a position near the bottom of the income distribution as children to a position near the top as adults. We may assume that, in many of these cases, the parents of these individuals, despite having failed to achieve economic success for themselves, have managed somehow to confer the attributes for success on their children.

In sum, there are "qualitative" dimensions of child care that have not been measured in research to date. Despite the importance of qualitative differences, however, it remains true on average that more is better than less. To be brought up in a family with (potential) income far below the median level is to be given a handicap that tends forever after to limit an individual's productive power relative to his or her peers.

We know, from research by psychologists, sociologists, and economists, that capacity at any age—as measured by IQ or achievement test scores, educational attainment, or success in market activities—correlates positively and quite strongly with capacity at any other age. Since equality of inputs in the process of elementary and secondary school education, if not yet a reality, is now generally accepted as a goal of American society,[22] the family emerges as the most logical target for assistance in any public program that would reduce inequality in America. Although norms relating to male-female sex roles and to the durability of the marriage contract are undergoing change—presumably they have always done so—the family remains the institution in which most children will spend their most formative years.

V

In recognition of the family's crucial nurturing role, the Carnegie Council on Children has called for a comprehensive national policy that would guarantee employment for at least one member of every family and, through a reformulated federal income tax, set a floor under every family's income, equaling approximately one-half of the median family income.[23] Under this system, the full-time care of a preschool child would be treated as a legitimate alternative to market employment, giving the single parent the option of withdrawing from the labor force, an option that is not financially viable under the present system. Moreover, temporary withdrawal for purposes of child care could not, under the new laws, result in loss of job or seniority within the firm.

By implication of these recommendations, the council holds that the development of capacity in young children depends (and should depend) principally on the inputs of parental time and market purchases *made out of family income*, and that the particulars of child care should be *left to the discretion of individual families* (except in the most extraordinary of circumstances, when direct intervention may be called for). The council proposes a system that would enable poor families to pro-

---

22 The goal is articulated in several recent, state-level court cases. See, for example, Serrano v. Priest, 483 P. 2d 1241, 1244 (Cal. 1971); Robinson v. Cahill, 62 NJ 473, 303 A. 2d 273 (1973); and Rodriguez v. San Antonio Independent School District, 337 S. Supp. 280 (WD Tex. 1971).

23 Keniston and the Council, *All Our Children*.

vide their children with more of the one input (market purchases) without having to sacrifice any of the other input (parental time).

Poverty, which by the council's definition afflicts one quarter of all American families,[24] has a debilitating effect on a child's development. As argued above, the disadvantaged child fails to acquire the learning skills that render educational investment, later in life, profitable. The problem of poverty is society's problem, though many would shift the blame onto the victims themselves. Existing programs for relieving poverty are generally demeaning, the direct descendants of seventeenth- and eighteenth-century poor laws. Moreover, partial programs directed narrowly at the *symptoms* of poverty are doomed to failure.

> Traditionally, American efforts to eliminate poverty and increase economic equality have dealt with everything but the fact of economic inequality and the economic system that allows and perpetuates it. All of these efforts have been unsuccessful: relative poverty has not decreased in over a century in America. As long as our economic system permits millions to live in poverty and as long as our political system is not committed to the elimination of poverty, no programs of personal reform, moral uplift, blame, therapy, philanthropy, or early education can hope to eliminate the enormous harm to the next generation that poverty causes.[25]

Only by attacking poverty directly and at its source, the family as cradle, can the nation hope to short-circuit the process that results in the replication of unequal distribution from one generation to the next.

---

24   The council's definition of poverty (income at or below one half the median family income, or $7,373 in 1974 for a family of four) diverges markedly from the official "poverty line" (arbitrarily set at $5,000 in 1974). By the government's more stringent standard, 11.6 percent of the American population (15.5 percent of American children) were "poor" in 1974. (Ibid., p. 27).

25   Ibid., p. 118

Western Schools in Non-Western Societies: Psychosocial Impact and Cultural Response

ROBERT A. LEVINE
Harvard University

The spread of the Western school in non-Western societies during the last century represents one of the most far-reaching instances of institutional diffusion in modern history; it continues today in New Guinea and other remote regions of the Pacific, Africa, and Latin America, with consequences that are probably irreversible and will be felt for centuries. Comparative sociologists have documented the effects of this diffusion: through rising literacy rates, on increased participation in large-scale systems of mass communication, national government, and industrial production; through the link between school and employment, on the development of occupationally based social strata; and through the communication of new cultural ·forms, on the erosion of traditional values in family life and other institutional domains. Their studies have taught us that the intellectual skills developed by literacy create in the individual an expanded awareness of environmental variation, alternative possibilities, and potentialities for choice—an awareness that raises doubts about tradition and increases receptivity to new norms of social participation.

In this article my interest centers not on societal outcomes of schooling or their bases in cognitive development, but on the place of the school in the social experience of non-Western communities. My goal is to suggest by way of illustration that as the school spreads, each society endows it with affective meanings derived from its cultural traditions,

This paper was presented at the American Sociological Association meetings in Chicago, September 1977. Field research among the Gusii during 1974-1976 was supported by a grant from the National Science Foundation (SOC 74-12692) and a Research Scientist Award from the National Institute of Mental Health.

meanings that determine community reactions to the school as an institution and its subsequent impact on social relationships. This is a phenomenological approach in that it focuses more on what school means to the children who attend it and their parents, less on its official goals in learning and social placement. These meanings often concern schooling as evaluation rather than learning, and therefore involve the collective processes by which social comparisons are made.

The introduction of a Western school system into a non-Western society, as I see it, often includes three *novel* institutional features: (a) a hierarchy of spatially segregated groups organized by attainment level, through which each individual child is expected to pass, (b) explicit evaluation procedures to assess his or her level of attainment and determine advancement to the next level, (c) selection procedures that assign individuals to higher and lower places in the educational hierarchy on the basis of evaluation outcomes, thereby affecting their subsequent placement in the socioeconomic order. As institutional innovation, such a system creates a highly visible arena in which the individual's performance is comparatively evaluated against that of his age-mates in a way that affects his future opportunities for success in life. The situation inevitably generates competition (due to selection and comparative evaluation), anxiety about being publicly and invidiously evaluated, and anxiety about the short- and long-term outcomes of evaluation. My hypothesis is that the reactions of a people to participation in this new institution are mediated by the cultural meanings they attach to competitiveness, public assertion of self, invidious comparison, and strivings for scarce resources (wealth, prestige). If traditional institutions have operated to conceal competition and personal strivings and to minimize self-assertion and invidious comparison, then these features of school life may be in opposition to existing norms and will arouse a great deal of anxiety in pupils and parents. The community will then have to deal with this anxiety by redesigning the evaluation procedures of the Western-model school, by changing the norms regarding the expression of competitive intent and self-assertiveness, by managing the anxiety intrapsychically as a stress reaction—or by all three.

I assume that in many non-Western societies there did exist cultural norms to minimize public expressions of competition and self-assertion, that the introduction of the school did in fact run counter to these norms, and that adjustments were indeed necessary, but that cultures differed (and continue to differ) in their solutions to this problem.[1]

1 My assumption is based on the view that the Western model of the school introduced in non-Western societies by missionaries and government administrators included norms favoring

Investigating these solutions in the context of the school as an institution represents a means of understanding each culture's norms of self-presentation in social encounters and its culturally constituted defenses for protection against psychic stress.

Although this problem has never been investigated in these terms (so far as I know), there is some evidence available concerning the reactions of non-Western peoples to the introduction of the Western school. Thirty years ago, for example, Leighton and Kluckhohn described the so-called shyness of Navajo children in classroom situations and explained it as a reaction to the competitiveness encountered there. For the Navajo child going to school for the first time, "being singled out from one's fellows for superior performance is embarrassing or acutely disturbing rather than rewarding." They related this to Navajo values concerning individual involvement and participation in a group: "To take initiative in any obvious fashion has for the Navajo the psychological meaning of separating him from the social group to which he looks for both support and recognition."[2]

The Japanese, as described by Vogel and Kiefer, have responded to a similar problem by redesigning the Western school system in a form they find more compatible. Examinations are impersonally organized on a national basis, thus removing from the face-to-face situation of the classroom the competitiveness that makes everyone involved uncomfortable. Being outside the evaluation process, the teacher never has to withdraw from the child the unconditional nurturance he or she has had at home; the male teacher can be seen by the child as a "motherly father," as Kiefer calls it. This keeps the classroom atmosphere and teacher-pupil relationship as warm and loving as the Japanese want it, but it nevertheless engenders great anxiety in the child, who must face those stiff and important national examinations. The Japanese solution to this is in the family, where mother works with the child on his homework, giving him the needed drill and practice in a totally supportive context. What is particularly interesting here is that in Japan, where Western schools were introduced in the 1870s, they were redesigned to accommodate the Japanese aversion to competitive display in face-to-face behavior.[3]

---

competition and invidious distinction that are extreme (though not necessarily unique) in their openness among societies of the world. This view can and should be tested in empirical investigation; I have not attempted a review of the existing literature in this article.

2 D. Leighton and C. Kluckhohn, *Children of the People* (Cambridge: Harvard University Press, 1948), pp. 68, 107.

3 E. Vogel, "Entrance Examinations and Emotional Disturbances in Japan's Middle Class," in *Japanese Culture: Its Development and Characteristics*, eds. R. Smith and R. Beardsley

The Gusii of Western Kenya, with whom I have worked, face a different problem; they have not had Western schools as long as the Japanese, but they have more control over them than the Navajo. They have also had to contend with opposition between their cultural code for regulating competitive interaction and the new standards of the Western school. To reap the benefits of Western schooling, they have changed their norms to some extent, accepting competitive evaluation in the heavily disciplined and regimented classroom if not in other face-to-face settings. But they also experience much anxiety about it, due to the particular meanings of competition in their society. For the Gusii, there is the assumption that the outcome of any competition will leave disgruntled losers whose jealousy might act through witchcraft and sorcery to kill the winners. This malevolent process of leveling is neither immediate nor uniform, but it is regarded as such a strong potential for danger in so many of life's arenas that a prudent person is well advised to conceal any advantage he has over anyone else. Any increase in the social visibility of material advantages, then, must be compensated for by an increase in interpersonal secrecy, concealing at least the advance information about such advantages, their magnitude, and whatever other details can be withheld from others.

This affects attitudes toward schooling because schooling is known to be linked to employment opportunities and because educational attainment is more visible socially than any other basis of invidious comparison. For the Gusii, jealousy and the fear of jealousy are located in the domestic group and the neighborhood (usually a localized patrilineage), where the men and women of childbearing years form reference groups of the same sex within which personal advantages are competitively calculated. The co-wives of a polygynist, for example, are always watching the distribution among them not only of the husband's favor and goods, but also of reproductive success, illness and death, and anything else that bears on their own health and welfare and that of their children. If one woman's child does well in school and another's does not, this becomes as much a source of jealousy and the fear of bewitchment as if it were deliberately arranged by the husband. Similarly, in the neighborhood of patrilineal kinsmen, if one man's herd of cattle is wiped out by disease and another's is not, the potential for malevolent jealousy is experienced as present. The expansion of schooling during

(Chicago: Aldine, 1962); and C. Kiefer, "Psychological Interdependence of Family, School and Bureaucracy in Japan," *American Anthropologist* 72 (1970): 66. For historical background on the introduction of Western schools in Japan see F. Jintaro, *Outline of Japanese History in the Meiji Era* (Tokyo: Obunsha, 1958), pp. 44-66, 147-57, 255-66.

the latter 1960s made educational attainment a major focus of invidious comparison among the Gusii as I had found it to be in more educationally advanced parts of West Africa earlier on. Once all children were going to school and taking their primary school examinations in a nationwide competition that determined admission to secondary school, the Gusii neighborhood was invaded by a new and powerful basis of invidious comparison. By the time children had reached their teens, they could be ranked by how far they had managaed to get in school, with those who gained admission to secondary school at the top. Each adolescent child could be seen as reflecting favorably or unfavorably on the future economic potential of his parents, who had new criteria, less ambiguous than ever, for comparing advantages within the local reference group. Parents tended to react with jealousy if their children did poorly and fear if their children did well. Thus, if a child who had performed well in school became ill, the parents were likely to assume he was being bewitched by jealous neighbors.

It seems that for the Gusii the locus of anxiety derived from Western schooling is somewhat different from that of the Japanese and Navajo. Whereas the Navajo child may experience competitive behavior in the classroom as an abandonment of those with whom he feels interdependent, and the Japanese may see competitive behavior as an aggressive display that disrupts the desirable appearance of nurturance in handling children, the Gusii are primarily concerned about socially visible inequality within the neighborhood reference group derived from differential school achievement. The situation generates so much fear of malevolent jealousy that the most popular local practitioner provides a medicine to protect parents whose preschool children are conspicuously obedient and responsible in domestic chores, the assumption being that such children will later do well in school.

The following case illustrates the problem as contemporary Gusii experience it and its solution. A man who was among the first from his area to be steadily employed in a modern occupation locally rather than in the city was determined that all his children, who were girls (which many Gusii in his cohort regarded as poor educational investments), would receive an education, and they went to secondary school and beyond, one of them gaining entrance to the university. The father died, and a few years later his wife died, while one of the daughters was still attending the university. There was strong suspicion that both deaths had been caused by the deceased father's brother, who lived next door and whose jealousy of his nieces' success was well known. In the aftermath of the mother's death, all of her many small children were sent to live with relatives living outside Gusiiland, and the family house was closed for the foreseeable future.

Although I have summarized this case in a very condensed way, it shows several typical features: (1) Educational success, in this case particularly exceptional because unexpected for a woman, arouses jealous feelings in neighboring kinsmen of the same generation; (2) the assumption is that the malevolent jealousy working through witchcraft or sorcery kills not only the successful individual but his entire domestic group; (3) the response is to move all surviving household members away from the neighborhood where neighbors reside. Thus, the Gusii solution is dictated by their definition of the problem. Insofar as the solution of emigration is widely adopted, residential segregation by socioeconomic status will develop among the Gusii; there are distinct signs that it is developing.

Both the problem and its solution seem to be culturally distinctive, at least when compared with non-African cases. Though the Gusii share with peoples like the Japanese and the Navajo an interpretation of the Western school as introducing disruptive forms of competition, they differ in what they regard its disruptive influence to be and how to cope with it. For both the Japanese and the Navajo, as I read the literature, the primary locus of disruption is the classroom where peer relations might be undermined, and, for the Japanese, the nurturant teacher-pupil relationship jeopardized, by overt competition. The Japanese solution has been to move competitiveness elsewhere.

For the Gusii the locus of disruption is the neighborhood and local descent group where schooling forces invidious comparison into a public realm it has been previously prevented from entering. In all cases, the Western school is a structural field that becomes infused with the meanings attached to overt competition in the indigenous culture.

On the basis of the above considerations, I propose the following formulation to be tested in future research: Every society has institutional means of regulating competition and self-assertion among its members. In some non-Western societies this regulation is effected through enforcement of a code of social interaction in which competition and self-assertion are publicly disavowed, banished from the field of face-to-face encounters to be pursued in a clandestine manner. It is not that individuals in these societies have no competitive or self-assertive tendencies, but that they have been socialized to disavow them rather than display them. Viewed from the institutional side, the enforcement of the indigenous code functions significantly in social control; viewed from the side of the individual, it affords him the safety and comfort of keeping from public sight tendencies of his own that are socially unacceptable and may represent inadmissible parts of the self. Thus the same pattern of social behavior that functions as part of an institutional system serves also as a culturally constituted defense mechanism for the individual[4] in what Inkeles and Levinson called *functional congruence* between personality and social system.[5] The introduction of Western schools into this situation leads to a case of what they called *institutionally induced noncongruence*, in which the Western norms of classroom interaction and public evaluation force individuals to bring their competitiveness and self-assertive tendencies out into the open. The anxiety thus aroused by the perceived threat to existing social relationships leads to one of two patterns of change: (1) If the bearers of the indigenous culture are in full control of the school system, they redesign its evaluation procedures to make them more compatible with their indigenous standards of self-presentation in face-to-face encounters. (2) If the school system is not under indigenous control, then bearers of the indigenous culture tend toward nonparticipation in school (truancy, dropping out), at least until a new generational cohort is socialized according to new standards of conduct modified toward a Western prototype.

4 M. Spiro, "Religious Systems as Culturally Constituted Defense Mechanisms," in his *Context and Meaning in Cultural Anthropology* (New York: Free Press, 1965).

5 A. Inkeles and D. Levinson, "National Character," in *Handbook of Social Psychology,* ed. G. Lindzey (Cambridge, Mass.: Addison-Wesley, 1954).

Families, Schools, and Communities:
An Ecosystem for Children

NICHOLAS HOBBS
Vanderbilt University, Nashville, Tennessee

Let me invite you to imagine a diagram. In your mind's eye, picture a large closed figure, generally circular but also sinuous, suggesting a vague boundary. Now put a circle in the middle of the figure and think of that as a child. Supply other small circles to represent sundry people like a mother and a father, and siblings, friends, teachers—a doctor, perhaps, or a social worker—all belonging to the child. Perhaps you should also put in TV characters, and perhaps a family dog or cat. Put in some places and spaces, like a kitchen and a classroom, a church or a community center, and make them big or small or friendly or threatening. Now stand back and look at it. What you have, if you are old fashioned and Lewinian, is a diagram of the life space of a child. Or, if you are up to date, what you have is an ecosystem defined by the being of a particular child.

But the picture is static, and that won't do. You must put in a time line. Children change, life spaces change, ecosystems change. So draw an arrow somewhere to suggest change, development. At the feather end of the arrow put zero, for birth; at the point end put eighteen, with fuzzy edges to suggest that we don't know much about when children become mature. In which direction should the arrow go? Which way does *time* flow? From left to right? Right to left? Downward? Upward? Diagonally? Or does time stand still while events change, giving the illusion of motion, like a passing train observed from a standing car? That seems too difficult, so draw your arrows to suit your own taste in such matters. But time and change are very important.

Now examine your diagram again, closely. Move the time frame back and forth from zero to the fuzzy eighteen and you will see two distinct

192

FIG. 1. Diagram of ecological system of a child. Each child's ecosystem is unique. A child is considered to be in trouble ("emotionally disturbed") when there is too much discord in the system caused by his own behavior or by inadequate support from others, or both. Efforts to help a child should address the system as a whole. The goal is to help make the system work in the interest of the child's development. The arrow emphasizes that the ecosystem changes with time.

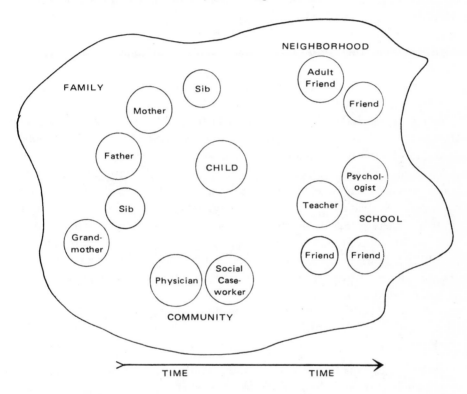

clusters of heightened activity in the ecosystem. By any measure—by time spent, for example, or by the number of people, or by dollars spent in the interest of the child, or by the significance for later development —these two clusters of activity are very important. One we call the home and the other the school. Of course there are other blips of activity here and there in the enclosure, involving a playground or a church or maybe a community center; these tend to be scattered and are not nearly so concentrated as in the clusters representing home and school. But neighborhoods and communities are important. Now examine the scene from age six on up to about sixteen or seventeen. You will notice something very peculiar: The two clusters of activity, called family and school, have almost no overlap and few or no connecting lines. One little blip of activity does connect the two clusters—the dreaded annual parent-teacher conference. Many schools regard parents as a nuisance; many parents regard schools as forbidding places in which they have no legitimate interest. How did these two clusters of activity, home and school, become so separated? What caused the grand schism?

Drawing on Rosabeth Kanter,[1] Tamara Hareven,[2] Samuel Bowles and Herbert Gintis,[3] and Sarah Lightfoot,[4] an apparently causal chain of events can be described as follows. The central phenomenon to observe is the role of the family in the transition of our society from a rural, handcraft economy to an industrialized economy. In the century prior to World War I, the family and the factory served each other. The family, for example, was the major recruiter of workers in many industries, channeling especially children and unattached women into particular factories and providing a source of discipline and of loyalty. With the rise of scientific management and the coming of child labor laws, the usefulness of the family in support of industry diminished. Indeed, managers came in time to insist on separation of family and work place in order to discourage conflicting loyalties. Today, while work and family clearly interact, the formal separation between the two is sharp and widely accepted. Contrast, for example, the formal separation of work and family in the United States with the solution developed in Japan where a unity between family and factory has been preserved in a sophisticated and highly functional fashion. Interestingly enough, as Bowles and Gintis delineate,[5] the public schools gradually followed the industrial model in defining the family-school relationships. According to Kanter:

> Schools, especially, sided with other organizations in their war against particularism and their desire to fit workers to the work place. Seeking discipline and wanting to legitimate their own authority claims, schools removed children from the family, set up a system of authority based on state sanction and expertise . . . and instituted a "work" discipline strikingly similar to that of adult organizations. . . . Today

1 Rosabeth Kanter, *Work and Family in the United States: A Critical Review and Agenda for Research and Policy* (New York: Russell Sage Foundation, 1977).

2 Tamara Hareven, "Family Time and Industrial Time: Family and Work in a Planned Corporation Town, 1900-1924," *Journal of Urban History* 1 (1975): 365-89.

3 Samuel Bowles and Herbert H. Gintis, *Schooling in Capitalist America* (New York: Basic Books, 1976).

4 Sarah L. Lightfoot, "Family-school Interaction: The Cultural Image of Mothers and Teachers," *Signs: A Journal of Women in Culture and Society* 2 (1977).

5 Bowles and Gintis, *Schooling in Capitalist America*.

the relations between schools and parents and between teachers and parents, despite alleged community control of schools, are not unlike the uneasy relation of corporations and families, with the family often unable to intervene in or influence organizational policies, even though these policies have great effects on their lives.[6]

Whatever the origins of the schism between home and school, all of us can attest to its reality by observation or personal experience.

Possibly as an expression of what Daniel Bell calls the post-industrial society,[7] there is evidence of a coming together of family and work place and of family and school. Goslin, for example, has organized visits of children to places of work,[8] and Bronfenbrenner has stressed the desirability of children's sharing their parents' work experiences.[9] The trend may be more pronounced for family and school than for family and work. In the past two decades families and schools in at least some communities have been coming together in many interesting ways. In some communities the two clusters of activities in the ecosystem can accurately be represented by substantially overlapping circles; in other communities the involvement is less extensive but bridges are being built between home and school that require at least some lines between them on our diagram. I propose now to describe some of these developments in what may be emerging as a new axis between families and schools.

Almost eighteen years ago several people at Peabody College became interested in inventing new institutional forms for helping emotionally disturbed children, work that subsequently came to be identified as Project Re-ED.[10] With a National Institute of Mental Health (NIMH) grant, we established two residential schools, one in Tennessee and one in North Carolina. Although we were partial to an educational idiom and a vocabulary of normalcy, instead of a clinical idiom and a vocabulary of pathology, we started out with the assumption, widely held at the time, that the emotional disturbance resided in the child. It was something a child "had." It was not long before we understood the complete inadequacy of this traditional view. It soon became clear that the only way we could help a child was to involve the child, his family, his school, and his community in a cooperative assessment of the prob-

6   Kanter, *Work and Family in the United States*, pp. 12-13.

7   Daniel Bell, *The Coming of Post-Industrial Society* (New York: Basic Books, 1973).

8   David Goslin, "Children in the World of Work," *New Society* 18 (1971): 409-12.

9   Urie Bronfenbrenner, "The Origins of Alienation," *Scientific American* 231, no. 2 (1974): 53-61.

10   Nicholas Hobbs, "Helping Disturbed Children: Psychological and Ecological Strategies," *American Psychologist* 21 (1966): 1105-15.

lem and a shared design for its solution. Borrowing the term "ecology" from field biology, where it refers to the study of interacting forces in complex natural systems, we began to talk about "ecological strategies in working with disturbed children." In time we came to define emotional disturbance in children as a symptom of acute imbalance, not in the child necessarily, but in the ecosystem that is defined by the child. So we gradually came to insist that four circles within the child's ecosystem had to overlap substantially: our special Re-ED school, the child's family, the child's regular school, and the community, with the child remaining the center of it all. In time, Cantrell and Cantrell and others reached the reasonable conclusion that for many children in trouble there is no need for a special residential school like Re-ED; some agent (we refer to them as liaison specialists) could facilitate the coming together of child, family, school, and community in the interest of restoring balance to the ecosystem.[11] The idea has been tested in several Tennessee school districts with good results. And the idea has subsequently been extended to other settings.

For example, Susan Gray, and a host of other investigators following her, demonstrated that early childhood development programs work best when mothers are actively involved in planning and carrying out learning projects.[12] Then Katherine Horton demonstrated that mothers could be trained to replace special technicians in teaching their hearing-impaired children communication skills.[13] Finally, in a progam that this year won the top prize of the American Psychiatric Association for innovative mental health programs, mothers are taught to be "therapists" for their unmanageable young children, using an operant conditioning paradigm.[14] One can begin to generalize: Participation by child, family, school, and community is essential to help children in trouble, whatever the cause of the difficulty.

The school's interest in families has been heightened in the past decade by studies by Christopher Jencks, Mia Kellmer Pringle,[15] and

11   R.P. Cantrell and M.L. Cantrell, "A Taxonomic Investigation of Children's Problems and Intervention Strategies: An Empirical Approach to Classification." Working paper, Prevention-Intervention Project, Tennessee State Department of Mental Health, Nashville, 1974.

12   Susan W. Gray and R.A. Klaus, "The Early Training Project: A Seventh Year Report," *Child Development* 41 (1970): 909-24.

13   Katherine Horton and F. McConnell, "Early Intervention for the Young Deaf Child through Parent Training," *Proceedings of the International Congress on Education of the Deaf* 1 (1970): 291-96.

14   Regional Intervention Program, "A Parent-implemented Early Intervention Program for Preschool Children," *Hospital and Community Psychiatry Journal* 27, no. 10 (1976): 728-31.

15   Christopher Jencks et al., *Inequality: A Reassessment of the Effect of Family and*

others, demonstrating the relationship between family background and subsequent school success. Schools that take their educational tasks seriously know now that they must extend their efforts to the family and to the earliest years of the child's life.

Interestingly enough, the civil rights movement has promoted a new liaison between families and schools. Until relatively recently, the public schools had unquestioned dominion over the life of the child while in school. The child could be promoted or held back, placed in a special class, or even excluded from school with only perfunctory involvement of the child's parents. The schools tended to be respectful of the wishes of middle-class parents, who have the competence and confidence to demand reasonable decisions about their children, but the schools have been singularly insensitive to the wishes of parents lacking skills in managing their institutional worlds. The Children's Defense Fund, for example, estimates that there are some 2,000,000 children who have simply been excluded from school, many quite arbitrarily.[16] Today court orders, legislation, and administrative guidelines require the informed consent of parents for decisions substantially affecting the well-being of a child. They also require provision of due process for decision making when parents and schools are in conflict. While some schools are circumventing these intrusions upon their traditional authority, enlightened schools recognize that these new requirements, though inconvenient perhaps, can be a source of a new reconciliation between the family and school and an enhanced educational experience for the child.

Public Law 94-142, Education for All Handicapped Children, contains a provision that can without extravagance be called revolutionary. The law requires that for a state to receive federal reimbursement for instruction provided handicapped children, there must be developed for each child each year an individually designed educational plan. The plan must be worked out cooperatively by teachers, supervisors, specialists when required, parents, and the child himself when he is old enough. The idea, applied first in special education programs, may in time be a requirement for all children. Naturally, some schools resist the plan, declaring it (without trial) impractical; other schools, however, are seizing upon the plan as a way of bringing together the now divided family and school in the interests of the child's fullest development.

Schooling in America (New York: Basic Books, 1972); and Mia Kellmer Pringle, *Deprivation and Education* (London: Longmans, 1965).

16 *Children Out of School in America*, Report by the Children's Defense Fund of the Washington Research Project, Inc. (Washington, D.C.: The Fund, 1974).

A related development fostering day-by-day working relationships between families and schools is the extension downward below age six of special provisions for education and health. The significance of this development, in historical perspective, has not been sufficiently emphasized. In the years between 1850 and 1900, the concept of compulsory education for all children, at state expense if desired, was firmly established. Massachusetts passed the first compulsory schooling law in 1852. We do not today appreciate how advanced a notion this legislation represented. It constituted, in the service of a unified society, a radical intrusion of the state into the previously private domain of the family. No other country had done anything like it. Still, for more than a hundred years there was preserved a period of early childhood largely free from state concerns. Children were registered at birth and again when they went to school. In the years between, children were the exclusive concern of the family, excepting only in situations of extreme neglect or abuse. In the past decade, the state has moved into the heretofore private years of zero to six in several programs, including education of the handicapped, Home Start and Head Start, and the Early and Periodic Screening, Diagnosis, and Treatment program. It is true that participation by families and children in these activities is not required, as it is in school attendance after age six. But the exigencies of life of poor families, especially, the number of women from all classes in the work force, and the vigorous outreach efforts built into several of the programs suggest that the years from zero to six are no longer sacrosanct. As early child development programs are further developed and refined, the challenge is to bring parents and public institutions closer together in the interest of enriched opportunities for children.

Clearly the most significant movement bringing families and schools together is the community school idea. Carolyn Cottom describes the movement this way:

> One approach to education which provides for citizen involvement in a way which has been acceptable to local school districts is Community Education. Community Education is an educational philosophy whose objective is to serve the entire community by providing for all the educational (and other) needs of all of its members. It seeks to relate the school to the community by opening up the schools, using the schools as the catalyst for bringing community resources to bear on community problems. Utilizing the leadership of a Coordinator assigned to the "community school," a community council is developed from leaders and citizens in the community. The council

becomes the instrument of the process of ongoing community assessment, identification and development of needed services, and community and school decision-making.

Community Education has grown from one school in Flint, Michigan, in the 1940s, to 1300 community schools in 970 school districts. Federal legislation, the Community Education Act of 1975, provides funds to plan, implement, and develop Community Education programs. In addition, six states now have legislation which provides matching money to local school districts which choose to develop Community Education programs in local schools. Research on Community Education, while scanty, has been generally positive: studies have found that Community Education programs have been accompanied by decreases in school vandalism, auto thefts, juvenile delinquency rates, convict recidivism, and high school dropouts. There are also indications that Community Education can increase political involvement, student achievement, student interest in school, and more positive attitudes of parents about numerous aspects of the school program.[17]

All of these developments describe or portend a new functional relationship between families and schools, a relationship involving heightened interaction with mutual benefits expected. I should like now to build on this emerging new pattern of shared responsibility between family and school to suggest a possible solution to the heretofore intractable problem of how to provide families and children with social and health services, as well as with educational services. The problem is well known: Services to families and children are fragmented, coordination is all but impossible, there is much duplication of effort, continuity of care is rarely achieved, and overhead costs are enormous. For decades this has been the litany of White House conferences, numerous commissions and committees, congressional inquiries, and editorials. Many solutions have been proposed, the most frequent one being the creation of a new coordinating superstructure from the White House to the neighborhood to ensure the orderly provision of services to families and children. The proposal has met massive opposition. The opposition to a coordinating superstructure leads me to a conclusion that responsibility for coordination of services to children must be lodged within some existing public institution. I propose, as was proposed by the Project on Classification of Exceptional Children,[18] that the public schools be assigned this co-

17 Carolyn Cottom, "The Community School" (Unpublished paper, 1976).
18 Nicholas Hobbs, *The Futures of Children* (San Francisco: Jossey-Bass, 1975).

ordinating function, with the family given a central role in making the system work.

The recommendation is that the public schools (in addition to their traditional educational responsibility) be made the locus of responsibility for the coordination of health and social services needed by families in the rearing of their children. The objectives are to reduce the fragmentation of services, to eliminate the needless expense of competing bureaus, to enhance continuity of care, to rationalize resource allocation and increase accountability, and to ensure for all children equitable access to services they need to grow up well. This pattern of service delivery to children is common in Western European countries and it has been tried successfully in several communities in the United States.

The arguments in favor of this recommendation may be summarized briefly:

1. Schools are where most children are—55,000,000 of them.

2. Schools are accessible, physically and psychologically, to nearly all children and their families. They are more favorably regarded than are the health, mental health, welfare, police, and corrections systems.

3. Schools are staffed by competent people who have dedicated their professional lives to children. There are nearly 3,000,000 teachers, 60,000 guidance counselors, 20,000 nurses, and 10,000 psychologists working in the schools. New patterns of staffing would be required but there is a solid base to build on.

4. Schools are supported by an established tax base involving local, state, and federal funds.

5. Schools have traditionally provided educational services on a universal basis; it is imperative that health and social services for children be provided on a similar basis.

6. Schools are already extending their educational services downward below the age of six in day care, Head Start, and programs for the handicapped, and upward in continuing education and community school programs.

7. Schools have a tradition of local control that should be sustained in the delivery of health and social services. Family and community involvement can and should be increased.

8. Schools have physical facilities that are already underutilized and that will become even more available as birth rates go down. There

are an estimated 91,000 public schools in urban and rural areas in the nation. They have buildings, playgrounds, transportation systems, record systems, food services, and other supporting services that are essential to a comprehensive health system for children.

9. The pattern of utilization of resources of schools (five days a week, part of each day only, for two hundred days a year) is a remnant of an agricultural economy long since past. Schools need more time—much more time—to achieve their educational objectives. By sharing overhead with health and social services, schools could gain resources needed to mount an educational program responsive to contemporary requirements.

10. Finally, several communities (including New Orleans, Galveston, and Cambridge, Massachusetts) have demonstrated that the plan is workable, efficient, and economical.

There are, of course, arguments against using the public schools as here considered, but the schools lead by far in comparison with other possible arrangements to provide comprehensive services to help parents rear children with sturdy bodies, quick minds, and humane sympathies.

It can be argued that public schools have been doing a less-than-satisfactory job in educating children because they are already overburdened with miscellaneous tasks having nothing to do with education. The argument here is that a new alliance between family and school in the service of the total development of children between the ages of zero and eighteen can be a source of revitalization of the schools and of enhanced educational effectiveness. It is one way, to cite a single advantage, to keep the schools open all the time, a primary condition for their effective and economical operation.

But no plan, including the one here proposed, will work without designing the system with the family as the unit of primary responsibility for its own members. I propose then that we think of a new ecosystem, deliberately designed and constructed to involve families and schools, in the context of caring communities, to provide an optimum array of resources for the rearing of our children.

To return again to our life space or ecosystem diagram: The diagram can be improved upon considerably if developments here described and advocated continue to unfold. In the diagram, draw the family as a large circle; draw the school as a somewhat smaller but still highly significant circle, and make them overlap a good bit. Depict somehow a caring community, a community appreciative of families, children, and schools.

Family, school, and community are the normal sources of support, af-
fection, instruction, discipline, and inspiration for children in our
society. So let's depict them—and keep the time line, the arrow, in the
picture. The new diagram looks like a pretty good way to help children
grow up.

Who Needs Parent Education?

URIE BRONFENBRENNER
Cornell University

In this article, I present an unconventional thesis; namely, that the groups most in need of parent education are those who do not yet, no longer, or never will have children. This paradoxical proposition grows out of an evaluation of the profound changes that have been taking place, over recent decades, in the structure and role of the family in American society, and the implications of these changes for what students of child development call socialization, or, in plainer English, the process of making human beings human.

THE CHANGING AMERICAN FAMILY

The changes that have occurred in the form and position of the family are all too familiar. We now hear about them daily from our mass media. Every report begins with the same or similar facts, but the interpretations vary. On the one hand, there are those who warn us that, unless we act now, the American family is in danger of falling apart—sentimental alarmists like Kenneth Keniston, Lawrence Fuchs, and the arch alarmist of them all, Urie Bronfenbrenner. On the other hand, there are those like Margaret Mead, Marvin Sussman, and Mary Jo Bane who counsel us to come to terms with new family forms, and to rest assured that, in one shape or another, the family is "here to stay." Finally, there are the reasonable middle-of-the-roaders, like Daniel Yankelovich, Nicholas Zill, and Paul Hare, who, sticking close to their survey data,

This position paper was prepared for a Working Conference on Parenting Education hosted by the Mott Children's Health Center in Flint, Michigan, and sponsored by the Charles Stewart Mott Foundation with cosponsorship from the Danforth Foundation, Lilly Endowment, Inc., W. K. Kellogg Foundation, C. F. Kettering Foundation, and the Flint Board of Education.

find most American families reasonably satisfied with their lives, but a minority, principally at the lowest income level, in serious trouble.

In keeping with my paradoxical stance, I shall argue, at least to start with, that all three lines of interpretation—the pessimistic, the optimistic, and the mixed—are correct, given the frame of reference of the interpreter. The critical factor is whether one views the family as a structure or as a functional institution; and, if the latter, what the function of that institution is in our society. Thus, from the perspective of structural sociology, there is little question that, so long as our society exists, there will always be large numbers of people living together who are bound by ties of blood or marriage, the usual definition of a family. And if one regards as a major function of the family the satisfaction of adult sex drives, then, for the majority of the adult population, this institution will continue to provide what Shaw referred to as "the maximum of temptation combined with the maximum of opportunity," though increasing numbers of Americans may also find other parties in other places even more seductive.

But for the student of human development, a primary function of the family remains nurturing the next generation. And it is when one looks at recent changes from this developmental perspective that it becomes difficult to maintain a rosy view of what the future holds in store. It is also this perspective that gives rise to my paradoxical proposition: Those in greatest need of parent education are nonparents.

To establish the basis for this contradictory conclusion, I must remind you once again of the nature of the changes that have been taking place in the structure and position of the American family. These have been recently documented in considerable detail in a report issued by the National Academy of Sciences[1] and published by a committee on which I was privileged to serve.

I shall summarize some of the committee's principal findings, but first a warning: We would be making a serious mistake if we interpreted the changes the committee documents as the source of the problem, or even as undesirable from the perspective of human development and family well-being. *It is not the changes within the family itself that impair the capacity of the family to function.* But we need to recognize and understand these changes if we are to understand where the crux of the problem and its possible remedies lie.

Based on an analysis of all the data they could put their hands on,

---

1   *Toward a National Policy for Children and Families* (Washington, D.C.: National Academy of Sciences, 1976).

both within and outside the government, the academy's committee found that, since World War II, there has been *progressive fragmentation and isolation of the family in its child-rearing role*. To begin with a familiar fact, every year more and more mothers are going to work—now, in 1978, well over half of those with school-age children, over 40 percent with children under six, and over one-third with infants under three, and, regardless of the age of the child, two-thirds of all these mothers are working full time.[2] A second change accompanies the first. As many more mothers go to work, the number of adults left in the home who might care for the child has been decreasing in two ways. First, what the sociologists call extended families, those that contain other adult relatives besides the parents, have been gradually shrinking and disappearing. But shrinkage and disappearance have been even more pronounced in the so-called nuclear family consisting of mother, father, and children. Today, more than one in every six children under eighteen is living in a single-parent family, with the one parent generally also being the head of the family and holding down a job, usually full time. This is often not a temporary state, since, on a national scale, the re-marriage rate, especially for women with children, is substantially lower than the rate of divorce in families involving children and this differential has been increasing over time. Finally, the fastest growing component in the increase of single-parent families has been the rocket rise in the number of unwed mothers; more young women are postponing the age of marriage, but an ever-larger number of them are already bearing children.

All these changes are occurring more rapidly among younger families with small children, and increase with the degree of economic deprivation and urbanization, reaching their maximum in low-income families living in the central core of our larger cities. Although levels of labor-force participation, single parenthood, and other related developments are substantially higher among non-whites than whites, those families residing in similar economic and social circumstances show similar rates of change. The critical factor, therefore, is not race, but the conditions under which the family lives.

But the general trend is not limited to the urban poor. It applies to all strata of society. For example, middle-class families in the cities, in suburbia, and in rural areas are changing in similar ways. Indeed, in terms of such characteristics as the proportion of working mothers, the

---

2   Appreciation is expressed to Howard Hayghe of the Bureau of Labor Statistics for supplying the most recent data. Parenthetically, there is no evidence of any complementary trend for more husbands to give up their jobs in order to stay home and take care of their children.

number of adults in the home, single-parent families, or children born out of wedlock, the middle-class family of today increasingly resembles the low-income family of the early 1960s.

So what? What are the implications of these trends—for families, for children, and for parent education?

Let us consider families first. Maybe it is all for the best? At least now a woman is no longer excluded from the job market, limited for a lifetime to the role of wife and mother, caring for, feeding, cleaning house for, not only children and husband, but a raft of relatives as well. Nor are a mismatched couple any longer bound to live out their lives imprisoned in a loveless marriage that should not have happened in the first place. What is more, a woman is now free to get a baby without having to put up with a husband in the bargain. Are not these new, and more honest, family forms? Perhaps so, but one cannot help wondering why honesty and innovation should be so heavily concentrated among the poor.

But remember it is happening to the nonpoor as well. And what does that mean? What does it mean for children in general that more and more mothers, especially mothers of preschoolers and infants, are going to work, the majority of them full time? What does it mean that, as these mothers leave for work, there are also fewer adults in the family who might look after the child, that in ever more families there is only one parent, who is usually also the breadwinner, living in an independent household and working full time?

Paradoxically, the most telling answer to that is yet another question: *Who cares for America's children? Who cares?*

As this reading audience knows all too well, at the present time, substitute care for children, care of whatever form—nursery schools, group day care, family day care, or just a body to babysit—falls far short of the need. In speaking of need, I have in mind not subjective feelings, but an objective situation in which there is no competent, responsible person available to care for the child. That kind of objective need can be measured in millions of children under the age of six, not to mention the millions more of school-age youngsters, so-called "latch-key" children, who come home to empty houses, and who contribute far out of proportion to the ranks of pupils with academic and behavior problems, who have difficulties in learning to read, or who are dropouts, drug users, and juvenile delinquents.

But we are getting ahead of our story. Unfortunately, statistics at a national level on the state of the child are neither as comprehensive nor as complete as those on the state of the family. In our census data, it is the taxpayer who counts, and gets counted. There is lots of information about parents; much less about children. Nevertheless, the available data do suggest a pattern that strikingly parallels the trend observed for changes in the family. Specifically, concomitant and consistent with shifts in the structure and position of the family are changes in indices reflecting the impaired well-being and development of children. Youngsters growing up in low-income families are, of course, at especially high risk of damage physically, intellectually, emotionally, and socially. The evidence also reveals disturbing secular trends, changes over time, indicated by declining levels of academic performance and rising rates of child homicide, suicide, drug use, and juvenile delinquency.

Ironically, many of these trends find their strongest expression in the institutions of society bearing primary responsibility for the preparation of children and youth for participation in adult society—the nation's schools. For example, consider the recent report of the Committee of the Judiciary of the United States Senate. The title tells the story: "Our Nation's Schools—A Report Card: 'A' in School Violence and Vandalism."[3] The report emphasizes that the pattern is not restricted to big cities and their slum areas; as the title implies, it is a national phenomenon. School vandalism is now as American as apple pie. Literally, the handwriting is on the wall.

The fact that the signs of progressive disarray are not limited to the poor and nonwhite is most clearly apparent from data on academic achievement. We are already familiar with a phenomenon widely reported in the press—the steady decline over the past dozen years in average performance on the Scholastic Aptitude Test (SAT) taken by the overwhelming majority of high school students who plan to go to college, and widely used as a basis for determining admission. Since 1963 there has been a decline of 25 points in the mathematics score and 44 points in the verbal score. Less well known is a comprehensive study sponsored by the Ford Foundation revealing that the decline in academic achievement is manifested among pupils from all segments of the society. The researchers analyzed time trends in data from seven major national testing programs, with an effort to take into account possible confounding influences resulting from changes in the test, pupil population, and other sources. Their conclusions are stated as follows:

Beyond doubt, beyond differences among assessment instruments, al-

3 U.S. Congress, Senate, Committee on the Judiciary, "Our Nation's Schools—A Report Card: 'A' in School Violence and Vandalism," Preliminary Report of the Subcommittee to Investigate Juvenile Delinquency (Washington, D.C.: U.S. Government Printing Office, 1975).

ternations in tests, or in pupil composition, achievement test scores have been declining for about a decade in all grades from five up-wards. Score declines are more pronounced in higher grades and in recent years. They are more severe for tests probing verbal than mathematics achievements. . . . these are the facts and they describe a national phenomenon. . . . we reported lowered test scores in diverse areas: English, writing, literature, vocabulary, reading, social studies, mathematics, and natural sciences.[4]

In speculating about the causes of the decline, the authors of the study point to the possible distracting influence of television and the decreasing emphasis on required basic courses. A more complex set of forces, however, is implicated by Dr. T. Anne Clarey, Chief Analyst for the College Entrance Examination Board, which administers SAT.

The SAT measures skills developed over a youngster's lifetime—both in and out of the school setting. It is evident that many factors in-cluding family and home life, exposure to mass media, and other cul-tural and environmental factors are associated with students' perfor-mance.[5]

Consistent with this broader perspective, a recent study conducted by the United States Office of Education reveals that the deficiencies are not confined to test scores but extend to skills required for everyday living. As reported in the *New York Times*,

The study found that 40 million more adults, one in every three, have just the minimum competence required to be effective citizens, consumers, wage-earners, or family members. Only about 55 million, less than half the total U.S. population aged 18 to 65, were found really proficient in reading, writing, computation, and problem-solving skills. . . . about 13 per cent—amounting to 15 million adults—were unable to address an envelope well enough to assure that the postal service could deliver it . . . and 14 per cent, equivalent to 16.5 mil-lion, were unable to make out a personal check correctly enough for a bank to process it.[6]

How are we to explain these changes over time for American families and their children? Is the progressive fragmentation and isolation of the

4 A. Harnischfeger and D.E. Wiley, *Achievement Test Score Decline: Do We Need to Worry?* (Chicago: CEMREL, Inc., 1976), pp. 115-16, 118.

5 College Entrance Examination Board, press release (New York: December 20, 1973).

6 *New York Times*, October 31, 1975.

family we documented earlier producing the decline in the intellectual and social competence of children and adults? Or are both the products of prior and deeper forces of disruption in contemporary society? The data themselves do not permit an answer to the question. We shall have to seek for explanations elsewhere.

In order to do so, I ask you to make an assumption about what the data I have presented mean. The assumption I am asking you to make is that they mean *trouble*, trouble for children and those responsible for their care.

If you are willing to make that assumption, then we are in a position to put the most important question before us: What can we do about it? What can we do to avert, or even only to reduce a little, the disarray that is growing in the lives of America's children and families?

What should our strategy be? Should we concentrate our energies on getting more day care? Seek legislation to provide families with a guaranteed minimum annual income? Put more money into preschool intervention efforts? Organize parent education programs on a national scale? All of these? None of these?

The answer depends on what you think the problem is.

At this point we pass from facts to interpretations, and I give you a second warning: Beware of interpretations, and those who make them. I shall now proceed to offer interpretations of available evidence bearing on four questions:

1. What do the data say about the needs of children?

2. What do the data say about how well these needs are being met?

3. What do the data say about the conditions that determine how well the needs of children are met?

4. What do the data say about how to improve these conditions?

The difficulty, of course, is that scientific findings bearing on these questions are incomplete. But we do have some information, so onward to data, interpretation, and, do not forget, skepticism.

ON MAKING HUMAN BEINGS HUMAN

What do the research data say about the needs of young children?

Here is what they say—to me. In order to develop physiologically, mentally, emotionally, motivationally, socially, and morally, a child requires, for all of them, the same thing:

Proposition I. In order to develop, a child needs the enduring, irra-

tional involvement of one or more adults in care and joint activity with the child.[7]

Question: What do I mean by irrational involvement?
Answer: Somebody has got to be crazy about that kid!

What do I mean by care? I mean by care what you mean by care—providing shelter, food, clothing, health services, protecting the child from harm, easing pain—physical and psychological.

What do I mean by joint activity? That is a little more complicated. It brings us to Proposition II.

Proposition II. The psychological development of the child is brought about through his continuing involvement in progressively more complex patterns of reciprocal activity with persons with whom the child develops a strong and enduring mutual emotional attachment.

That part at the end, that is the irrational part. Let us now analyze it rationally.

What do I mean by a strong and enduring mutual attachment? I mean a love affair that does not break up—that lasts a long, long time. How long? and why an irrational involvement? Answer from a Soviet colleague: "You can't pay a women to do what a mother will do for free." As you probably know, communist propaganda about sexual equality notwithstanding, so far as women's liberation is concerned, the Soviet Union has a long way to go. Of course, so do we, but more of that later.

We are considering enduring, irrational involvement—love that lasts. But as Bruno Bettelheim has emphasized in the text, and title, of one of his books: "Love is not enough."

Notice that my Soviet colleague did not say "love"; he said "do":

---

7 Evidence and argument in support of this and subsequent propositions are contained in the following published articles by the author: "When is Infant Stimulation Effective?" in *Environmental Influences,* ed. D.C. Glass (New York: Rockefeller University Press, 1968); "On the Making of New Men: Some Extrapolations from Research," *Canadian Journal of Behavioural Science* 1 (1968): 4-24; "The Dependency Drive As a Factor in Infant Learning and Development," *Schweizerische Zeitschrift fur Psychologie und Ihre Anwendunger* 23 (1970): 218-23; "Development Research and Public Policy," in *Social Science and Social Welfare,* ed. J.M. Romanshyn (New York: Council on Social Work Education, 1973); "A Theoretical Perspective for Research in Human Development," in *Childhood and Socialization: Recent Sociology, No. 5,* ed. H.P. Dreitzel (New York: Collier-Macmillan, 1973); "Social Ecology of Human Development," in *Brain and Intelligence: The Ecology of Child Development,* ed. F. Richardson (Hyattsville, Md.: The National Education Press, 1973); *Is Early Intervention Effective? A Report on Longitudinal Evaluations of Pre-school Programs,* vol. 2 (Washington, D.C.: Department of Health, Education, and Welfare, Office of Child Development, 1974); and "Toward an Experimental Ecology of Human Development," *American Psychologist* 32 (1977): 513-31.

"You can't pay a woman to *do*, what a mother will *do* for free." Love must involve action, specifically care, and our new friend "progressively more complex . . . activity" with the child.

In fact, Proposition II implies not that love generates care and action, but the reverse: It is *after* the child engages in intensive reciprocal activity with someone that he then develops a strong and enduring emotional attachment. This brings us to Proposition III.

Proposition III. The involvement of caretaker and child in patterns of progressively more complex reciprocal activity generates an emotional bond, enhanced motivation, and cognitive and manipulative skills that are mutually reinforcing to both participants, are then reflected in the child's competence and cooperation in other situations, and thereby facilitate the child's future development.

We have been examining answers to our first question: What do the research data say about the child's needs? We are by no means done, for each answer poses new questions. For example, what is the concrete nature of these activities? What exactly does one do? And who is to do it, mothers, fathers, day-care workers, baby sitters, the government?

Paradoxically, these secondary queries cannot be answered until we consider the remaining three of our four primary issues. So let us turn to our second major question: How effectively are the child's needs being met?

Answer: Not very.

In fact, less and less effectively each year, in *my* judgment. Each year there is less and less joint activity, therefore less care, and less emotional involvement.

Do I mean that parents do not love their children as much? I suspect so, but there is really no direct evidence on that.

By now you should really be uneasy; you should be asking: "What is your evidence for all these statements?" I would have to answer that it is not very good. In fact, most of it is in all those statistics I began with.

How do I get to such a conclusion from that evidence?

You remember what the child needs—"enduring reciprocal joint activity in progressively more complex situations, generating mutual irrational attachment," and so forth.

Now activity requires an *occasion*. Progressively more complex activity requires not just one occasion, it requires *time*. And joint activity requires *somebody to be there*.

Finally, the development of an irrational, mutual, emotional attachment takes even more occasions, even more time, and, if the attachment is to be mutual, it not only takes somebody to be there, it takes the *same* somebody.

That is asking a lot nowadays. As a young married woman put it in a recent conversation: "You gotta be crazy to have kids these days."

And my young friend is not the only one who feels this way. The popular columnist Ann Landers received a letter from a mother who expressed the same sentiment. Finding the letter quite disturbing, Ms. Landers invited reactions from her readers. She received 10,000 replies from parents, 70 percent of them expressing regret about the children they had had. Of course, it is a biased sample—7,000 strong!

It is becoming increasingly difficult to provide children with the conditions necessary for their normal, just normal psychological development.

What are the conditions that determine how well children's needs can be met? What do the research data say?

Here is what the data say—to me.

Proposition IV. To develop the enduring involvement of one or more adults in care, activity, and so forth, requires social policies and practices that provide opportunity, status, encouragement, example, and approval for parenthood.

And that's not all—parenthood not only on the part of parents, but also on the part of relatives, older children, all the members of the household; and on the part of day-care workers, preschool personnel, social workers, teachers, all those who deal professionally with children and their families. This list is arranged in an order of increasing importance. We are about to go from the vital to the even more critical: not only relatives or professionals, but friends, neighbors, work associates, that is, people who do not carry any direct responsibility for the care and well-being of children or families.

And, finally, we take the giant step, the quantum leap. We pass from the invaluable to the absolutely essential: not only on the part of individuals, but of *institutions*.

Again, I have in mind not the institutions that directly serve children and families, such as schools and social agencies, but the truly powerful systems—both formal and informal—that really determine what happens to human beings in our society: business and industry, federal, state, and local government, mass media, the legal system, the distribution of goods and services, patterns of recreation and social life, transportation facilities, means of communication, working hours, shopping facilities, the organization of residential and business areas. There are of course many more. But it is possible to sum up all these factors under two main headings. There are two major contexts in which the quality of the next generation of Americans will be determined: the *neighborhood* and the *world of work*. And, in the United States of America, the latter mainly means *companies and corporations*.

We have come a long way from the cradle to the corporation. But we have arrived at our destination, for here is where the crux of the problem lies. The issue is not who cares for children but *who cares for those who care?*

CARING FOR THE CARETAKERS

What is my evidence for that assertion? Some comes from systematic research, but much more is based on experience in our own and, especially, in other societies. Let me give you some examples.

Some time ago I gave a lecture in Stockholm, Sweden. It evoked considerable interest. The next day there was a front-page article about it in Sweden's biggest morning newspaper and, on the following day, I was invited to a meeting with the prime minister of that country. He spent more than two hours of the late afternoon talking about Swedish national policy on families and children, and, as he spoke, I was struck by the concern for and commitment to families and children exhibited on the part of the entire society from its leaders on down. Some of the policies and practices the prime minister, and his country, were committed to I would not wish to see prevail in our own society, but there was no doubt that the commitment was there.

Evidence? Much of our conversation dealt with two laws the prime minister and his party had introduced in the Riksdag, the Swedish parliament. The first of these laws had passed by a wide margin. The second had just failed of passage.

The law that had passed authorized sick leave for working parents whenever a child was ill, *provided* that half of the allotted leave time was taken by the father.

The law that failed would have permitted parents with a child under three to work a six-hour instead of an eight-hour day, with the remaining two hours paid for out of social security, again provided that half of the released time was taken by the father.

The prime minister had been spending the whole day talking with representatives of the groups that had defeated the bill, trying to persuade them to change their position on it. The groups were of two kinds:

1. unions, who argued that passage of a bill establishing a six-hour

day for working parents of young children would destroy any hope for legalizing a six-hour day for everybody, and

2. certain women's groups, who opposed the bill on the ground that it placed responsibility for the care of children on parents rather than providing for substitute care by professionals or paraprofessionals. In their view, anyone who was not interested in and trained and paid for child care should not be placed in the position of having to care for children.

"You can see," said the prime minister, "they do not understand the crucial importance for the child's development of what you call 'irrational attachment.' "

I replied that, nevertheless, his society had at least recognized the importance of a problem and was prepared to do something about it.

"No," he responded, "you overestimate our progress. We still have a long way to go. Let me give you an example."

He then recounted an incident that had occurred on the previous day. It had been his first evening off in many weeks, and he was just settling down to enjoy it when the doorbell rang. There stood a worker from the local day-care center with two young children, and a tale of woe. The parents had failed to pick up the children at the closing hour, so the worker had taken them to their home herself only to find that no one was present except a teenage son and his friends, all of them drunk.

"What happened then?" I asked.

"I took my young son with me; he is eighteen. We got those teenagers out, cleaned up the children, fed them, and I left my son there to wait until somebody got home. You see, our people still do not understand that when you are dealing with children, you cannot expect to work on a fixed time schedule."

So much for anecdotal evidence. What about research findings?

Some time ago, in connection with my responsibilities as a member of the Advisory Committee on Child Development for the National Academy of Sciences, I completed a review of systematic research on the effects of early intervention programs conducted for children from disadvantaged backgrounds.[8] The studies covered a wide variety of projects ranging from group preschool programs in the manner of Head Start, through tutoring efforts, to home visits involving both mother and child. Some strategies did turn out better than others, but, in my judgment, the most important finding concerned certain factors that,

8 Bronfenbrenner, *Is Early Intervention Effective?*

when they occurred together, predicted how successful any program would be regardless of the method or content involved. Here are some of the conditions that emerged as critical in this regard:

1. the employment status of the breadwinner for the family;
2. the level of family income;
3. the number of children per room in the household;
4. the presence in the home of another adult besides the principal caretaker;
5. parents' education.

When the breadwinner was unemployed, the family income below the poverty line, many children crowded into a small space, and only one parent present—and he or she without much schooling—when all, or even just two or three, of these conditions occurred together, no intervention program, whatever the strategy employed, was able to be very effective. Conversely, children from families that were not subjected to these stresses all at once were more likely to benefit from whatever opportunities were provided.

In short, as we discovered at the very outset of our inquiry, the critical factor is the conditions under which the family lives. And these conditions are usually not in the family's power to control. For example, take the problem of finding a job. Clearly, our national policy on unemployment rate has implications for what happens to children.

It is important to recognize what these conditions mean in concrete terms. As a case in point, we may take the more than two million children under six whose mother is a single parent and also the family head. What are the economic facts of life for these families? For comparative purposes we may look first at the situation of all six-year-olds living in two-parent families. Based on the latest available data from the United States,[9] the median income for such families was $14,563. But for all the nation's six-year-olds whose mothers are single-parent heads of families, the median family income was only $4,015. I mention the $15.00 because, at that level, it can make a difference. An instructive contrast is provided by the median income of single-parent fathers who have children under six; the corresponding figure was $8,005, twice as much for being male.

The median figure of $4,015 for single-parent mothers with children

---

9 Appreciation is expressed to Howard Hayghe of the Bureau of Labor Statistics for providing the most recent median family income figures here cited.

under six is an overall average including both those who work and those who don't. Nonworking mothers with children under six have to get along on even less—$3,546. Under these circumstances, it is not surprising that the majority of these mothers (55 percent) with young children are in the labor force. Many of them, however, cannot find work. The unemployment rate for single-parent mothers with children under six is one of the highest and least publicized in the nation—19 percent.

But the group that is worst off by far is that composed of single-parent mothers under the age of twenty-five who head independent families. Such mothers, when all their children are small (i.e., under six), must make do with a median income of only $3,021. Yet a quarter of all single-parent mothers with children under six are living under these circumstances, and they constitute the fastest growing group in the maternal population.

But about well-to-do families? Maybe they don't have these problems?

Professor Mavis Hetherington of the University of Virginia has just completed a brilliant investigation of "The Aftermath of Divorce" among families well above the poverty line. Hetherington compared the experience of mothers, fathers, and their four- to six-year-old children in matched samples of divorced and intact families. Initially, it was the fathers who were hardest hit by the experience of separation. Feeling anxious, insecure, and inadequate, they engaged in a desperate search for a new identity in a variety of activities. But within a year the crisis had abated, primarily because they had established a new heterosexual relationship. The problems experienced by the mothers and the children had a longer course, and were not so readily resolved. Placed in the unaccustomed position of a family head, the mother usually also finds it necessary, because of her reduced financial situation, to look for work or for a more remunerative job. At the same time, she must care for the house and the children, not to mention making a new personal life for herself. The result is a vicious circle. The children, in the absence of the father, demand more attention, but the mother has other things that have to be done. In response, the children become more demanding. Hetherington's data reveal that in comparison with youngsters from intact families, the children of divorce are less likely to respond to the mother's requests. Nor does it make it any easier that similar requests are complied with when made by the divorced father. And even when the child is responsive to her, the divorced mother is less likely to acknowledge or reward the action. Professor Hetherington sums up the net effect by a quotation from one of the mothers: "It's like being bitten to death by ducks."[10]

Once again, it is important to repeat the warning signal. Such findings do not mean that there is anything wrong with single-parent families as such. Rather, as Professor Hetherington points out, the data reflect how we treat divorced mothers with children in our society; existing support systems are removed, and no substitute structures are provided.

But what of the intact, two-parent family? How is it faring in our contemporary society? Some light is shed on these questions from a pilot study my colleagues and I have just completed in connection with a new five-country study we have initiated on the impact of family support systems on family functioning and the development of the child. The research is supported by grants from the Lilly Endowment, the National Institute of Education, and the Kettering Foundation. The pilot study was designed to pretest an instrument for assessing sources of stress and support experienced by families with young children. The study, which is just being completed, involves a sample of ninety-six families, each with a three- to five-year-old child, stratified by family structure (one vs. two parents), family size (one vs. two or more children), occupational status (three levels), and sex of child. Utilizing an interview specially designed for the purpose, the investigation revealed, as anticipated, that families living under certain social circumstances appear to be especially vulnerable to feelings of distress. What was not expected, however, was that under certain conditions, two-parent families experienced even greater stress than single-parent families living in comparable conditions. For example, the families reporting greatest strain across a variety of areas were intact blue-collar households with two or more children. It would appear that, for families at the bottom of the occupational ladder, the advantages of having the husband at home may be offset by the problems of finding the necessary resources to house, feed, and provide for a second adult. Respondents' comments also suggested that when two parents cannot between them provide the needed family resources, the situation produces tension and resentment.

But the lowest occupational level was not the only context in which single-parent mothers appeared to be better off than their counterparts

10 E.M. Hetherington, M. Cox, and R. Cox, "Divorced Fathers," *Family Coordinator* 25 (1976): 417-42; and E.M. Hetherington, M. Cox, and R. Cox, "The Aftermath of Divorce," in *Mother-child, Father-child Relations*," eds. J.H. Stevens, Jr., and Marilyn Mathews (Washington, D.C.: National Association for the Education of Young Children, in press).

in intact families. The same pattern also appeared at the top of the job ladder, but in this instance for households containing only one child. The content revealed that the major source of tension for these families centered around the demands of a job on which the person's career depended, sometimes for the wife as well as for the husband. To state the finding in a provocative form: It would appear that a woman who is having her first child and is married to a professional may, under present circumstances, be better off if she herself had a profession and not a husband.[11]

It is noteworthy, in connection with the foregoing finding, that of the twelve areas covered in the interview, "conditions at work" ranked second only to "family finances" as a source of stress affecting the parent's capacity to function in a child-rearing role. Other areas of special strain included television and the neighborhood. Especially critical for the family's perceived well-being was the availability of satisfactory child-care arrangements, regardless of type. In the absence of arrangements regarded as adequate, mothers were substantially more likely to report difficulties in a variety of areas including job situation, housework, and obtaining needed help and advice. They also felt less adequate in their role as parents, and had a less favorable view of the child and the prospects for his or her future.

Taken as a whole, the results of this pilot study suggest a sobering possibility; namely, we may be creating a society in which it is more difficult to sustain a family than to dissolve it. The forces impinging from the outside are often too powerful for the family to withstand.

ENDS AND MEANS OF EDUCATION ON PARENTHOOD

Virtually nothing of what I have been talking about belongs in a course for parents—not because the information isn't relevant, but because most parents know it already. After all, it was *they*, the parents, who gave *us* scientists the information in the first place. It is *we* who are ignorant—ignorant not only because we do not know, but because we have been misinformed. Thus, we have been taught that most of the problems experienced by families have their origin within the family and therefore ought to be solved by the individual family member pri-

11 In the absence of longitudinal data, this interpretation remains necessarily speculative, although it is based on two not unlikely assumptions: first, that most single-parent mothers who work as professionals previously had husbands who were also professionals; second, that these women felt under at least as much stress before they separated from their husbands as those who remained married. Unfortunately, no information bearing on these points was obtained in the interview, but it will be in the future.

marily concerned. To be sure, that person may need to go to a counselor or a therapist, but it's mainly his own responsibility to solve the problem. If he succeeds, it's to his own credit; if he fails, it's probably his own fault. Helping too much won't work. He shouldn't be coddled. He has to learn "to try harder," "to face reality," "to stand on his own two feet." Witness the American ideal: the Self-Made Man.

But there is *no such person*. If we can stand on our own two feet, it is because others have raised us up. If, as adults, we can lay claim to competence and compassion, it only means that other human beings have been willing and *enabled* to commit their competence and compassion to us—through infancy, childhood, and adolescence, right up to this very moment. What we need to learn, in our national ignorance, is that there is no other way.

We also need to learn the truth of something we affirm as a national principle but deny in national practice—that "all men are created equal," that every human being has the potential to contribute to the lives of others and to the community in which he lives. If he doesn't, it's because he, or she, is prevented by existing circumstances. And if these circumstances are changed, the human potential can be fulfilled. We still have to learn the validity of that hard reality and experience the creative power it can release in our society.

In sum, we as a nation need to be reeducated about the necessary and sufficient conditions for making human beings human. We need to be reeducated not as parents, but as workers, neighbors, and friends; as members of the organizations, committees, boards; and, especially, the informal networks that control our social institutions and thereby determine the conditions of life for our families and their children.

And so we arrive at our paradoxical answer to the opening question: Who needs parent education? From the perspective of our analysis, the priority response emerges as nonparents, or, more precisely, the actual and potential decision makers in all segments of our society and those to whom they are supposed to be, and often are, responsive—the general public.

But some difficult questions still remain. With such an expanded and diverse student body, what should we use as our curriculum? What shall we teach them, and where, when, and how?

The first of these questions seems deceptively easy to answer at first blush. If parent education is what they need, that is what we should give them. But, if our analysis is correct, the curriculum must be concerned not so much with the process of parenting as with the *conditions of parenthood*. We need to communicate an understanding of the circum-

220

stances under which families are living in different segments of our society, how these circumstances affect the capacity of the family to function, and, most important of all, how these circumstances might be altered so that the family's magic power can be enhanced, so that its full potential can be realized.

And here we encounter our first major obstacle. It is of substantial proportions, being no less than the magnitude of our ignorance of the subject at hand. As one who has the dubious honor of having been identified by Shep White as a member of the "Child Development Mafia," I shall presume to speak for the profession in pointing out what we do know and what we don't. We know a great deal about children's behavior and development, and quite a bit about what can and does happen inside of families—parent-child interaction, family dynamics, and all that. But we know precious little about the circumstances under which families live, how these circumstances affect their lives, and what might happen if the circumstances were altered.

There is, however, a way to get this knowledge. As my friend and colleague Professor Moncrieff Cochran puts it, the knowledge is "out there." Those who know most about the conditions under which families live, about the needs of families, and even about the ways in which these needs might best be met are families themselves.

Before we can engage in parent education of the kind here proposed, we have to learn a good deal more than we know at present about the actual experience of families in different segments of our society. Our efforts to assist families, to improve their condition, should rest on such knowledge and, in turn, should be carried out in such a way as to correct and extend such knowledge as we already possess.

So it is that the first recommendation I offer you on the theme of parent education is another paradox: a call for first priority not to teaching about parenthood, but to rigorous research on the conditions in which families live, the way in which these conditions affect the capacity of the family to function, and how these conditions might be altered to enhance that capacity. Many may feel that such a recommendation is more properly addressed to the granting agencies, public and private, that support research in our society, and thereby determine its character and content. I would remind you, however, that a funding organization can only approve the ideas that come before it—and we, the professional community, are primarily responsible for those. One has only to become familiar with a small fraction of the proposals that deluge the desks of our colleagues in foundations and federal agencies to realize that the scientific community does not as yet accord much status to studies of the human condition as it occurs outside the laboratory or the testing room.

To be sure, there are signs of welcome change. But one cannot wait for science to mature in the face of pressing human needs. There is some information already available that can and should be disseminated. More important, there is new information that can be gathered in the process. How can this be done? I offer four additional recommendations:

1. *Television and the World of the Family* For some years, I have been attempting, without much success, to persuade the major television networks, public as well as private, to take a new approach to programming on the family. Up until now, the family has been presented on the nation's television screens primarily as farce, fairytale, or psychiatric orgy. Moreover, all three of these modes of presentation focus principally on the inner workings of the family rather than on the circumstances in which families live out their lives. As a result, the American public is deprived of a major source of information about the state of families and children in our nation. To fill this knowledge gap, I have suggested to program producers that they consider presentations of two kinds. The first would be a much-needed transformation of the accusing voice and threatening vista that asks viewers nightly: "Do you know where your children are?" The intent would be to document what the environment is like for today's children and youth in America: where the children are, what they are doing, and what places, and especially people, are available to them. The presentation would then move further to describe the circumstances of life for those who care for children—or might care, if social policies and practices were altered; in other words, what life is like today for parents, teachers, youth workers, policemen, judges, bus drivers—all those who, by decision or default, find themselves responsible for the well-being and nurturance of the next generation.

A second type of programming moves from present practice to possibility by calling attention to innovative departures from prevailing trends—imaginative programs, and, equally important, naturally occurring situations in which circumstances have evolved that enable children and their caretakers to realize their potential. In point of fact, such instances are occurring daily in hundreds of communities scattered across the country; as of now, they are experienced with joy by the participants, and a happy smile from passersby. But they could be writ large across the land through television's magic mirror and then instead of having today's newscast followed by a rash of bomb scares, we would have a small epidemic of human happenings in their stead. At the very least, the nation would be obtaining an education about the present reality and future potential of life for families and children in our land.

2. *Family Impact as Process versus Product* Since we began working together a year ago, I have been urging Sidney Johnson and my colleagues in the Family Impact Seminar to relegate to a subordinate or even nonexistent status our assigned objective of producing a "statement" of probable disasters, following in the established pattern of our protectors of the environment. Instead, I urged emphasis on family impact as a process—getting persons and organizations in various segments of our society to think about and become aware of their present and potential role in relation to the lives of families and children.

From this perspective, family impact becomes an educational process rather than a political document. As such, it should of course be applied not only within the government, but, even more extensively, in the private sector.

3. *A Community Audit on Families and Children* It is not necessary to wait for scientific research to provide the knowledge necessary for educating one's own community about the conditions and needs of families and children. Following the pattern introduced by Kurt Lewin for raising the consciousness of a community about its minority citizens, local groups could undertake audits to find out what is happening to their children and those responsible for their care. The audits should not be conducted only by those who care for children—the parents, the teachers, the people in the schools and social agencies. All segments of the community should be involved—the businessmen, professionals, skilled workers, retired people, everyone. And don't forget the children themselves, for they are likely to be the best source of information about what their world is like. As you get the results, have them reported in the local newspapers, TV and radio stations, and then provide opportunities for public discussion.

4. *Curriculum for Caring* It is now possible for a young person eighteen years of age to graduate from an American high school without ever having had to do a piece of work on which someone else depended. And if that person goes on to college, the experience may be postponed for another four years, and beyond to the completion of a Ph.D. Equally disastrous from our present perspective, it is possible for a young person, female as well as male, to graduate from high school, college, or university without ever having held a baby in his or her arms for longer than a few seconds, without ever having had to care for someone who is old, ill, or lonely, without ever having had to comfort or assist another human being who really needed help. Yet all of us, sooner or later, will

desperately need such comfort and care, and no society can sustain itself unless its members have learned the motivations, sensitivities, and skills that such caring requires.

For some years I have been advocating the introduction in our schools, from the earliest grade onward, of what I call a curriculum for caring. The purpose of such a curriculum would not be to learn about caring, but to engage in it; that is, children would be asked to take responsibility for spending time with and caring for others—old people, younger children, the sick, and the lonely. It would be essential that such activities be carried on under firm supervision, and this supervision could not be provided by already overburdened teachers. Instead, the supervisors should be drawn from persons in the community who have experience in caring—parents, senior citizens, volunteer workers, and others who understand the needs of those who need attention, and the requirements on those who would give it. Obviously, such caring activities could not be restricted to the school—they would have to be carried on in the outside community. It would be desirable to locate caring institutions, such as day-care centers, adjacent to or even within the school, but it would still be important for the care-givers to come to know the environments and the people in the lives of their charges. For example, older children taking responsibility for younger ones should come to know the latter's parents and become acquainted with the places where they live and play by escorting them home from school. In this way, the children would come to know firsthand the living conditions for the people in their community.

If educational measures such as the foregoing can become part and parcel of our way of life, we may have some hope that the kind of changes we documented at the outset of this article will themselves undergo a change: The divorce curves will do a turnabout, juvenile delinquency will experience the dropouts, and families and communities can effectively perform the functions for which, from an evolutionary point of view, they are most needed and best adapted—the process of making human beings human.

The Parent Education Game: The Politics of Child Psychology in the 1970s

STEVEN SCHLOSSMAN
Radcliffe Institute. Harvard University

This essay is a critical overview of the ideology, politics, and implications of recent federal initiatives in parent education. The essay is in two main parts. Part one examines the intellectual and political context in which federal programs first emerged in the early 1970s; part two analyzes two of these programs, less to evaluate their immediate impact than to critique their original design. My goals are to explain why parent education has become so popular a tool of social reform, and to point up the inherent weaknesses of parent education programs as vehicles for social change.

WHEN DREAMS ARE SHATTERED, WHO GETS THE BLAME?

For many academics and child development "experts" in Washington, parent education became the social panacea of the 1970s. Particularly at the Office of Child Development (OCD) and the Office of Education (OE), parent education was acclaimed as the most effective method yet devised to equalize educational opportunity for children of the poor. Moreover, it was also asserted that parent education would add new dignity to the domestic pursuits of the everyday citizen-mother, whose role was being debunked in the woman's movement. Parent education was therefore doubly valuable: It would "save the children" (to

This paper is part of a larger study, under the sponsorship of the Childhood and Government Project, Boalt Law School, University of California, Berkeley, on the relationship of the state to children and families. For enthusiastic discussion of the themes contained herein, I wish to thank especially W. Norton Grubb of Berkeley and Alison Clarke-Stewart of Chicago. Responsibility for errors in fact or interpretation is, of course, my own.

use the old rallying cry of the Children's Bureau) and, at the same time, conserve and upbuild the family. To comprehend the growing appeal of parent education, however, we need to look beyond the particular objectives of diverse programs and examine, more generally, the political viability of the parent education concept at a particular moment in time. In this regard it is instructive to compare parent education with its immediate predecessor in the sympathies of child development experts: compensatory education, best represented by Head Start, and, to a lesser extent, "developmental" day care.[1]

At first glance, programs in parent education appear to derive quite naturally from the oft-expressed concern in the 1960s for "parent involvement" and "parent input" in all aspects of education.[2] A noteworthy feature of Head Start (and of some day care centers), for example, was that at all stages of design and implementation funding was contingent on consultation with parents; in addition, parents were often integrated into advisory and instructional roles. The appearance of continuity is, however, deceiving. Recent enthusiasm for parent education is better understood in political terms as more a rejection of, than an evolution from, 1960s compensatory education.

Programs in compensatory education and parent education are both conceived, in equal measure, as strategies of child development and poverty prevention. Their ultimate goals are similar: Each seeks to remove handicaps to school learning acquired in early childhood that, it is assumed, are largely responsible for the educational and occupational failure poor children commonly experience.[3] In spite of this similarity, each educational strategy proposes a fundamentally different method of eliminating childhood handicaps. Parent education represents what can be termed a "facilitative" solution; compensatory education represents, by contrast, an "interventionist" solution. In the former the policy focus is on poverty parents rather than on their children. Parents become the principal agents of educational change: Mothers

1 My approach to these subjects has been much influenced by discussions with W. Norton Grubb, and by several of his unpublished papers, for example, "Alternative Futures for Child Care," Working Paper # 11, Childhood and Government Project, Boalt Law School, University of California, Berkeley. See also W. Norton Grubb and Marvin Lazerson, "Child Care, Government Financing, and the Public Schools: Lessons from the California Children's Centers," *School Review* 86 (November 1977): 5-37.

2 This aspect of 1960s educational and welfare reform thought has been nicely parodied in Daniel Moynihan, *Maximum Feasible Misunderstanding* (New York: Free Press, 1969).

3 For background see, for example, Sar Levitan and Robert Taggart, *The Promise of Greatness* (Cambridge: Harvard University Press, 1976); and Sar Levitan and Karen Alderman, *Child Care and ABC's Too* (Baltimore: Johns Hopkins University Press, 1975).

learn scientifically approved child-rearing techniques so that they can raise their children to compete on equal intellectual terms with middle-class youth. The facilitative approach, then, is parent centered and home based. The interventionist strategy, on the other hand, is child centered and center based. Poor children are the direct recipients of supplementary education, provided in new learning environments, and designed to compensate for their relative (and continuing) intellectual deprivation at home.

I do not draw these distinctions in order to argue for the inherent superiority of one or the other strategy in equalizing educational opportunity. It is still much too early to judge—despite the confident assertions of many psychologists—whether either approach is dramatically more effective in the long run, or, indeed, whether either produces any significant impact on adult intellectual or occupational achievements. But these distinctions are nonetheless important for their political implications. Consider the following. When, early in the Nixon administration, the much-heralded compensatory programs of the 1960s were widely attacked as failures, the burden of blame fell primarily on the programs' inadequacies. The squandering and insufficiency of financial resources and the insensitivity of pedagogical theories and methods were the aspects most criticized. Blame, in short, rested mainly with the programs themselves; the clientele (the children) were seen as innocent victims of academic and bureaucratic bungling in theory, design, and implementation. If, however, ongoing programs in parent education are similarly adjudged failures in the future (a result, I shall argue, that is almost inevitable), the conclusion about who is primarily to blame will surely be different. These programs, after all, view poverty mothers rather than professional educators as the critical agents in developing their children's intellectual potential. How well or poorly mothers stimulate their children's minds daily at home becomes the key variable in explaining the children's later success or failure in school and work. Parent education programs thereby shift the burden of accountability for failure from the government-sponsored professional educator to the poverty parent. In William Ryan's terms, they sharply increase the likelihood of "blaming the victim" in rationalizing the inability of federal programs to equalize educational opportunity.[4]

For these reasons, I believe, the shift in emphasis from compensatory education to parent education should be viewed primarily in terms of its political implications. Washington child development experts, assisted

4   William Ryan, *Blaming the Victim* (New York: Random House, 1971).

by some of the nation's leading psychologists, successfully promoted an educational "reform" which had the effect of diminishing government responsibility for future failure. In retrospect, perhaps, this change in strategy is not very surprising. The compensatory programs of the 1960s, after all, had made politicians and child development specialists unusually vulnerable to criticism and directly accountable for the scientific validity of their proposals. The parent education programs of the 1970s, on the other hand, decentralized responsibility for educational outcomes by isolating poverty mothers as the principal agents of change. From a political standpoint, then—without ascribing specific motivation to any of the key decision makers—the switch from compensatory education to parent education represented "smart" social policy indeed.

It is one thing to point up the political attractiveness of parent education, quite another to trace the *process* by which parent education replaced compensatory education as the preferred national policy for equalizing opportunity among children of the poor. Washington's growing preference for parent education can best be explained as a response to three interrelated developments: first, the attack on compensatory education fueled by the report of the Westinghouse Learning Corporation in 1969; second, the subtle shifts in developmental psychology that undermined the theoretical base of compensatory education; and third, the organizational necessity for OCD to find a *raison d'être*.

A. THE WESTINGHOUSE REPORT

Until the publication of the Westinghouse report, Head Start remained a remarkably popular program throughout the country and especially in Washington. But the report deflated the naive dream of many psychologists, politicians, and community organizations that at last an educational panacea for poor children had been found. More concretely, the report led to the withdrawal of promised presidential support for major expansion of compensatory education, and to efforts by experts in Washington and academia to save face, intellectually and politically.[5]

The Westinghouse report made three main points: first, the later children entered Head Start programs, the less they benefited; second, the positive effects of Head Start dissipated soon after children left the program; and third, the more actively parents participated, the greater and longer lasting were the children's gains. The first finding surprised child development specialists least; in fact, it was quite consistent with

5 I have found Gilbert Steiner, *The Children's Cause* (Washington, D.C.: Brookings Institution, 1976), pp. 32-35 and passim very useful in charting the relevant chronology and politics.

the original mandate for Head Start. Washington had already anticipated and attempted to defuse this criticism when, in 1967, it created three dozen Parent and Child Centers for poor children under age three (we shall return to these centers again shortly). The second Westinghouse conclusion received the most publicity and did much to undermine support for compensatory education among behavioral scientists. In truth, though, Washington accommodated rather quickly and easily to this challenge by creating a new program, Follow Through, to extend Head Start benefits to children after they entered regular public schools. Follow Through, in other words, provided more of the same.[6]

Washington adjusted least easily to the third main criticism of the Westinghouse report, that concerning parent participation, due to the political volatility of the entire issue of parent involvement in the continuing community school controversies.[7] Eventually, though, this third point evoked the federal government's most original response. Essentially, Washington child development experts blunted the criticism by transforming it into a call for new federal action. What was needed, they argued, was not simply more parent participation in existing programs but, instead, a new policy orientation that focused on the poverty mother at home as the instrument of educational reform. The mother's influence was omnipresent, the experts affirmed, and hence was inevitably greater than the intermittent instruction provided by the professional teacher. Rather intriguingly, then, child development specialists in Washington transformed a direct rebuke of their 1960s program into a mandate for new and different programs in the 1970s. Their goal was still to equalize educational opportunity and their concentration was still on early childhood as the critical period; but their method was different: a facilitative strategy was substituted for the recently maligned interventionist approach.

B. FROM "NAIVE ENVIRONMENTALISM" TO THE "NEW DOMESTICITY"

Two trends in developmental psychology laid a theoretical base for using the Westinghouse report as a spur for new programs in parent education. First was the increasing attention psychologists were paying to children's social, as opposed to intellectual, development. Head Start had taken its

---

6   Ibid., pp. 54-59, 82.

7   The depth of emotion generated by the role of parents in community schools in the late 1960s is vividly recaptured in Diane Ravitch, *The Great School Wars* (New York: Basic Books, 1974).

theoretical cues largely from Benjamin Bloom's authoritative synthesis of previous research, *Stability and Change in Human Characteristics*,[8] which concentrated almost entirely on cognition and environmental deprivation. By the late 1960s many psychologists were coming to believe that Bloom's concerns were unnecessarily narrow and potentially harmful in promoting children's overall growth. As Edward Zigler, first chief of OCD, has recalled: "When the history of compensatory education in the Sixties is finally written, it will be reported that our early efforts embraced a cognitive emphasis tied to a naive environmentalism."[9] Equal attention should be paid to children's physical, social, and emotional maturation, the psychologists now said. Given this drift in psychological research, it was natural to look to the child's own home rather than to the preschool center as the appropriate setting for stimulating development of "competence" and of the "whole child."

Even more influential on new policy formulations, though, was psychological research that retained the focus on cognition but scorned "naive environmentalism," emphasizing instead the family supports necessary to sustain children's cognitive growth. Earl Schaefer has traced the evolution of ideas as follows:

> I think the early research suggested a need for early education. At that point, some of us thought that if we educated in the early years, that was sufficient. It turned out that early education was not enough. Then we began to realize the need for continued education through Follow Through and other programs, but continued education in the schools was not enough. Then we began to see the need for parent-centered education and for involving the parent in the child's education from birth to maturity. That is the concept which Home Start [to be examined shortly] is working on.[10]

Drawing on the latest psychological research, one commentator after another—university scholars, Washington child development specialists, and politicians alike—argued that compensatory education, while kind-

---

8 Benjamin Bloom, *Stability and Change in Human Characteristics* (New York: John Wiley, 1964).

9 Edward Zigler, "Head Start and Home Start: Their Past and Their Future," in *Report of a National Conference on Home Start and Other Programs for Parents and Children* (Washington, D.C.: U.S. Department of Health, Education, and Welfare, 1975), p. 60. See also Edward Zigler, "Project Head Start: Success or Failure?" *Children Today* 2 (November-December 1973): 2-7, 36.

10 Earl Schaefer, "Summary of Research on Parent-Focused Child Development Programs," in *Report of a National Conference on Home Start and Other Programs for Parents and Children*, pp. 53-54.

hearted and expressive of good intentions, embodied a naive theory of learning. The most effective way to improve the life chances of poor children, they asserted, was to teach mothers how to improve their children's intellectual promise at home.[11] The publication of Urie Bronfenbrenner's *Is Early Intervention Effective?* appeared to confirm this viewpoint as the new conventional wisdom among psychologists,[12] and encouraged leading government officials, for example Commissioner of Education Terrel Bell, to view parent education as critical to the survival of public schools as levers of social mobility. "The key to dramatic progress in American education," Bell stated, "is to gain a rededication to learning in the home."[13] Providing "equal education in the home as well as in the school" became the new rallying cry of reformers in Washington child-development circles.[14]

I term the psychological ideas underlying federal parent education programs the "new domesticity." My intent is not to deride their foundations in scientific research but to draw out their social implications, something that psychologists, in the interest of maintaining scientific distance and objectivity, are usually unwilling to do.[15] Implicit in the new domesticity, I believe, are a conservative social philosophy, a parochial view of the family's relation to larger social, economic, political, and historical forces, and a stereotypical image of woman's social

11   The literature is voluminous. See, for example, David Weikart, "Implications for Education from a Decade of Early Intervention Research" (Paper presented at the American Educational Research Association meeting, April 1976); David Weikart, "Parental Involvement through Home Teaching," in *High/Scope Report of 1974-75* (Ypsilanti, Mich.: High/Scope Educational Research Foundation, 1975), pp. 2-5; Earl Schaefer, "Parents as Educators: Evidence from Cross-Sectional, Longitudinal and Intervention Research," *Young Children* 4 (April 1972): 227-39; May Aaronson, "Review of Early Childhood Education Studies Funded by the National Institute of Mental Health" (Paper presented at the American Educational Research Association meeting, March 1975); and May Aaronson, "Future Directions in Parent Education Research" (Paper presented at the Society for Research in Child Development meeting, April 1975).

12   Urie Bronfenbrenner, *Is Early Intervention Effective?* (Washington, D.C.: DHEW Publication No. [OHD] 76-30025, 1974). As will soon become apparent, though, I believe that Bronfenbrenner was selectively misquoted by enthusiasts of parent education.

13   Terrel Bell, quoted in report of the *National Conference on Parent/Early Childhood Education* (Denver: U.S. Department of Health, Education, and Welfare, 1975), p. viii.

14   Schaefer, "Parents as Educators," p. 238.

15   I am presently engaged on a book, tentatively entitled *For Mothers' Sake? Feminism, Science, and the "Modern" American Parent*, which will develop this theme in historical perspective. My general approach is exemplified in three pieces: Steven Schlossman, "G. Stanley Hall and the Boys' Club: Conservative Applications of Recapitulation Theory," *Journal of the History of the Behavioral Sciences* 9 (April 1973): 140-47; idem, "The 'Culture of Poverty' in Antebellum Social Thought," *Science and Society* 38 (Summer 1974): 150-66; and idem, "Before Home Start: Notes toward a History of Parent Education in America, 1897-1929," *Harvard Educational Review* 46 (August 1976): 436-67.

role. Of course not all modern psychologists think alike on these issues; they vary considerably in their social awareness and sensitivity to the political implications of behavioral science research. Bronfenbrenner, for example, is careful to align his support of "family centered intervention" with recommendations for "major changes in the institutions of the society and the invention of new institutional forms." He further observes:

> The first and most essential requirement is to provide those conditions which are necessary for life and for the family to function as a childrearing system. These include adequate health care, nutrition, housing, employment, and opportunity and status for parenthood. These are also precisely the conditions that are absent for millions of disadvantaged families in our country.[16]

But many other psychologists are considerably less sophisticated, socially and politically, in their applications of new psychological research to federal educational policy. The single most important example for present purposes is Harvard University's Burton White (not to be confused with Sheldon White, also at Harvard). White has played a major personal role at OCD and OE in generating interest and legitimating investment in parent-education programs.[17] The social and political implications of his work consequently merit serious consideration.

White contends that psychologists like himself hold the key to equalizing opportunity in our society; social reform is less a matter of providing the poor with new economic resources than of teaching poverty mothers scientific child-rearing methods. Viewing American family life in near total isolation from the rest of society, he holds mothers wholly responsible for the intellectual development and competence of their children. Children who fail in school do so mainly because of their mothers' prior neglect. Almost needless to add, White's work is incredibly demanding and anxiety producing for women. White judges women as shortsighted and overly self-involved if they fail to see that child rearing is the most challenging and fulfilling social role possible. No ra-

16 Bronfenbrenner, *Is Early Intervention Effective*, p. 55. See also idem, "Developmental Research, Public Policy, and the Ecology of Childhood," *Child Development* 45 (March 1974): 1-5.

17 I reach my conclusion about White's influence not only on the basis of his published work and his promotional activities at government-sponsored parent-education conferences, but also from conversation with several major administrators at OCD and observation of the number of White's published and unpublished papers reprinted and widely available at OCD. For an important critique of White's work, see Alison Clarke-Stewart, "Dr. White's Patent Elixir for Parents," *The Review of Education* 3 (March/April 1977): 101-11.

tional woman, in his view, would sacrifice the privilege and joy of child rearing for alternative sources of employment or pleasure, or shirk her responsibilities by relying primarily on day care during the child's early years.[18] In White's work, despite the scientific jargon, one sees a clear parallel to the nineteenth century "cult of domesticity," which placed women on pedestals as objects of reverence so long as they confined their energies to domestic pursuits.[19] Under the sponsorship of experts like Burton White—whom I have singled out only because of his direct influence and continuing role in federal programs—parent education not only tends to blame the victim; it places an inordinate share of the blame on women alone.

C. A LESSON IN ORGANIZATIONAL SURVIVAL

When OCD came into being in 1969, it ostensibly embodied the Nixon administration's commitment to expansion of children's services and comprehensive welfare reform; the two were seen as going hand in hand. It soon became apparent, however, that the president's commitment to children's services was highly problematic, and that his so-called family assistance plan would never be fully developed or implemented. Gilbert Steiner has astutely recalled what this meant for OCD:

> Expecting to marry Head Start's concern for children to its broader interest in workfare-in-lieu-of-welfare, the Nixon administration had quickly created the child development office to spotlight the children's side of that plan. Welfare reform, so called, never came to pass, leaving the administration stuck with an OCD of its own making.[20]

And, one might add, leaving OCD with no special purpose.

OCD inherited Head Start from the Office of Economic Opportunity just as the Westinghouse report was beginning to weaken its prior support. To be sure, Head Start was far from being dead and maintained considerable congressional and grass-roots appeal; but it was clearly headed for a period of no growth and was consequently not what a new

18 See Burton White, *The First Three Years of Life* (Englewood Cliffs, N.J.: Prentice-Hall, 1975); and idem, "Reassessing Our Educational Priorities (To Put More Emphasis on Parent Education)" (Unpublished paper, edited version, presented to the Educational Commission of the States' Task Force on Early Learning, August 1974).

19 Barbara Welter, "The Cult of True Womanhood: 1820-1860," *American Quarterly* 18 (Summer 1966): 151-74; Anne Kuhn, *The Mother's Role in Childhood Education* (New Haven: Yale University Press, 1947); and Kathryn Sklar, *Catharine Beecher* (New Haven: Yale University Press, 1974).

20 Steiner, *The Children's Cause*, p. 60.

federal agency needed to establish a distinctive identity. OCD inherited two additional programs that represented other potential sources of organizational identity—the previously mentioned Parent and Child Centers, and Community Coordinated Child Care. Within a year, however, it became clear that these programs were, respectively, too politically suspect and too hazy in conception and operation to make systematic evaluation possible.[21] Thus by the early 1970s OCD was very much in search of a new set of ideas and programs. Obviously parent education suited OCD's organizational needs quite well, and Zigler, in rapid succession, approved three new, varied parent education programs: Parent and Child Development Centers (PCDCs), for children under age three; Home Start, for children age three to six; and Education for Parenthood, for young teens in grades seven to twelve. (This is not to say, of course, that OCD saw the issue this way or did not genuinely believe that the new programs were more scientifically valid; it is simply to point up a coincidence in time between an organization's survival needs and policy proposals, leaving questions of motivation ambiguous.) By the end of 1971 OCD could at last claim a unique purpose, a distinctive set of programs, and a secure place among the avant-garde in developmental psychology.

Considering OCD's growing identification with parent education in 1971, it is not surprising that some of its leading spokespersons were quick to rationalize the president's December veto of the Comprehensive Child Development Act, which would have vastly increased Washington's commitment to center-based children's services.[22] The veto was, from OCD's political standpoint, a blessing in disguise; it eliminated competition from educational/welfare programs representing different psychological assumptions and strategies. OCD believed that parent education, not Head Start or developmental day care, embodied the best scientific knowledge available. Nixon's veto sharply politicized the latest child development research by giving Washington's imprimatur to the new domesticity. Of course OCD did not seek the Nixon veto. But the president's action nonetheless provided OCD with a mandate for programs to which it had already committed itself. Nixon's veto, in short, buttressed OCD's *raison d'être* at a critical time in its search for organizational identity.

21   Ibid., pp. 46-59.
22   On the act and its political downfall, see Margaret Steinfels, *Who's Minding the Children?* (New York: Simon and Schuster, 1973), especially pp. 185-215. For a different viewpoint see B. Bruce-Briggs, " 'Child Care': The Fiscal Time Bomb," *The Public Interest* 49 (Fall 1977): 87-102.

EQUALIZING OPPORTUNITY THROUGH PARENT EDUCATION:
PCDCS AND HOME START

I turn now to a brief examination of two of the more important federal programs in parent education: PCDCs and Home Start. Both programs originated on the premises that compensatory education failed to improve the life chances of poor children because it offered too little too late, and because it insufficiently recognized the significance of the mother-child relationship in fostering and sustaining cognitive growth.

PCDCs evolved out of the Parent and Child Centers. From the start, these centers were beset by conflicts between child development specialists in Washington and the dispersed community action organizations that administered the centers. The experts wanted the centers to serve as scientific pilot projects to test the value of center-based educational services for very young children. The community action organizations, on the other hand, minimized research goals, objected to the elitism of the experts, and stressed delivery of concrete social services to poverty mothers. The result—according to critics of the centers and sponsors of PCDCs—was that the centers were nearly worthless: Their design was inadequate to generate scientific knowledge about infant learning; they were operated so unsystematically that they were impossible to evaluate; they delivered minimal services at exceptional cost; and, judging from the responses of parents who participated, they created more child-rearing anxieties than they relieved.[23]

PCDCs, then, were seen as alternatives to the Parent and Child Centers, their principal goal being to verify, integrate, and disseminate the psychological discoveries of the new domesticity. The first step was the creation in 1971 of three pilot projects in Houston, New Orleans, and Birmingham. The projects were organizationally varied and designed to compare the relative merits of center-based versus home-based delivery systems. Of the three pilots, for example, the one in Birmingham was wholly center based, the one in Houston employed home visiting the first year and a center-based program the second year, while the one in New Orleans compared a three-year home-visiting arrangement with a three-year center-based program. The clientele in each instance were relatively poor; in Houston the mothers were Mexican-American, in New Orleans entirely black, and in Birmingham mixed black and white.

---

23   Steiner, *The Children's Cause*, pp. 54-59; and Mary Robinson, "Parent/Child Development Centers: An Experiment in Infant-Parent Interventions and Systematic Testing of Social Innovations" (R&D Planning Memorandum, Office of Research Plans and Evaluation, Office of Economic Opportunity, 1971-1972), pp. 15-17.

In each of the settings, though, the emphasis—in accord with the new domesticity—was on the mothers' interaction with their children. Mothers were shown alternative ways of coping with specific behaviors, were taught the rudiments of child-development literature, and were introduced to a variety of toys and materials they could use to stimulate their children's development. Based on highly optimistic evaluations of the three pilot projects, the PCDC concept began to be replicated in scattered locations throughout the country in 1976.[24]

PCDCs are sustained politically by various psychological, economic, and philosophic rationales, all geared to prove that parent education is a scientifically superior substitute for compensatory education. According to Mary Robinson, the leading Washington expert associated with them, the PCDCs were a direct outcome of "the disappointing experience with remedial preschool and subsequent school-based compensatory education interventions." The Westinghouse report, she believed, merely confirmed what the Coleman report had stated several years earlier, namely "that the factors that contribute most strongly to later school achievement lie largely outside the school and are concentrated in the home . . . ." And both of these reports corroborated on a large scale what developmental psychologists were demonstrating in small experiments with young poverty children—"the importance of parent-child interaction as a shaper of the child's early intellectual, social, physical development and as a major determinant of his subsequent IQ and school and economic success."[25] Or as the Houston project summarized the relevant psychological literature: "Tutoring the child without helping the parent to develop her teaching abilities, formally or informally, was a waste of time."[26]

Economic arguments further buttress the view that poverty mothers ought to be at home devoting themselves full-time to the intellectual development of their children. According to government analysts, only 12 percent of the PCDC target population is employed full-time, and the costs of child care for working women—especially given the types of jobs for which poor women tend to be qualified—are high. The opportunity costs of participating in PCDCs are thus relatively low, and

---

24   Office of Child Development, "Parent Child Development Centers: An Experiment in Model Building and Model Replication, Description and Status Report" (U.S. Department of Health, Education, and Welfare, April 1976), p. 1.

25   Robinson, "Parent/Child Development Centers," pp. 5, 10.

26   Dale Johnson, *Houston Parent-Child Development Center* (Washington, D.C.: Office of Child Development, Final Report, Grant No. DHEW-90-C-379, 1976), p. 19.

PCDCs, consequently, are considered cheaper as well as more effective than the chief alternative, developmental day care for infants.[27]

Other rationales for PCDCs are more dubious, and highlight OCD's tendency to see parent education as the quintessential antipoverty strategy. For example, spokespersons argue that lower-class children do less well in school and later life than middle-class children mainly because of their mothers' ignorance of intellectually stimulating child-rearing techniques. Robinson predicted, for instance, that through wide sharing of "the infant development knowledge base" with poverty mothers, OCD "stood a good chance of closing the knowledge and skill gaps between the middle- and low-income parents. . . . direct and indirect access to such knowledge had served through time as a major cumulative influence shaping middle-class maternal behaviors and thus had contributed significantly to the difference in competence between poor and non-poor children."[28] In other words, according to Robinson, the lower competence of poor children derives less from differential access to economic resources than from differential access to scientific child-rearing knowledge. By distributing that knowledge equally, she believes, the federal government will be taking a great step forward in assuring that every child enjoys equal educational opportunity.

Equally dubious are what might be termed the "populistic" rationales for PCDCs. Proponents claim to be speaking against elitism and for the masses in challenging the implicit assumption in compensatory education programs that only experts working directly with poverty children can stimulate their intellectual development.

> The idea that garden variety, low-income parents might become as good as, or perhaps better agents of their own children's development than paid child-care professionals and para-professionals flew in the face of much long established conventional European and American thinking which had long allocated critical educational roles to "experts" and challenged the emergent vested interests of an ambitious child-care establishment.[29]

It is further claimed that PCDCs have populistic, grass-roots political goals. Experience in the PCDCs will so sensitize mothers to the importance of healthy home environments for young children that the mothers will become vocal advocates of social change at the community

27 Robinson, "Parent/Child Development Centers," pp. 18-27.
28 Ibid., p. 9. See also Johnson, *Houston Parent-Child Development Center*, p. 1.
29 Robinson, "Parent/Child Development Centers," p. 6.

level. As the Houston project puts it: "The parent is in a position to be the child's best advocate."[30]

It seems ironical at best for PCDC advocates to have adopted this populistic stance. These were, after all, the same Washington experts who, in the controversies surrounding the Parent and Child Centers, had scorned the stress of community action organizations on delivery of services and upheld scientific research as the only worthy use of pilot projects. Indeed, the final irony is the argument that child development specialists are snobs and that the "child-care establishment" is self-seeking; for this is precisely what PCDC proponents had been accused of by defenders of the Parent and Child Centers! The populistic rationale, then, is best understood as a politically oriented promotional device clearly belied by the genesis and operation of PCDCs.

Current expectations for PCDCs remain as grand as at their origin. Restated in 1976, prior to the funding of replication projects:

> By sharing the lore of child development with parents, especially mothers, in low-income families to enable them to become effective agents of their own children's social, emotional and intellectual development during the years from birth to three, it was hypothesized that much of the environmentally based, cumulative disadvantagement of low-income children could be prevented.

> Other benefits were also expected to accrue to participating parents, children and families, including: the acquisition of a wide range of social skills and intellectual competencies on the part of mothers; more positive attitudes and motivations; increased potential for employment of mothers when infants reach school age; involvement of fathers and their increased understanding and psychological support of mothers in the child-rearing task; greater family solidarity; positive effects on older children and on subsequent infants born to participant families.[31]

Based on evaluations of the pilot projects, OCD feels that these goals have substantially been realized: The child-rearing abilities of participating mothers have significantly improved and their children show development in cognitive and social-emotional areas that promise their future success in school. In addition, PCDC mothers "feel less restricted

---

30 Johnson, *Houston Parent-Child Development Center*, p. 18.
31 Office of Child Development, "Parent Child Development Centers," p. 2.

by child rearing and home making tasks; find children more interesting and enjoyable."[32]

It is difficult for a layman to judge the validity of a fairly rigorous behavioral science experiment like the PCDCs. Nonetheless, it is readily apparent that OCD's congratulatory self-evaluation skirts a number of critical issues.[33] For example, the problems of measuring the social and cognitive capacities of infants are obvious; it is highly problematic to predict, on the basis of such measures, children's future levels of accomplishment. Also, the reliability of program evaluations that do not constantly monitor the home activities of parents and children are suspect. In the PCDCs, as in many behavioral science experiments, the tendency is to attribute all positive results to the educational program when any number of other undetermined causes or simple "maturation effects" may be responsible. Finally, OCD's evaluation plays down the matter of cost-effectiveness, a crucial consideration given the fact that PCDCs cost considerably more to operate than other forms of parent education or traditional center-based programs. None of my reservations is meant to deny that for many parents and children PCDCs have produced positive and welcome results, but simply to point up the danger—witnessed time and again in the evolution of the behavioral sciences—of publicizing early results as scientific truth when methods of evaluation remain uncertain, and of hiding legitimate doubt under the cloak of science.[34]

For my purposes, moreover, the unstated social assumptions underlying PCDCs are most important. Whether scientifically valid or not, PCDCs reinforce stereotypes about women and lay a groundwork for blaming the victim. Interestingly, the Houston project recognizes the latter possibility but dismisses it.

> Calling attention to the family's role in the child's school achievement has been described by some as "blaming the victim." It is seen as shifting attention from the quality of schooling offered, or from the role of society at large in providing for all of its citizens, to the family as the source of the problems. This misses the real point

---

32   Ibid., p. 6.
33   For a discussion of these basic, and often unacknowledged, methodological difficulties, see Alison Clarke-Stewart, *Child Care in the Family* (New York: Academic Press, 1977); and Alison Clarke-Stewart and Nancy Apfel, "Evaluating Parental Effects on Child Development," in *Review of Research in Education*, AERA, ed. L. Shulman (Itaska, Ill.: F.E. Peacock, 1978, in press).
34   See Schlossman, "Before Home Start," for historical examples of these tendencies.

which is that home and school must both be involved in the child's education, sharing skills and knowledge in the best interest of the child.[35]

True enough; indeed, this statement could serve as a springboard for sophisticated analysis of educational configurations in modern America. It is only a short conceptual step from recognizing the interdependence of home and school to recognizing the impossibility of evaluating either home or school apart from the larger social environment. But neither OCD nor the Houston project follows through in this direction; they raise larger issues only to retreat from them. As we have seen, PCDC proponents contend that the assistance provided poverty mothers is sufficient to enable their children to compete on equal terms with middle-class youth. Should children whose mothers participate in PCDCs fail to achieve at equal levels, the likely inference is apparent: Their mothers must have shirked their domestic/educational duties. The blame, in other words, must lie in lax implementation by uncaring poverty mothers. Similarly for the Houston project: Despite sensitivity to the blaming-the-victim issue, they also view PCDCs as genuine equalizers of educational opportunity. Witness, for example, the following hypothesis, which their evidence purports to substantiate:

If the environment is encouraging, rewarding, rich with verbal interaction and responsive to the child's developing curiosity, as is presumed to be the case in the middle- or upper-income home, then the child's intellect is expected to thrive. Given the presence of these environmental conditions, irregardless of family income, we would expect the child to do well.[36]

Here, then, in the jargon of science, is a round of applause for the "virtuous poor" and for parent education as an effective substitute for more direct means of reducing social inequities. PCDC advocates assume that middle-class mothers rear smart, successful children while lower-class mothers rear stupid, unsuccessful children primarily because the former are more attuned to the dictates of science. Their solution to poverty is to reduce the knowledge gap between middle- and lower-class mothers and thereby provide "equal opportunity in the home." "Irregardless of family income, we would expect the child to do well": a more succinct revelation of the Pollyannish thinking underlying parent-education programs can hardly be imagined.

35 Johnson, *Houston Parent-Child Development Center*, p. 6.
36 Ibid., p. 126.

While it is difficult to evaluate a sophisticated social experiment like the PCDCs, it is easier to judge a much less rigorous program like Home Start. Fifteen Home Start projects began in 1972 with the intent of bringing the benefits of Head. Start to children of the same age range but without removing them from their homes. Home Start operates by sending "home visitors" into family settings, to teach parents—almost always mothers—about child development, to assist in specific child-rearing tasks, and to serve as "a sympathetic listener, a helper, an adviser, and *friend* to the entire family being served."[37] So that home visitors will share the community, class, racial, and language characteristics of families they befriend, Home Start hires mainly indigenous nonprofessionals and gives them brief periods of training, generally a few weeks. Home Start carries OCD's hopes for an alternative to center-based preschools that is cheaper, more effective educationally, and more viable politically than compensatory education.[38]

Funding patterns for Home Start suggest that OCD saw it more as a substitute for than as an addition to Head Start. Thus Washington did not authorize Home Start programs to begin anew; instead they had to be operated by existing Head Start centers or by other community organizations authorized to receive Head Start funding. This proviso accomplished two things: It placed the weight of OCD on the side of Home Start and set a financial ceiling on potential federal involvement. An OCD directive in 1973 indicated to Head Start centers that the burden of justifying existing center-based programs would fall on them:

Continuation of the present five-day-per-week, center-based classroom format will be optional. Communities electing to continue this format are free to do so provided that they demonstrate through a careful assessment of their needs and capabilities that continuing the present program is in the best interest of the individual children and families served. If this assessment indicates that the present format is not adequately meeting local needs, the program is to consider whether these needs could be met more effectively by one or more of the other options.[39]

By so phrasing the choice, OCD doubtless hoped that Head Start centers

37   Office of Child Development, *A Guide for Planning and Operating Home-Based Child Development Programs* (Washington, D.C.: U.S. Department of Health, Education, and Welfare, 1974), p. E-3.

38   On the genesis of Home Start, see Steiner, *The Children's Cause*, pp. 79-85.

39   Office of Child Development, *A Guide for Planning and Operating Home-Based Child Development Programs*, p. H-6.

would get the message: The way to avoid review was to adopt the Home Start concept in whole or in part.

To OCD's chagrin, relatively few Head Start centers chose to adopt any aspect of the home-based approach, much less to convert entirely to Home Start. By late 1976 only 13 percent of enrolled children were partaking in home-based options—a total of 12,179 children, mainly between ages three and five. Of these, 20 percent were handicapped youth for whom center-based programs were inappropriate and who could be reached in no other way. Though OCD has staged several major conferences to demonstrate the superiority of Home Start, the great majority of parents who use Head Start have refused to switch.[40]

Are these parents obstinately and irrationally attached to the status quo? Are they selfish enough not to want to forgo the use of Head Start as government-financed babysitting? Are they simply ignorant of the latest behavioral science research on child development? Are the professionals and paraprofessionals who operate Head Start centers calculatingly protecting a vested interest? Or—while not necessarily denying any of the above—is there good reason for poverty parents to doubt the vaunted superiority of Home Start to Head Start, and to continue to place their hopes and trust in center-based programs? My review of Home Start, as idea and reality, suggests that there is good reason indeed for poor parents to distrust it and to conclude that Head Start is unquestionably the safer bet.

The promotional literature for Home Start emphasizes innumerable benefits for participating mothers and children. For the same amount of money as Head Start centers usually spend, it is claimed, Home Start will provide significantly lower staff-clientele ratios and more personal, individualized service. Better yet, Home Start will educate children not formally enrolled in the program, especially older siblings; it will even extend to "neighbors, and friends [who] may be getting development services as a result."[41] These purported spillover effects are obviously appealing at a time when Head Start is in a period of no growth. In addition, Home Start is flexible enough to reach isolated rural families; unlike Head Start, it can bring services to needy people wherever they are (more populism). Home Start will involve fathers more actively than Head Start, since home visitors can arrange to meet with families on

40 Ann O'Keefe, *Head Start Home-Based Programs: A Preliminary Report* (Washington, D.C.: U.S. Department of Health, Education, and Welfare, 1976).

41 Office of Child Development, *A Guide for Planning and Operating Home-Based Child Development Programs*, p. 7.

weeknights and weekends. Home Start will also provide career access for participating mothers, who will learn skills necessary to become operators of family-based day-care centers. Finally, and still more heroically, Home Start will strengthen the (presumably) declining family spirit among the poor by getting all family members to recognize their mutual responsibilities, and by revitalizing family life into such an enjoyable experience that no rational mother would ever want to leave the family hearth.

It is still too early to judge the long-term impact of Home Start on the school and occupational performances of poor children. But the intrinsic conceptual and operational weaknesses of Home Start raise serious doubts about its potential, and that of parent education generally, as an antipoverty strategy.[42] At its core Home Start embodies pedagogical methods so anachronistic it is remarkable they were advanced as original in the 1970s. It is as if Home Start were trying to reinvent casework as it was practiced before the turn of the century; the home visitors bear an alarming similarity in function to the "friendly visitors" who dispensed love, religion, and advice on child care and household management as cure-alls for poverty.[43] Of course there is a great deal that is new and appealing about having indigenous community members serve as the principal teachers of poverty mothers. But considering the magnitude of their tasks and the extraordinary expectations for Home Start, the role devised for the home visitors seems nothing short of impossible. Failure is virtually built-in. Having only the ability to dispense advice at their disposal (and only ninety minutes per week at that), the home visitors are expected to teach mothers how to become "child development specialists," to rear their children so that they can compete on equal intellectual terms with middle-class children, and to adopt "a positive, 'preventive' approach . . . so that the atmosphere and attitudes conducive to a happy home environment are encouraged."[44] But home visitors must accomplish all this without dealing directly with the material deprivations that defined the Home Start clientele in the first place. The "happy home" approach smacks of trying to convince the

---

42 My judgments derive from reading the aforementioned sources on Home Start plus Office of Child Development, *The Home Start Demonstration Program: An Overview* (Washington, D.C.: U.S. Department of Health, Education, and Welfare, 1973); and Office of Child Development, *Report of a Joint Conference: Home Start/Child and Family Resource Program* (Washington, D.C.: U.S. Department of Health, Education, and Welfare, 1974).

43 See Roy Lubove, *The Professional Altruist* (Cambridge: Harvard University Press, 1965), chap. 1; and Steven Schlossman, *Love and the American Delinquent* (Chicago: University of Chicago Press, 1977), chap. 4.

44 Office of Child Development, *Home Start Demonstration Program*, p. 8.

poor to adapt to their poverty by altering the dynamics of intrafamily life, holding out to poor parents only the hope of a better future for their children.[45] In short, Home Start seeks to change attitudes and assumes that the right attitudes will obviate the effects of poverty on children's social and economic achievement.

In view of the startling gap between means and ends in the Home Start design, it is not surprising that so few Head Start centers have adopted a Home Start component, and that the majority of parents have refused to switch out of Head Start.[46] Home Start symbolizes on a small scale the conservative social philosophy that has triumphed in Washington and the rest of the nation in the 1970s.[47] This philosophy redirects responsibility for failure toward the victims of social injustice, focusing blame for unsuccessful child rearing on poor families rather than on extrafamilial institutions. By citing "scientific" evidence that poverty mothers alone hold the key to their children's intellectual potential, it becomes impossible to hold social institutions accountable for educational outcomes. Home Start is symptomatic of a new politics of child psychology in America, which relies on science to defuse the need for more thorough reforms of social institutions and which absolves government of responsibility for glaring disparities in achievement between lower-class and middle-class youth.[48]

CONCLUSION

Implicit in the recent federal enthusiasm for parent education is a remarkably anachronistic view, namely, that parents wholly determine their children's futures. Today more than ever, as Lawrence Cremin argues in his theory of modern educational configurations, this view is absurd.[49] It is fruitless to try to isolate the impact of individual educational institutions—whether the family, the school, or the television—and assign them full responsibility for educational outcomes. The in-

•

45   Along these lines see the rather embarrassing "national Home Start song," discussed by Steiner, *The Children's Cause*, p. 84.

46   For a sampling of parents' specific complaints about Home Start, see Office of Child Development, *A Guide for Planning and Operating Home-Based Child Development Programs*, pp. 7, 32.

47   See Kenneth Keniston, *All Our Children* (New York: Harcourt Brace Jovanovich, 1977), for a lucid analysis of how this has affected American family policy.

48   For imaginative discussion of related themes, see Christopher Lasch, *Haven in a Heartless World* (New York: Basic Books, 1977); Mary Jo Bane, "A Review of Child Care Books," *Harvard Educational Review* 43 (November 1973): 669-80; Edgar Friedenberg, "Save the Children!" *The Review of Education* 3 (July/August 1977): 256-60; and Arlene Skolnick, "The Myth of the Vulnerable Child," *Psychology Today* 11 (February 1978): pp. 56, 58, 60, 65.

credible variety of institutions that socialize children, and the complex manner in which they touch, overlap, and interact, demands that we exercise considerable caution in parceling out blame for educational failures. To subscribe to "parent determinism" or "school determinism" or "television determinism" is to indulge in that characteristically American sport Richard Hofstadter called the "educational jeremiad," whose goal is to exorcise devils rather than to increase understanding of institutional relationships.[50] After reviewing the development of parent education programs in the 1970s, I am not so much against them as appalled by their pretense as social panaceas.[51] If parent education programs engaged adults in appraising the role of the family as educator today, or in assessing the utility of educational reform as a means of reducing social inequities, then they might serve a valuable public purpose.[52] But to the extent that such programs hold poverty mothers mainly responsible for their children's later failures, I believe they do a grievous disservice. It is no sport at all to increase the burdens of the poor.

49   Lawrence A. Cremin, *Public Education* (New York: Basic Books, 1976); and idem, *Traditions of American Education* (New York: Basic Books, 1977).

50   Richard Hofstadter, *Anti-Intellectualism in American Life* (New York: Random House, 1962).

51   Not only am I not unalterably opposed to parent education, but I have been working for the National PTA to develop more socially responsible forms of parent education. See Steven Schlossman, ed., *Today's Family in Focus* (Chicago: National Congress of Parents and Teachers, 1977).

52   See Hope Jensen Leichter, ed., *The Family as Educator* (New York: Teachers College Press, 1976); and Henry Perkinson, *The Imperfect Panacea* (New York: Random House, 1968).

CONTRIBUTORS

URIE BRONFENBRENNER is Professor of Psychology and of Human Development and Family Studies at Cornell University. He is the author of *Two Worlds of Childhood: U.S. and U.S.S.R.*, and is currently coordinating a five-nation research program on the Comparative Ecology of Human Development that attempts to study the impact of family support systems on family functioning and child development.

ELIOT D. CHAPPLE, who is currently associated with the Rockland Research Institute, has been studying the anthropology of organizations and of human interaction since 1940. He is the author, among other works, of *Culture and Biological Man*.

LAWRENCE A. CREMIN is Frederick A. P. Barnard Professor of Education and President at Teachers College, Columbia University. His most recent books are *Public Education* and *Traditions of American Education*.

J. W. GETZELS is the R. Wendell Harrison Distinguished Service Professor in the Department of Education and of Behavioral Sciences, The University of Chicago. He is coauthor of *Educational Administration as a Social Process* and *The Creative Vision: A Longitudinal Study of Problem Finding in Art*.

NICHOLAS HOBBS is Professor of Psychology and of Preventive Medicine at Vanderbilt University and Director of the Study of Families and Children of the Vanderbilt Institute for Public Policy Studies. Among his publications is *The Futures of Children*.

HOPE JENSEN LEICHTER is Elbenwood Professor of Education and Director of the Elbenwood Center for the Study of the Family as Educator at Teachers College, Columbia University. Her book, with William E. Mitchell, *Kinship and Casework: Family Networks and Social Intervention* was recently issued in a second edition. She also edited *The Family as Educator*.

ROBERT A. LEVINE, Roy E. Larsen Professor of Education and Human Development at Harvard University, is a psychological anthropologist who has been conducting research on African patterns of child rearing and development since 1955. He is the author of *Culture, Behavior, and Personality*.

MARGARET MEAD (1901-1978) was Curator Emeritus of Ethnology at the American Museum of Natural History and Adjunct Professor of Anthropology at Columbia University. Her many published works include *Culture and Commitment: A Study of the Generation Gap* and *Letters from the Field, 1925-1975*.

245

PETER R. MOOCK is Associate Professor of Economics and Education at Teachers College, Columbia University. He is a coauthor of *Higher Education and Rural Development in Africa* and of a book that will appear later this year entitled *The Determinants of Educational Outcomes.*

STEVEN SCHLOSSMAN, Assistant Professor in the Department of Education at the University of Chicago, is currently on a two-year leave as a research associate at the Radcliffe Institute. He is the author of *Love and the American Delinquent: The Theory and Practice of "Progressive" Juvenile Justice, 1825-1900.*